Flex Appeal

The Changing Face of
’70s Skateboard Culture

gestalten

Contents

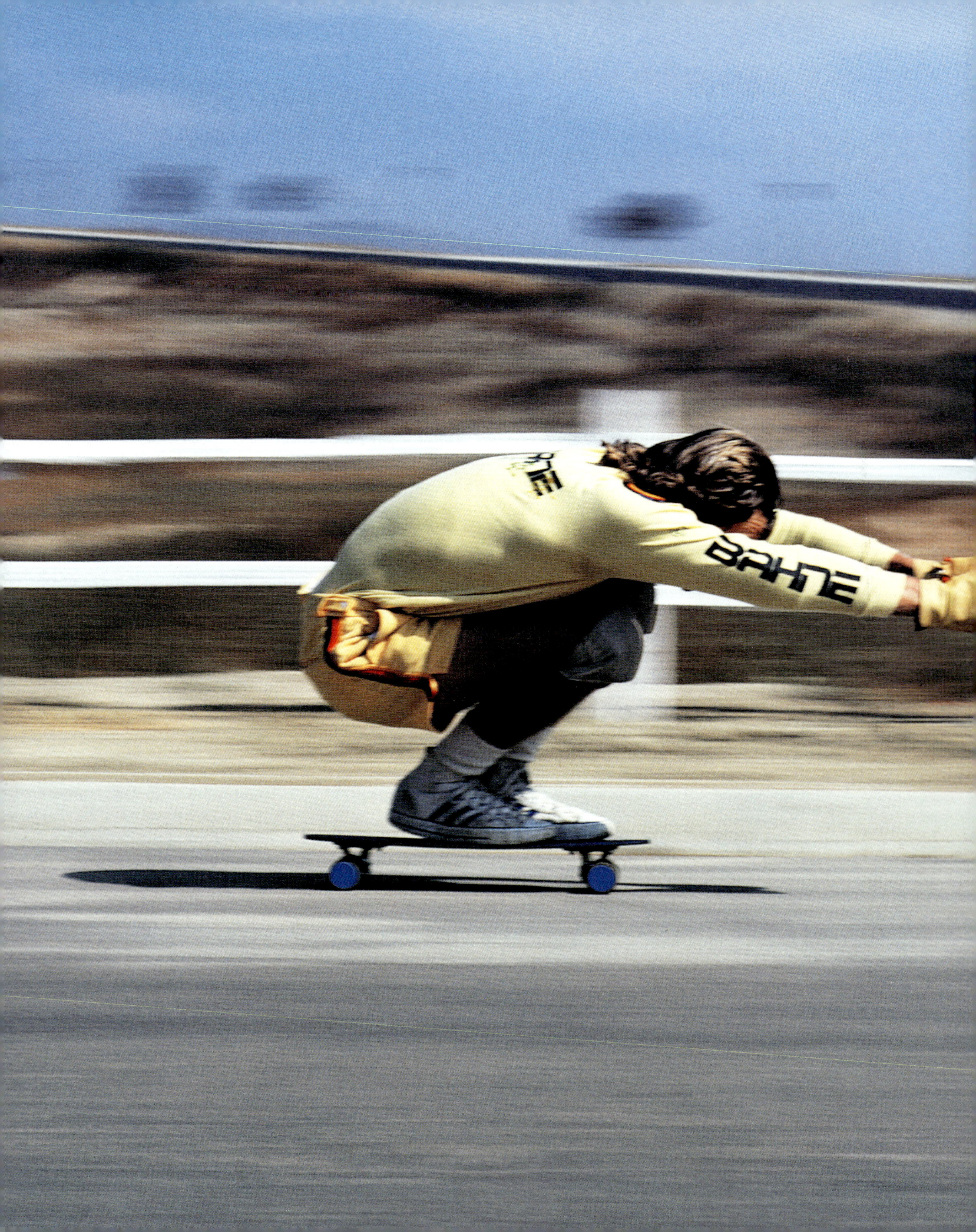
BAHNE

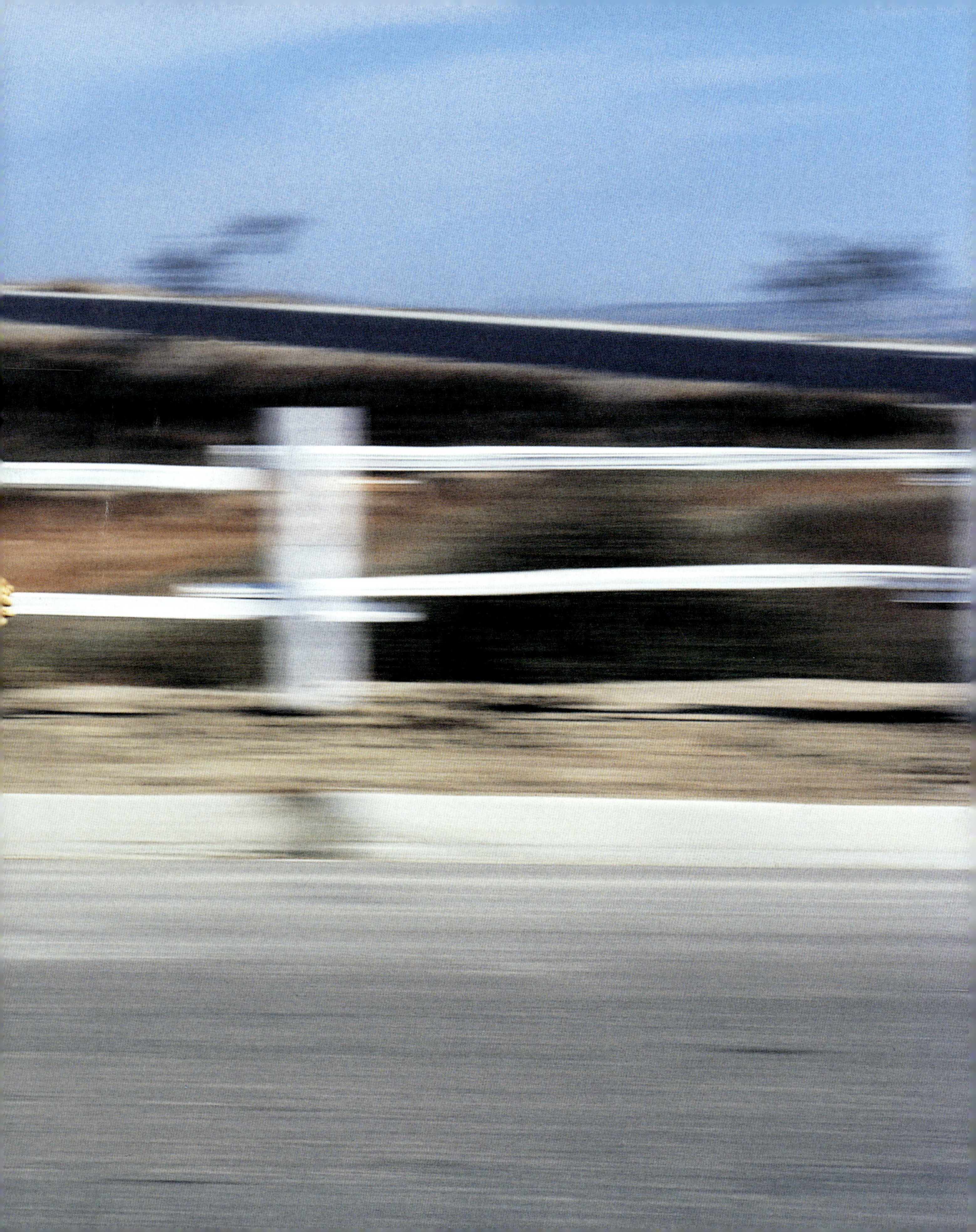

The Thrill of the Chase

by Stefan Ytterborn

A chance encounter with an original FibreFlex skateboard reconnected Stefan Ytterborn with a brand that, during the mid-to-late 1970s, stood at the intersection of design, engineering, and performance. What began as a moment of nostalgia quickly became a deeper exploration of a formative period in skateboarding. Over time, Ytterborn, a longtime skater, collector, product guy, entrepreneur, and brand builder, assembled an unrivaled collection of FibreFlex models from these years. Every item in his archive, whether restored or pristine, reflects a distinct moment in the sport's rapid evolution.

Growing up in Sweden as a teenager, I always dreamed of owning a FibreFlex skateboard. Back then, I rode early decks from brands like Newporter and Logan, but as skateboarding shifted toward a more vertical style in the late 1970s, I moved on to Dogtown and Santa Cruz boards. Still, the longing for a FibreFlex lingered in the background: it belonged to that shimmering Californian universe I connected to only through the pages of *SkateBoarder* magazine, which for kids like me in Scandinavia felt like a portal straight into that world. We consumed every issue until the pages softened at the folds, studying the culture, the riders, the brands, the gear, the skateparks, the ads, and the team photos. Even then, what struck me about FibreFlex was that it meant more than just boards: there were the fiberglass layups, the engineered flex patterns, the way form and function kept evolving from model to model. Someone was thinking about these objects the way an engineer or a designer would, and that registered with me long before I had the language for it. Looking back, I was part of a global community of teenagers who didn't know each other – yet we were all somehow connected by those pages.

Decades later, while still skateboarding, a chance encounter brought that era back to life. My wife and I were donating clothes to charity when I spotted a late-1977 blue FibreFlex Freestyle with yellow-and-red YO-YO wheels. It immediately transported me to my childhood, and I knew I couldn't leave it there, so I brought it home, planning merely to clean it up a little. Despite this, I quickly found myself restoring it entirely, an impulse that sparked obsession. Soon, I began looking for used original FibreFlex decks and reissues, exploring collector groups and scrolling eBay deep into the night. Before I knew it, what had begun as nostalgia had transformed into something much, much bigger: a collection.

Flex Appeal is therefore an examination of both the very fabric of my obsession – the boards themselves – as well as a celebration of FibreFlex and its history. On every page, I hope to demonstrate not only the cultural value of the items I've collected – a complete selection of FibreFlex's output from 1975–79 – but why the San Diego–based brand was so important during this formative era of skateboarding. Through images and texts, with the collection at the core, I'm excited to share the story of skateboarding's rapid evolution in the late '70s. What still fascinates me most is how much of that evolution was driven by design, engineering, material experimentation, and the constant search for better performance. That mindset stayed with me and, in many ways, shaped how I would later think about product development, brand building, and innovation.

But this book reaches well beyond my shelves. FibreFlex also makes more sense when seen in relation to its mother brand, Gordon & Smith (G&S), which emerged from the West Coast surfing scene in the mid-20th century to give the first "sidewalk surfers" something worth riding. It means looking at how decks were built, how wheels evolved, and how quickly shapes, setups, and materials responded to riders pushing harder into pools, ramps, and the contest circuits that defined the era. And it means knowing the names: Henry Hester, Steve Cathey, Doug Saladino, Greg Taie, Chris Yandall, Ellen O'Neal, and Dennis Martinez, skateboarders endorsed by FibreFlex whose riding shaped both the brand's identity and the history unfolding around it. Whether you're a FibreFlex devotee or coming to all of this for the first time, my hope is that these pages bring you closer to understanding why this sport, and this brand, still gets a fully grown human being out of bed in the morning.

Indeed, my collection is, at heart, the crux of the matter – an undertaking that has evolved. Having quickly accepted, for instance, that my fascination with FibreFlex as an adult was more than just a passing fancy, I set about restoring and customizing my acquisitions. The seven earliest decks I worked on, therefore, all received sky-blue bottoms, with some needing only light touch-ups and others requiring structural repairs, such as rebuilding portions of the wood. That was Phase One. Phase Two began when I received a rare FibreFlex as a gift from my colleagues: an out of the box "NOS" (new old stock) Greg Taie Slalom Signature model. That board changed everything. From then on, I only wanted originals or NOS FibreFlex decks – nothing less. And then there was Phase Three. Driven by perfection, I subsequently encountered the extraordinary restoration work of Mark Mayers, whose ability to resurrect FibreFlex decks into factory-perfect condition made me rethink my approach to collecting once more.

After this, I stopped thinking of my collection in phases and accepted the fluctuations and changes as my interests and focus have continued to shift. One consistent element is that all the boards in my collection date from 1975 – when G&S relaunched the brand following its decline since the boom of the 1960s – to 1979, the end of its golden era. Regardless, each item is either NOS or an original restored by Mark Mayers to its exact period appearance. The sole exception to this is the first board I found, the Mother Ship, which remains in its sky-blue custom finish. Collecting is an art too, one in which research becomes its own reward. In my efforts to ensure every board I acquired was fitted with period-correct trucks and wheels, I dug through old magazines, catalogs, price lists, interviews, online forums, and obscure archival scans. I wanted to know how many plies of wood certain decks used, the positions of the holes used to fit the trucks, how shapes and setups changed from model to model, and how all of this related to performance. My goal was to assemble every model FibreFlex sold in this period, and I wanted to make sure I was doing the brand justice. In the end, this aim was achieved through painstaking attention to detail: as the following pages make clear, I have assembled, give or take a few variations in size, a comprehensive tribute to this pivotal period in skateboarding.

In addition to the FibreFlex collection, I have gathered the brands, decks, and complete boards that most influenced my teenage years. This collection serves to fully materialize the time and space of that period.

Flex Appeal is an homage, a historical survey, and a record of compulsion, made for people who already know this world well and, I hope, for others who may feel its pull through these pages. With the help of photographer Jörgen Brennicke and designer David Gonzalez (both skateboarders themselves), this book was created so that these boards can be seen, understood, and appreciated as the beautifully crafted, designed, and engineered objects they are – objects that continue to resonate far beyond their original moment. Furthermore, if it hadn't been for my "by chance" outreach to Michael Brooke after reading his piece on the history of FibreFlex that I found online, the result would have been limited. Michael has been an invaluable and inspiring speaking partner, a hub of information, and the gatekeeper for Warren Bolster's photography. Through this, my hope is that, by browsing these pages, you will understand – and perhaps even experience – some of the wonder I felt as a teenager dreaming of riding a FibreFlex.

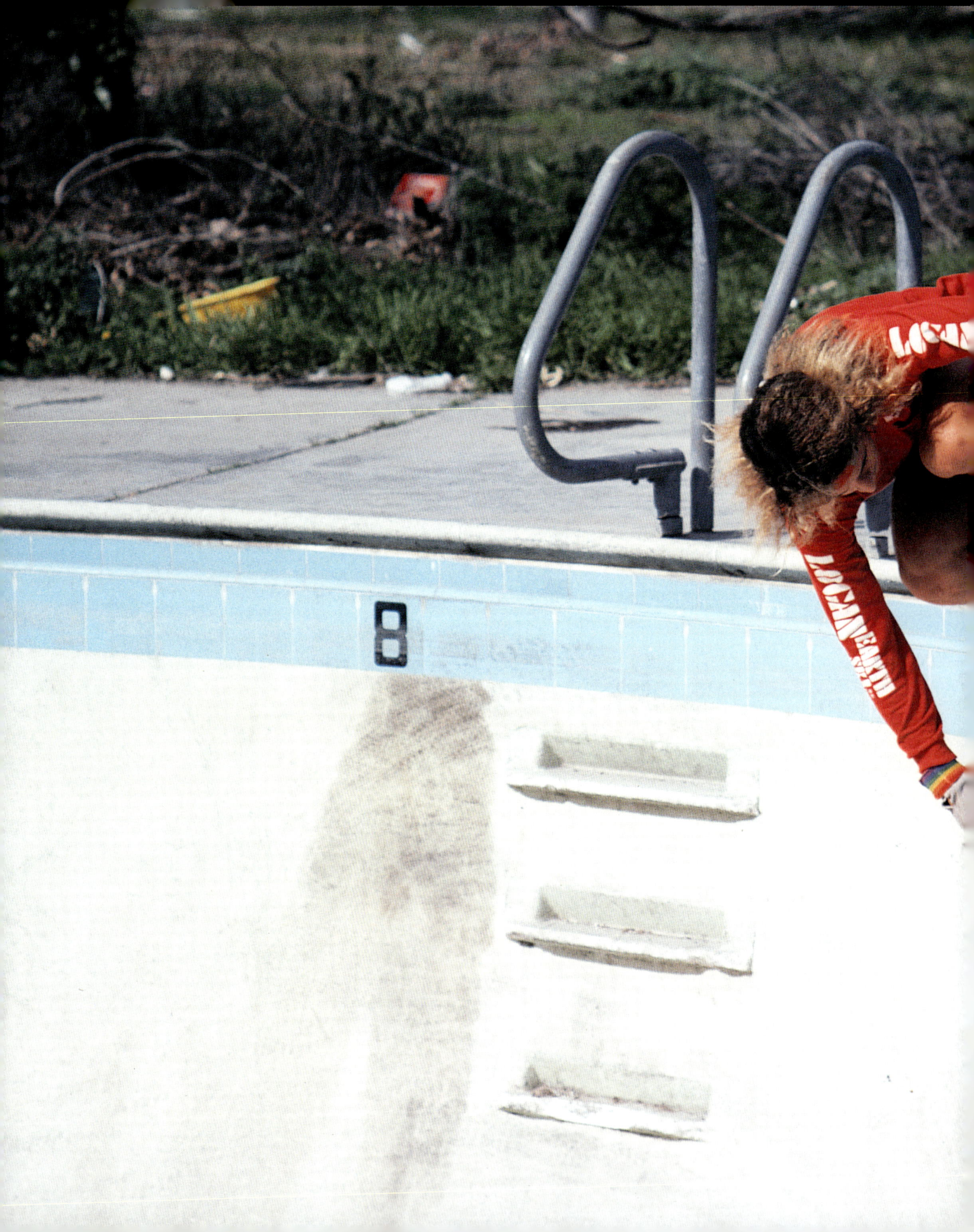
8

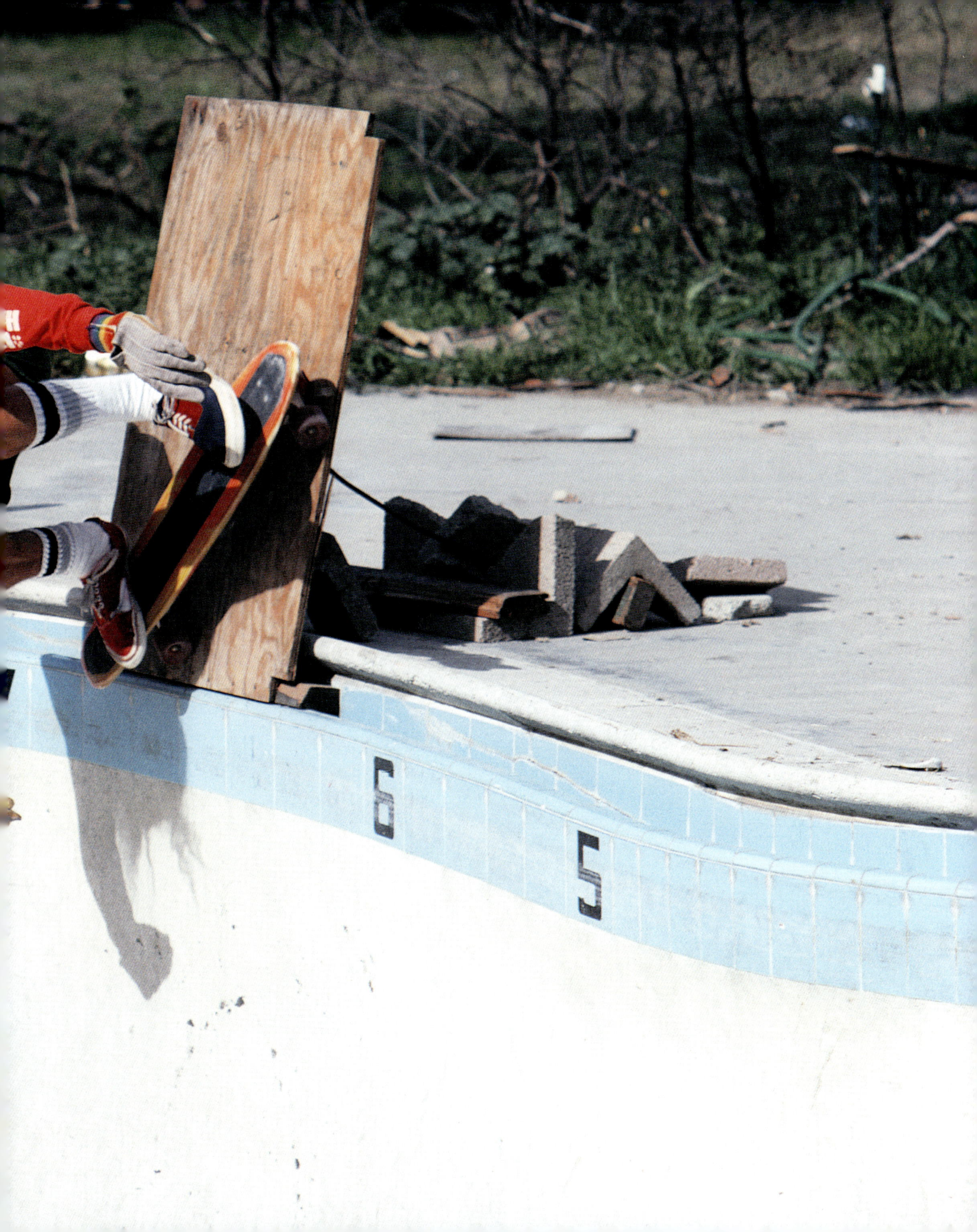
6
5

The Story of the Gordon & Smith FibreFlex Skateboard

by Michael Brooke

Skateboarder and Author of *The Concrete Wave: The History of Skateboarding*

Who could have predicted that the sports of archery and skateboarding would one day connect to create one of the most popular skateboards ever produced: the FibreFlex?

The FibreFlex was manufactured by Gordon & Smith. The roots of Gordon & Smith go back to the late 1950s. Surfer Larry Gordon was studying chemistry in college when he teamed up with Floyd Smith. The two began making surfboards in the corner of the Gordon Plastics factory, run by Larry's father and two uncles. Eventually, Larry and Floyd moved out of Gordon Plastics and into Floyd's garage. In 1962, Larry left school and went into manufacturing surfboards full-time. The company was known as Gordon & Smith Surfboards. In the summer of 1964, Larry's cousin Mike returned home from college, where he had been studying business and chemistry.

Archery and Skateboarding

At the time, skateboarding was gaining in popularity, and Larry came up with a brilliant idea. He took a material called Bo-Tuff and combined it with a wood core to create a skateboard deck. Bo-Tuff was a fiberglass-reinforced epoxy used to make bows for the archery industry, and it had some amazing physical properties. For example, a bow that incorporated Bo-Tuff set a world record for shooting an arrow. It went over one mile.

By combining Bo-Tuff with a maple wood core, Gordon & Smith developed a skateboard that offered an extremely responsive ride. The camber, or arc, of the board also added to its responsiveness. If you pushed down on a FibreFlex, it would spring back into place immediately. It was the first laminated skateboard.

In an interview for *SkateBoarder* magazine in 1978, Larry Gordon described the skateboard scene in the mid-1960s. "Slalom racing was the most exciting aspect of the sport at that time, and we felt we had a better idea for a skateboard design," Gordon stated.

Larry teamed up with his friend Jim Hovde and formed a company to make FibreFlex skateboards. They made a few at a time and eventually produced a thousand boards using a hand-screw press. Over time, a FibreFlex slalom team was put together.

Surfers like Skip Frye, Willie Phillips, John Haywoods, Tommy Ryan, Denis Shufeldt, and Mike Hynson dominated the First Annual Skateboard Contest held in Anaheim in May of 1965.

But most skateboarders in the mid-1960s were content to ride on wooden boards that gave little to no flex. The FibreFlex's highly advanced technology was lost on most skaters, who were still struggling with the challenges of clay wheels. When the skateboard craze died in late 1965, so did the production of the FibreFlex. It would take close to ten years before another one was manufactured.

500 FibreFlex Per Day

Larry and Mike decided to resume production in 1974 in a garage with the same equipment that had been used in the 1960s. On average, Mike was producing about 25 boards a day. Eventually, Mike decided to return to Gordon Plastics with his uncle. He also moved his FibreFlex equipment from the garage to the factory, where there were more presses.

The introduction of the urethane wheel in the early 1970s brought with it several skateboarders who were enthralled by slalom skating. The speed and smooth, flowing motion achievable on a FibreFlex made it an extraordinary skateboarding experience. Skateboard magazines featured numerous ads and articles on slalom pros Paul Engh, Henry Hester, and Chris Yandall, who were winning contests on FibreFlex skateboards.

By the mid 1970s, the factory was churning out 500 FibreFlex boards a day, which still was not enough to meet demand. Dave McIntyre, head of the sales division at that time, vividly recalls having six months' worth of orders.

Based on the success of the slalom skateboard, Gordon & Smith soon introduced other FibreFlex models. There was a freestyle model with a rocker, the reverse of camber, and a 25 to 27-inch kicktail model that proved very popular. In 1977, they released a stiffer model called the Bowlrider, which offered the flex of fiberglass and the stability of a wood board.

A Timeless Inspiration

The next benchmark for G&S arrived in the form of a solid-wood board, also known as a deck, made from ash or oak, depending on what was available. There were two models: a flat wooden board and the Warptail, which had a slightly raised rear kicktail and was the signature model of skateboarder Stacy Peralta, the Tony Hawk of his day. In the course of 18 months, 110,000 Warptail boards were sold. The Warptail II model, which incorporated layers of maple veneer, was significantly lighter. Gordon & Smith also marketed the Rockit deck, similar in construction to the Warptail II.

In 1978, after their success with both fiberglass and wood models, the company introduced the Teamrider, the widest and largest FibreFlex they had ever made. It was one of the most versatile boards, and countless photos show it being used in both vertical and freestyle riding.

Over time, however, skateboard manufacturers like Gordon & Smith moved away from fiberglass. Slalom riding took a backseat as more skaters became interested in halfpipes, bowls, wooden ramps, and concrete skateparks. By 1979, the FibreFlex line was replaced by strictly plywood-type boards, although the Teamrider model was still available. The G&S Proline, Dennis Martinez's Flying Ace, and Doug Saladino's Pine Design were all vertical boards.

Finding an original FibreFlex board nowadays is difficult. The ABC Company licensed the Gordon & Smith Skateboards trademark and reissued FibreFlexes, allowing riders to once more experience the ultimate cruising and carving experience. However, in 1998, Larry Gordon decided to begin producing a longboard FibreFlex, an incredibly responsive ride, making FibreFlex one of the most enduring names in skateboarding.

After six decades, FibreFlex remains one of the most enduring names in skateboarding.

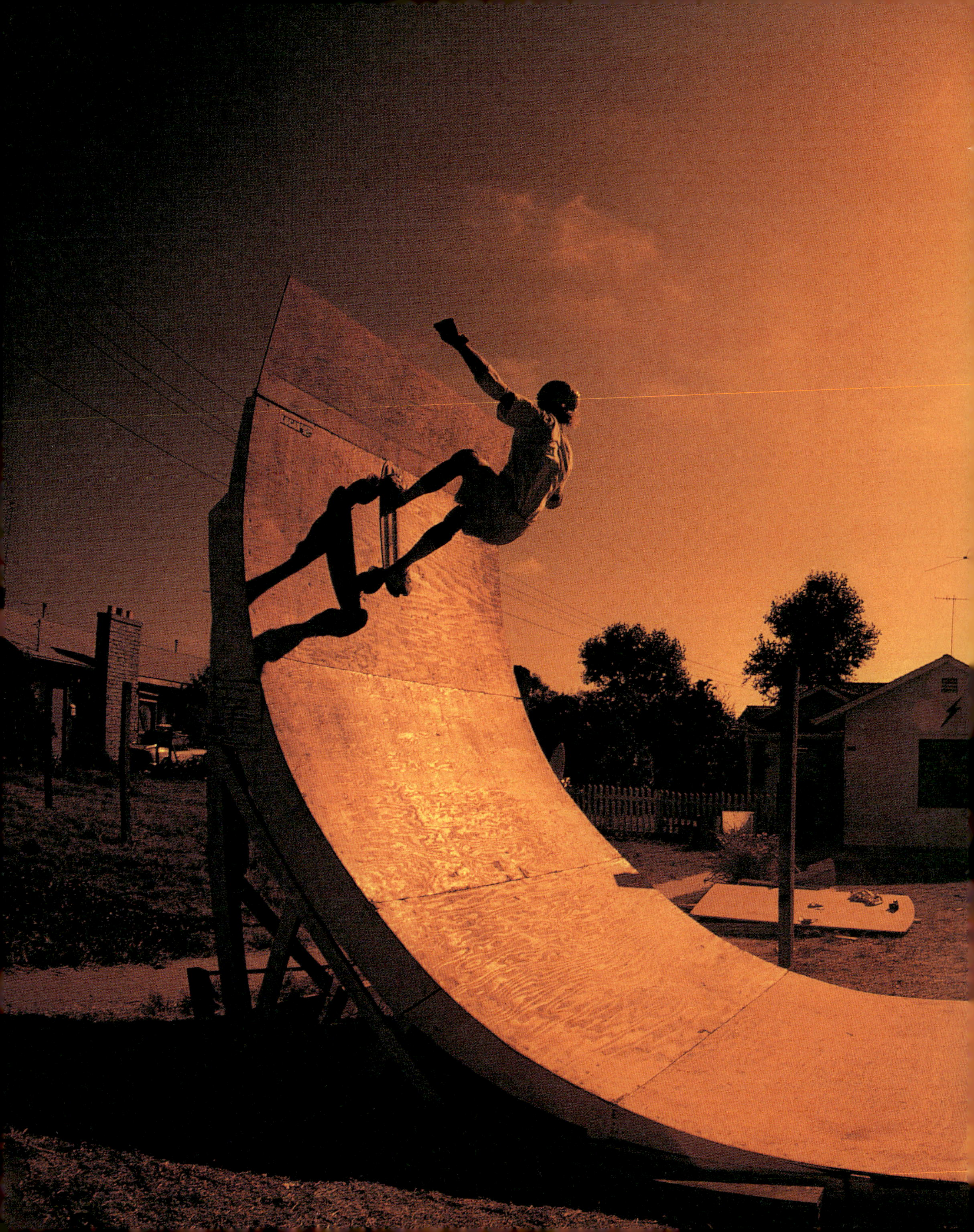

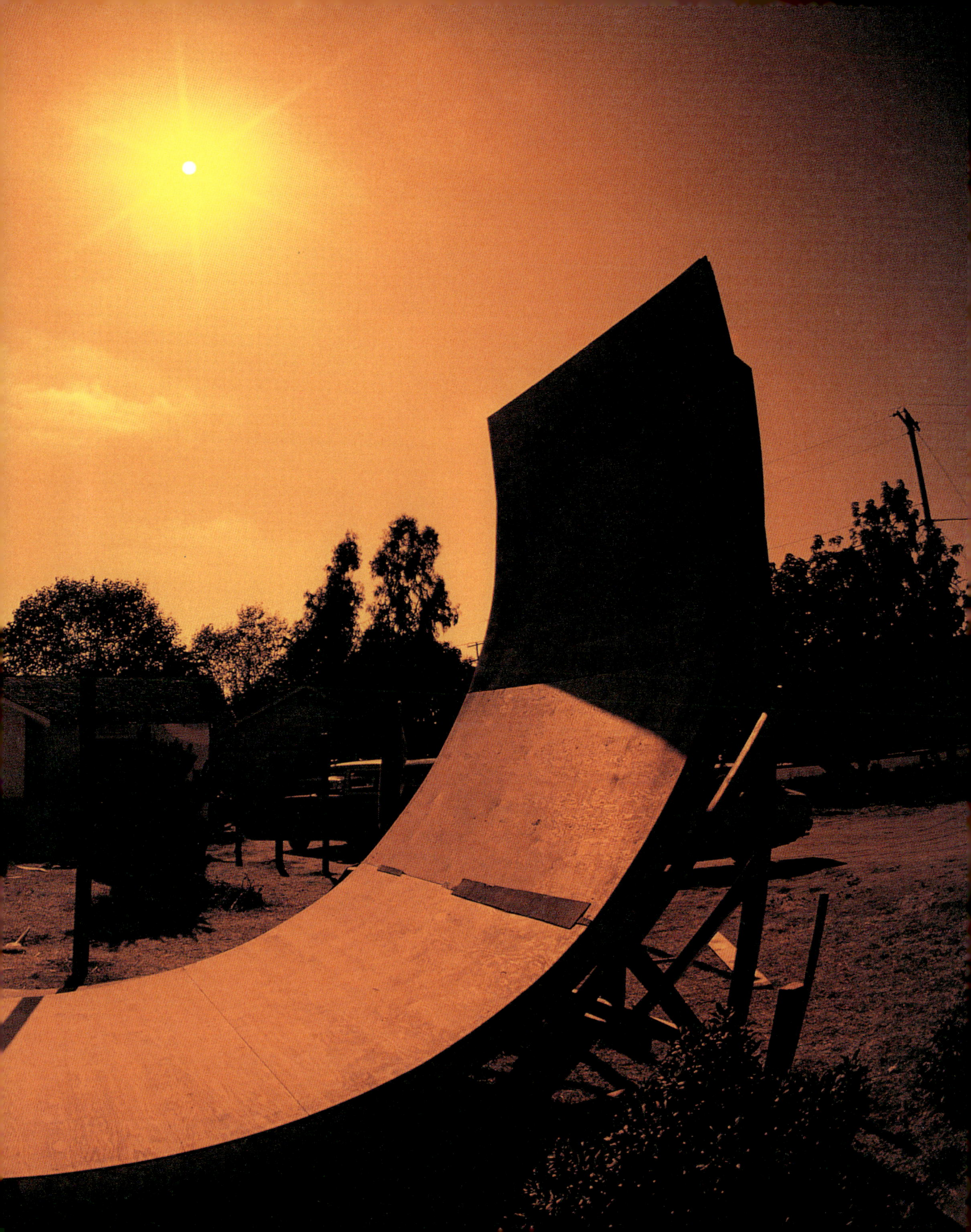

The Blues

The sky-blue boards are where my entire project of collecting 1970s FibreFlex boards began. They are a mix of original and reissued decks, all restored by me. The deeper I went into collecting—and the more I learned—the narrower my definition of what qualifies as part of the core collection became. Aside from one board—"the Mother Ship," as I like to call it, as it was my first acquisition—these blue skateboards now sit just outside the official collection.

Nonetheless, I've put a lot of effort and affection into these boards, and they carry a great deal of personal meaning. I will always keep them and look upon them fondly.

The Blues

1976 OG Cut Out board with OG Gullwing Split Axle trucks and NOS OJ Slalom wheels

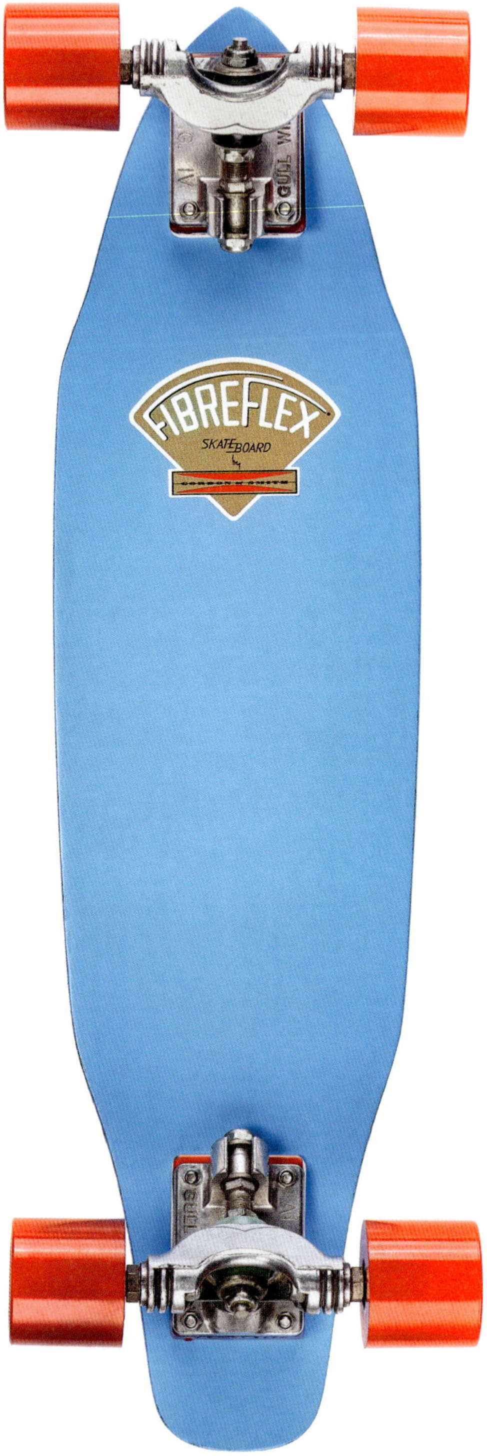

1977 OG Freestyle board with OG ACS 500s trucks and NOS Sims Pure Juice wheels

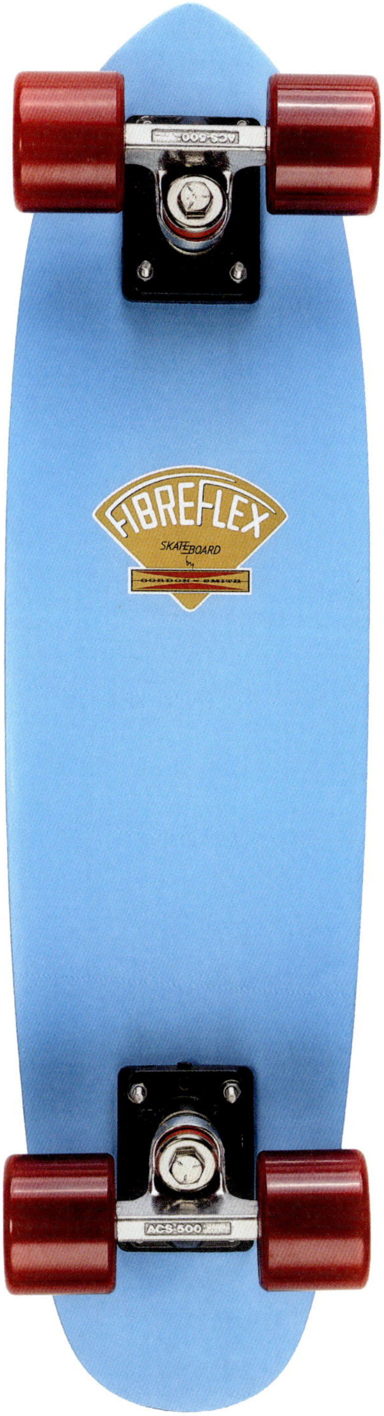

1977 OG 29" Bowlrider with OG Gullwings and NOS Yandall Bowl Roll wheels

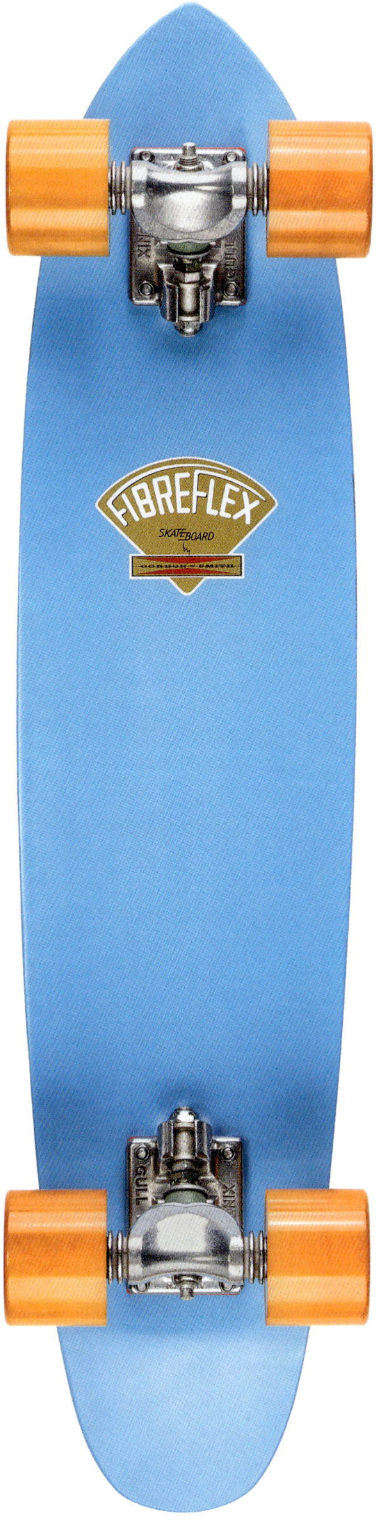

1978 OG 27" Bowlrider with mid tracks and Pacific wheels

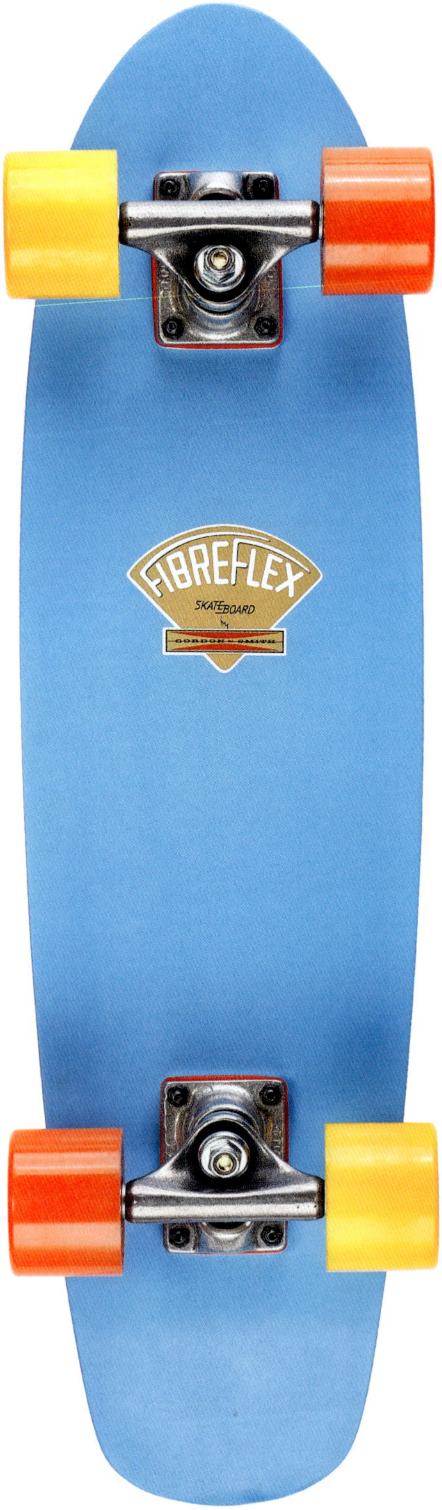

2015 Henry Hester reissue with reissue Tracker Ex trucks and NOS Road Rider 4 wheels

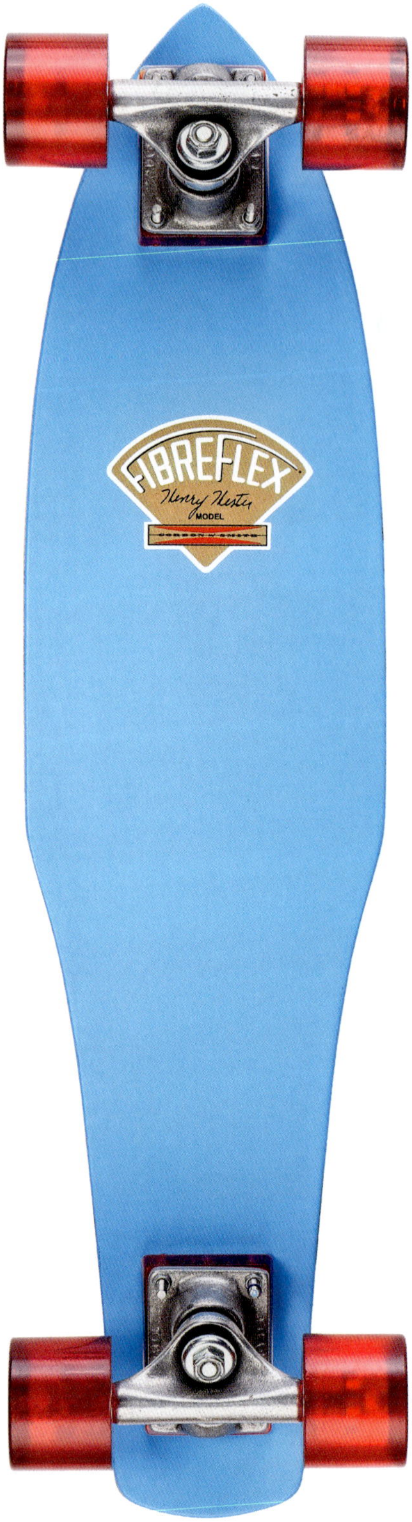

2015 Teamrider reissue with reissue Tracker Ful truck and NOS Powerflex 5 wheels

2005 Dennis Martinez Flying Aces reissue with reissue Six Trucks and NOS green Kryptonic wheels

The Collection

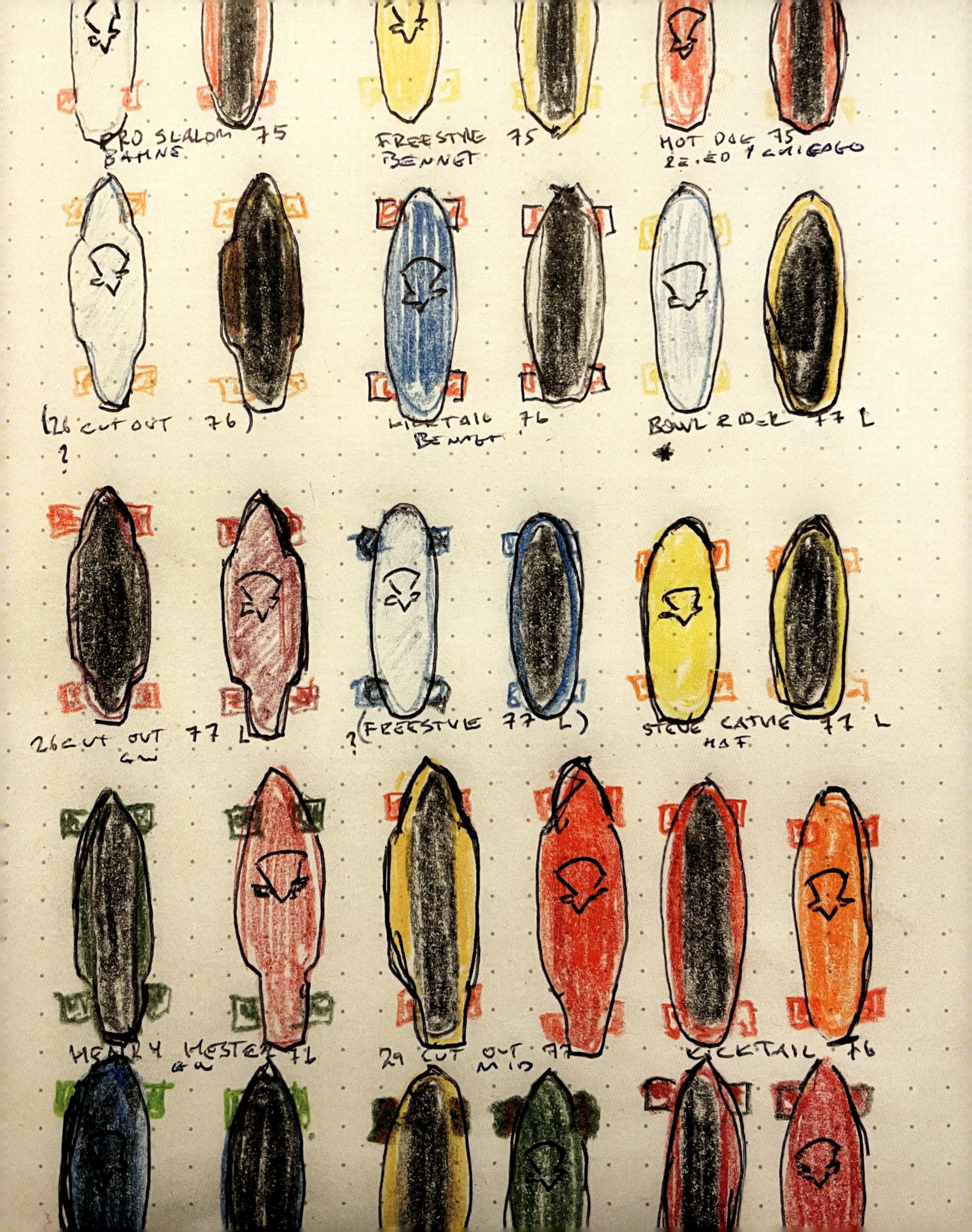

PRO SLALOM 75
BAHNE
FREESTYLE 75
BENNET
HOT DOG 75
(26 CUT OUT 76)
?
KICKTAIL 76
BENNET
BOWL RIDER 77 L
26 CUT OUT 77 L
GW
?(FREESTYLE 77 L)
STEVE CATHIE 77 L
HAF
HENRY HESTER 76
GW
29 CUT OUT 77
MID
KICKTAIL 76

1975 Pro Slalom

"The Beginning"

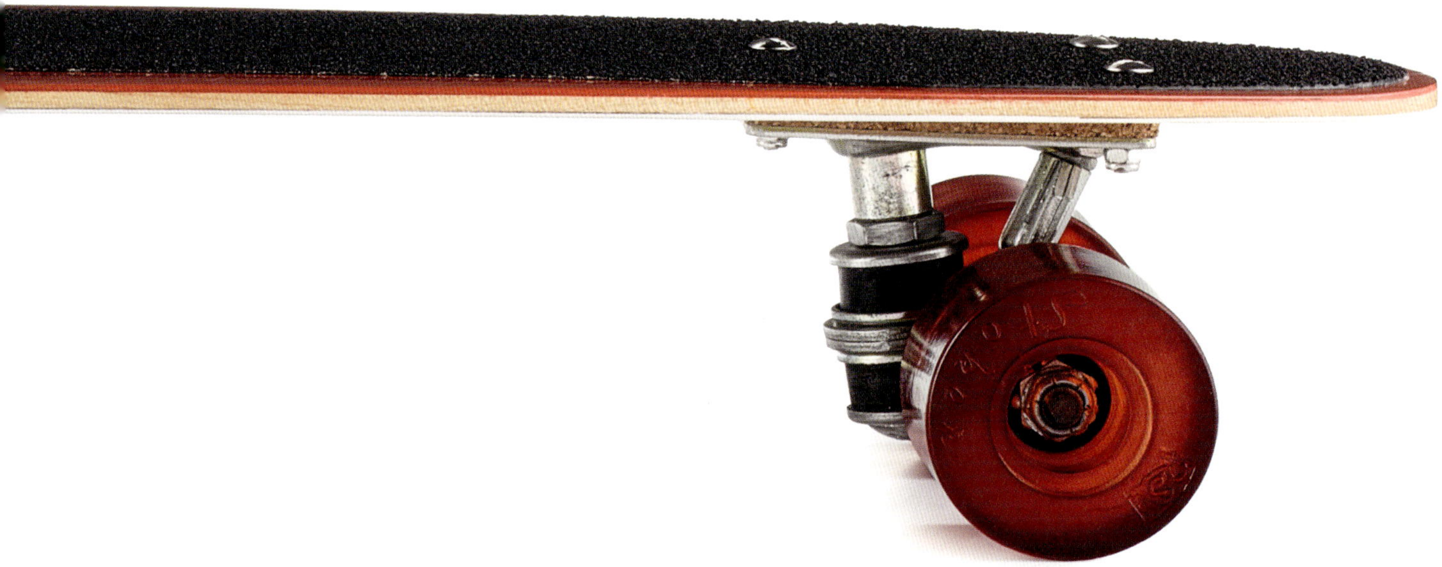

This is the board that put FibreFlex on the map. When the company relaunched in 1975, its focus was on downhill and slalom—the popular styles of skating at the time—and the Pro Slalom quickly became one of the dominant race boards of its era, sharing the podium with the competitor brand Bahne. It was also the first FibreFlex model advertised in the relaunched *SkateBoarder* magazine during summer 1975, marking the true starting point of the brand's impact. This board is set up with Bahne All Steel trucks, cork risers, and RSI Stoker wheels.

Provenance

This 1975 single-ply Pro Slalom was acquired from the English restorer Mark Mayers and refurbished to period-correct condition. The Bahne All Steel trucks are first-generation slalom trucks (Fall 1975), sourced from a California collector; the NOS Roller Sports Stoker wheels match the FibreFlex model shown in the Summer 1975 *SkateBoarder* ad, and were sourced in Australia.

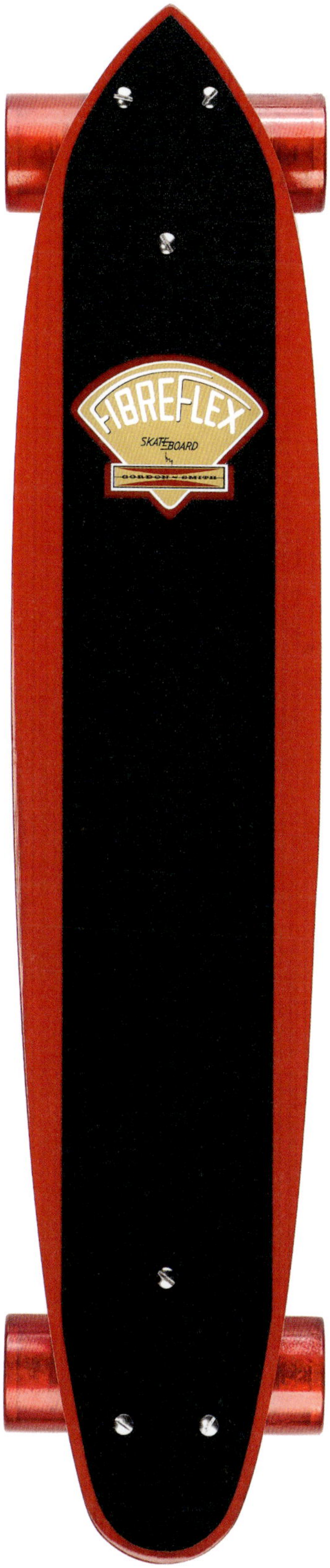

1975 Pro Slalom Specs

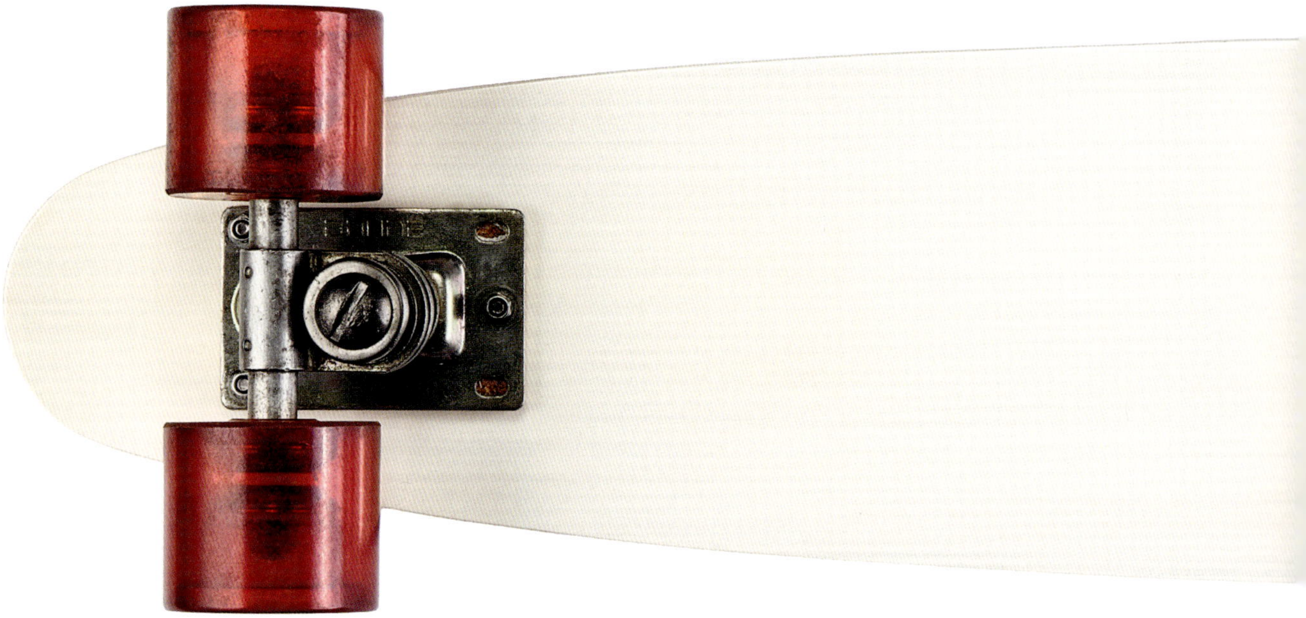

Deck

- Original FibreFlex Pro Slalom
- Maple single ply between two layers of Bo-Tuff
- Length: 28" (71cm)
- Width: 6" (15cm)
- Thickness: ¼" (6.35mm)
- 3M rubber grip tape

Trucks

- NOS Bahne All Steel zinc-chromate slalom / downhill trucks
- Cork risers

Wheels

- NOS RSI Stoker wheels from Roller Sports Inc.
- Diameter: 2.16" (55mm)
- Durometer: 78A
- Loose ball bearings

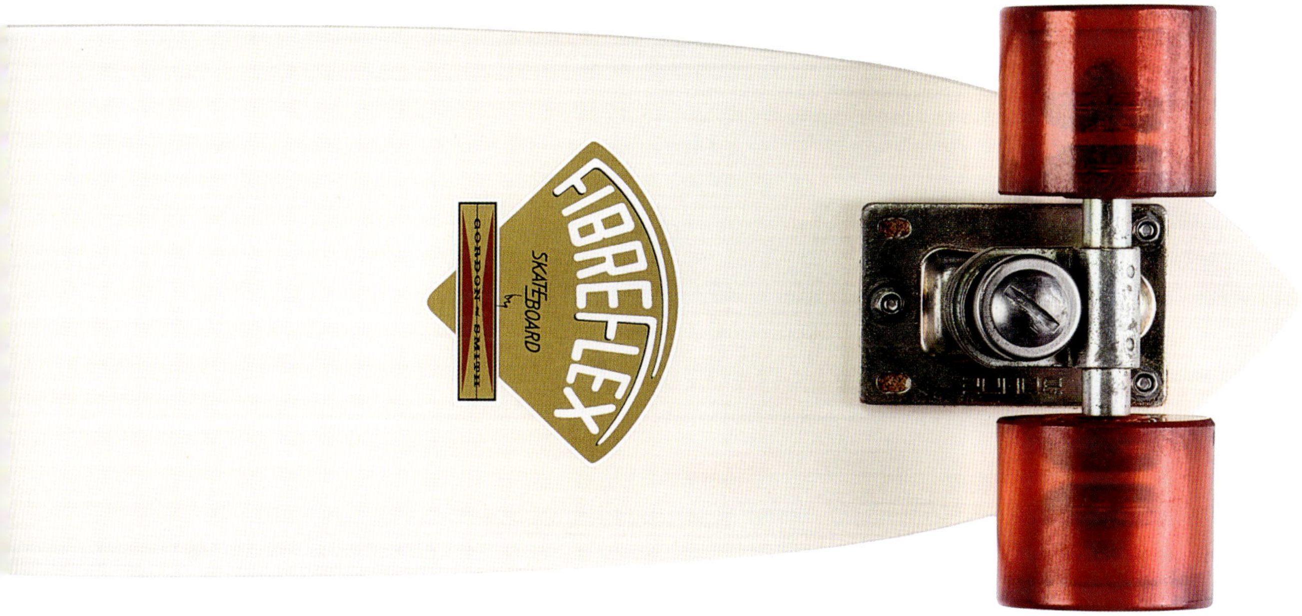

1975

24" Slalom

"The Cheat"

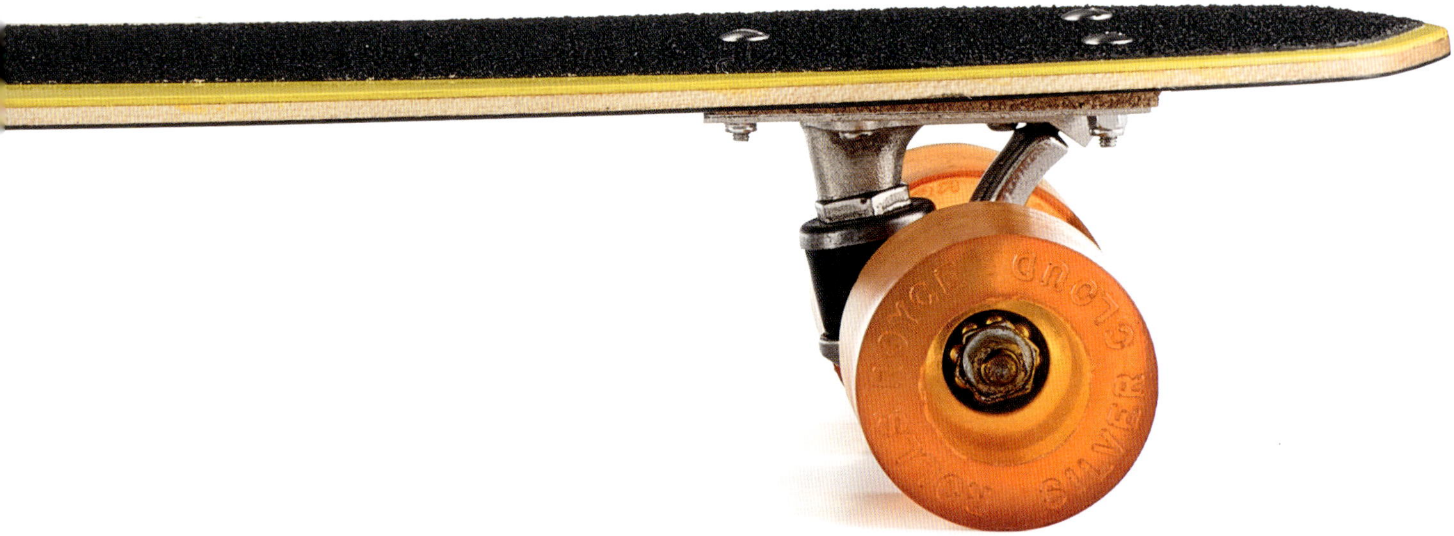

The 24" Slalom was the second FibreFlex deck to be commercialized, and is by far the rarest of them all. Only an estimated 14–20 originals are known to exist globally. Most are flat; a few rare specimens show a slight camber. It was never pictured in advertising, and only mentioned in the Summer 1975 FibreFlex ad in *SkateBoarder* as "Also available in a 24" version." This complete "setup" (i.e. skateboard) uses OG Chicago trucks with cork risers and NOS Rolls Royce Silver Cloud wheels. In addition to this model, there was also the 28" Pro Slalom version.

Provenance

I call this setup The Cheat, because the donor board is, I believe, actually a 1975 Freestyle that was refurbished into an identical copy of the original 24” Slalom. It’s fitted with OG Chicago trucks from a US collector and NOS 1975 Rolls Royce Silver Shadow wheels from an Australian seller. Loose ball bearings complete the setup.

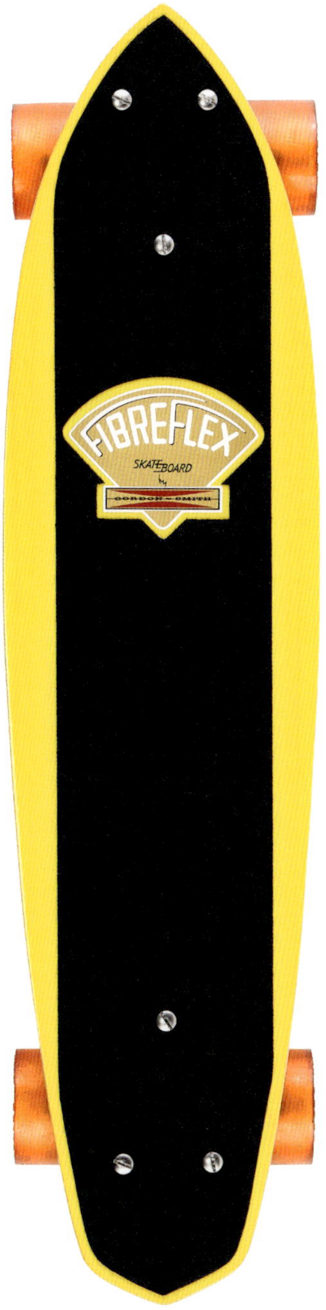

1975 24" Slalom Specs

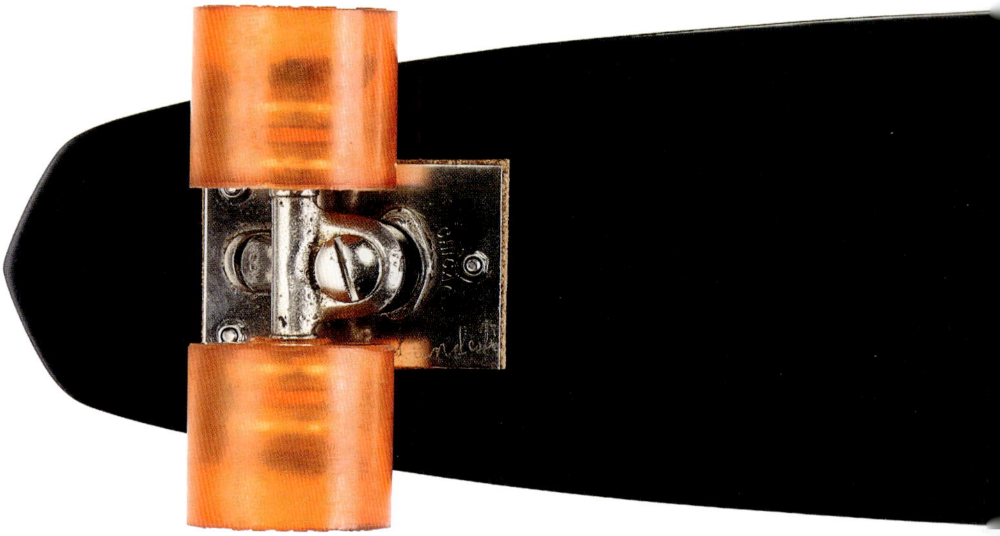

Deck

- Donor FibreFlex, probably a Freestyle, reshaped to a 24" (61cm) Slalom
- Maple single ply between two layers of Bo-Tuff
- Length: 24" (61cm)
- Width: 6" (15cm)
- Thickness: ¼" (6.35mm)
- 3M rubber grip tape

Trucks

- OG Chicago trucks
- Cork risers

Wheels

- NOS Rolls Royce Silver Cloud
- Diameter: 2.2" (56mm)
- Durometer: High 70s
- Loose ball bearings

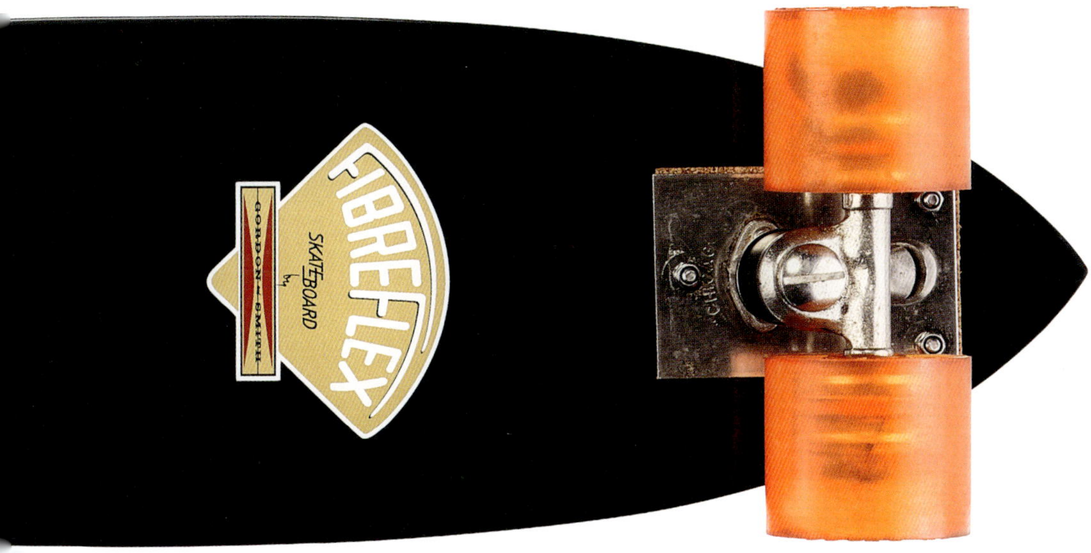

1975 Freestyle

"A Streaker"

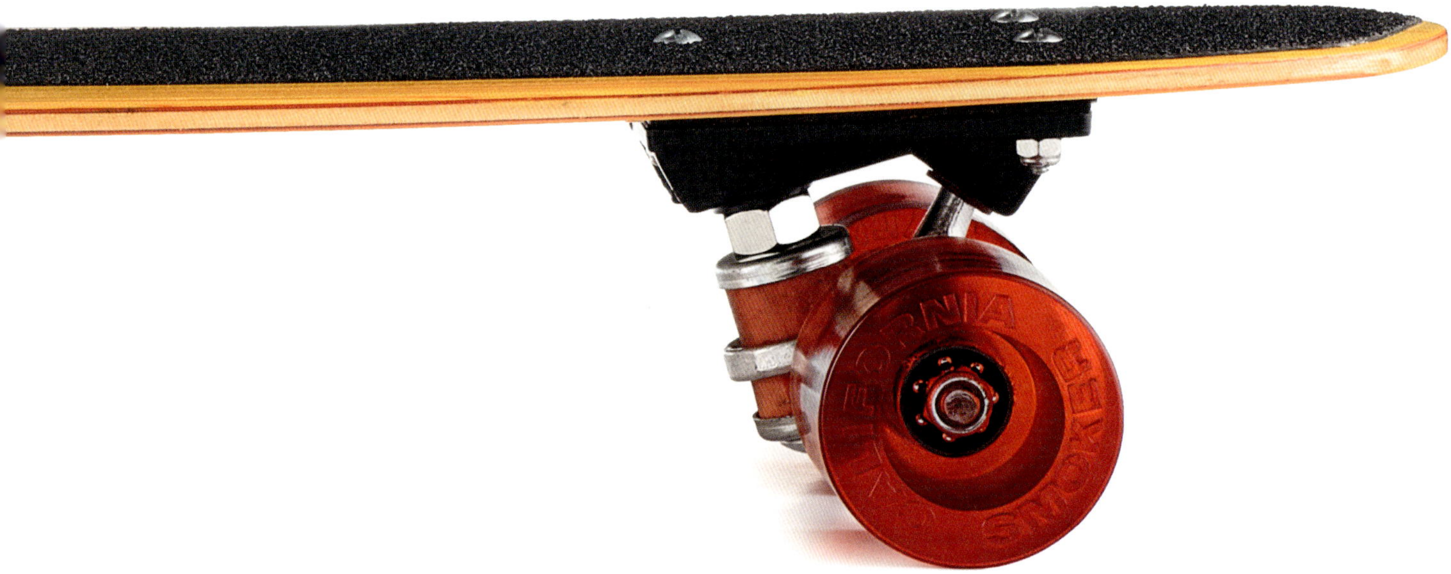

The third board in the 1975 FibreFlex lineup is a freestyle deck. It has no kicktail, just a flat outline with a slight spoon "rocker" (i.e. a dip in the middle). It was advertised in the fall 1975 issue of *SkateBoarder* as a board for "freeform and trick performance: 360s and wheelies." The color on this example has been fully restored, revealing the rare "streaker" deck striping. It's set up with original Bennett Hijacker trucks—one of the first truly modern skateboard trucks—with rubber risers and NOS California Smoker wheels on loose ball bearings.

Provenance

Acquired from an Australian collector, who sold it with OG Bennett Hijackers and NOS Silver Shadow wheels. Although I initially believed the board to be NOS, it is in fact a refurbished original, restored by English restorer Mark Mayers.

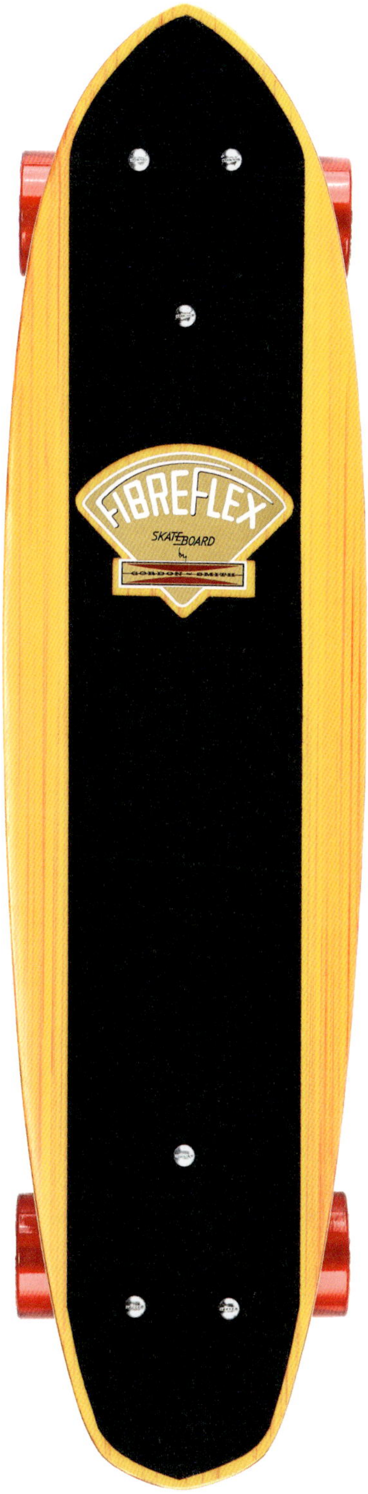

1975 Freestyle Specs

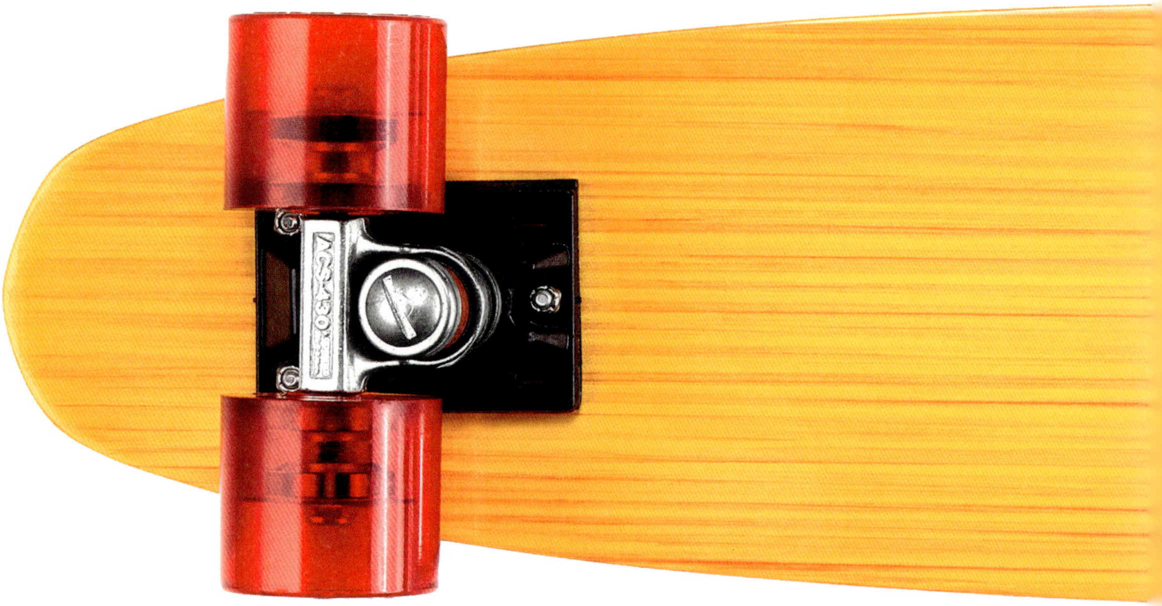

Deck

- OG FibreFlex Freestyle
- Maple single ply between two layers of Bo-Tuff
- Length: 26” (66cm)
- Width: 6½” (16cm)
- Thickness: ¼” (6.35mm)
- 3M rubber grip tape

Trucks

- OG Bennett Hijackers
- Rubber risers

Wheels

- NOS California Smoker
- Diameter: 2.2” (56mm)
- Durometer: High 70s
- Loose ball bearings

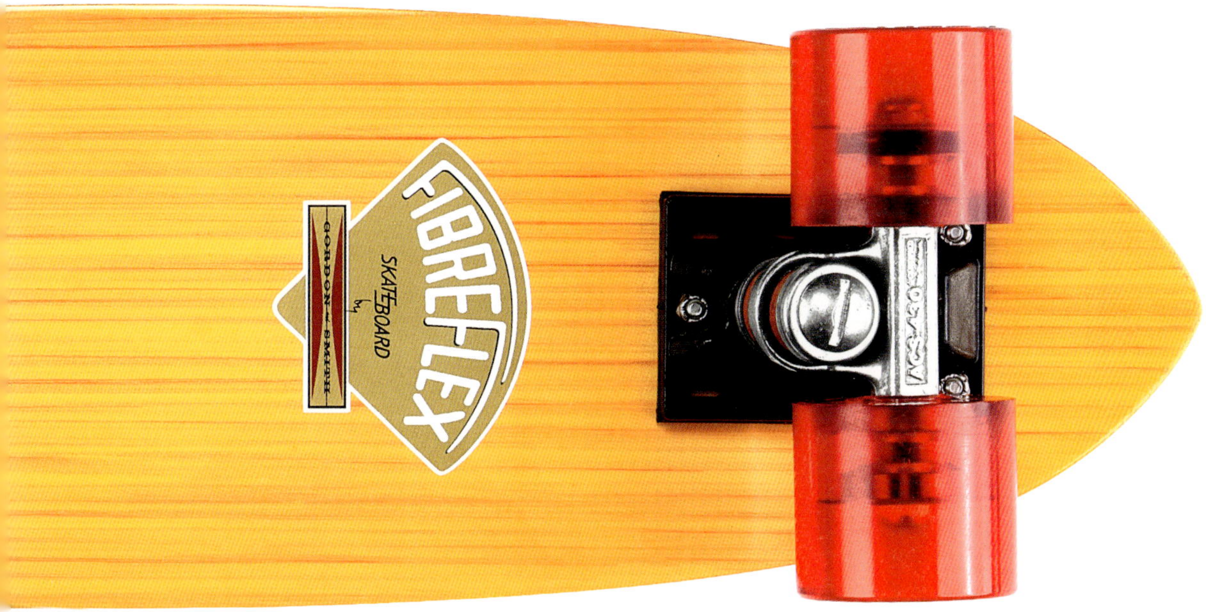

1976

Kicktail

"The Flippy Kicktail"

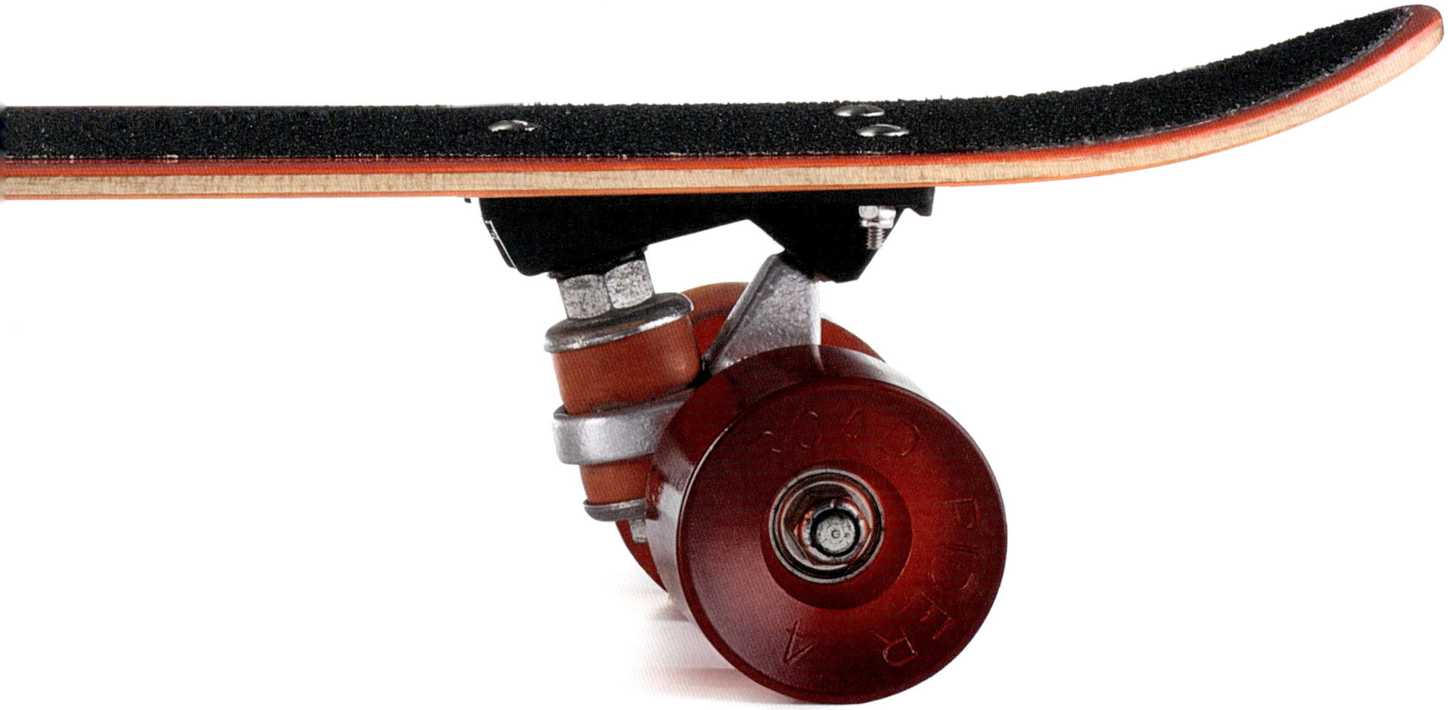

This was FibreFlex's first freestyle deck with a kicktail. It is a narrow 6" (15cm) board with a distinct, snappy tail. Initially it had a square tail, before developing a round one. In 1976, most FibreFlex models used single maple cores, even though a dual-core concept was advertised. By late 1976, the first triple-ply cores may have appeared, but this deck is single ply. This complete is set up with Bennett Hijackers, no risers, and Road Rider 4 wheels on sealed SKF bearings.

Provenance

The deck was acquired, restored to its original colors, from Pacific Coast Vintage in Paris. Restorer Mark Mayers returned it to a factory-like condition. The trucks OG Bennett Hijackers and NOS Road Rider 4 wheels were purchased from US and French collectors, respectively.

1976 Kicktail Specs

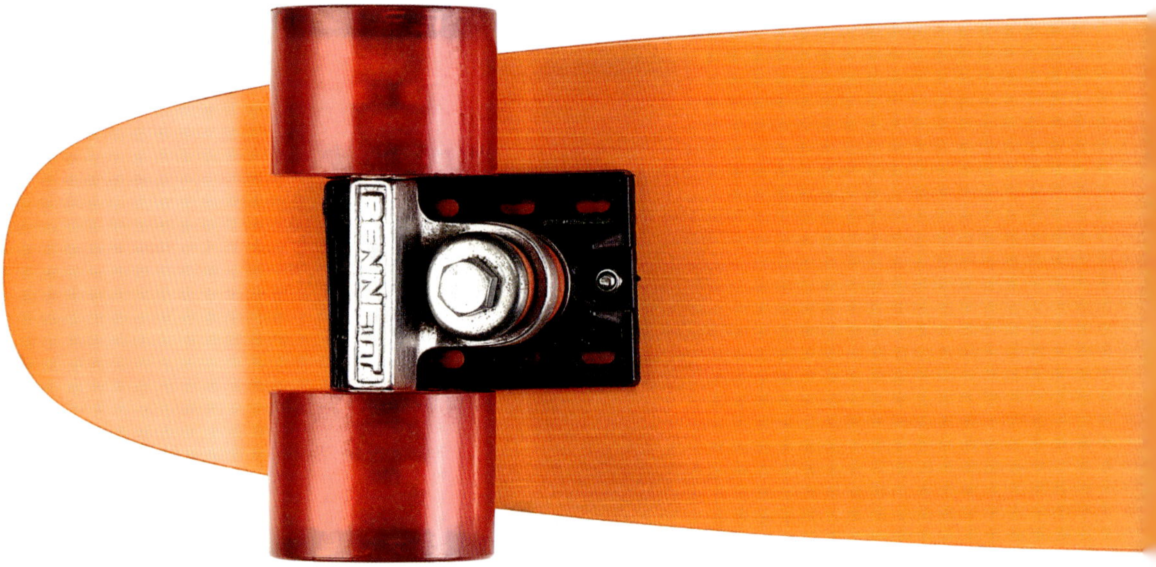

Deck

- OG FibreFlex Kicktail ("flippy tail")
- Maple single ply between two layers of Bo-Tuff
- Length: 26" (66cm)
- Width: 6" (15cm)
- Thickness: ¼" (6.35mm)
- 3M rubber grip tape

Trucks

- OG Bennett Hijackers
- No risers

Wheels

- NOS Road Rider 4
- Durometer: 2.36" (60mm)
- Diameter: 78-82A
- Sealed SKF bearings

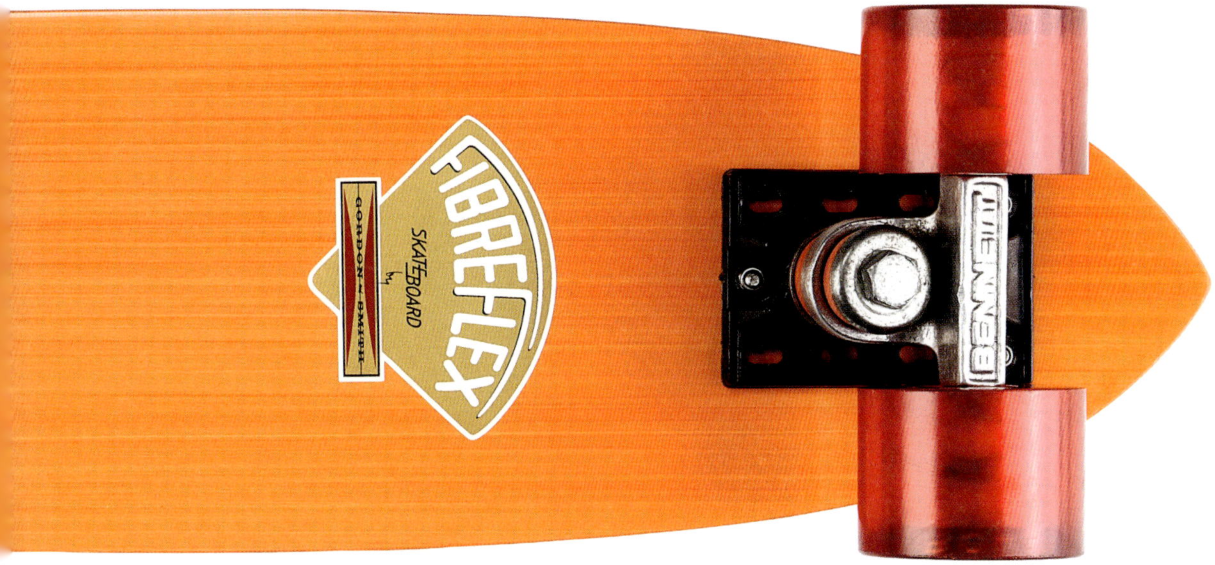

1976 Henry Hester

"The Speed Machine"

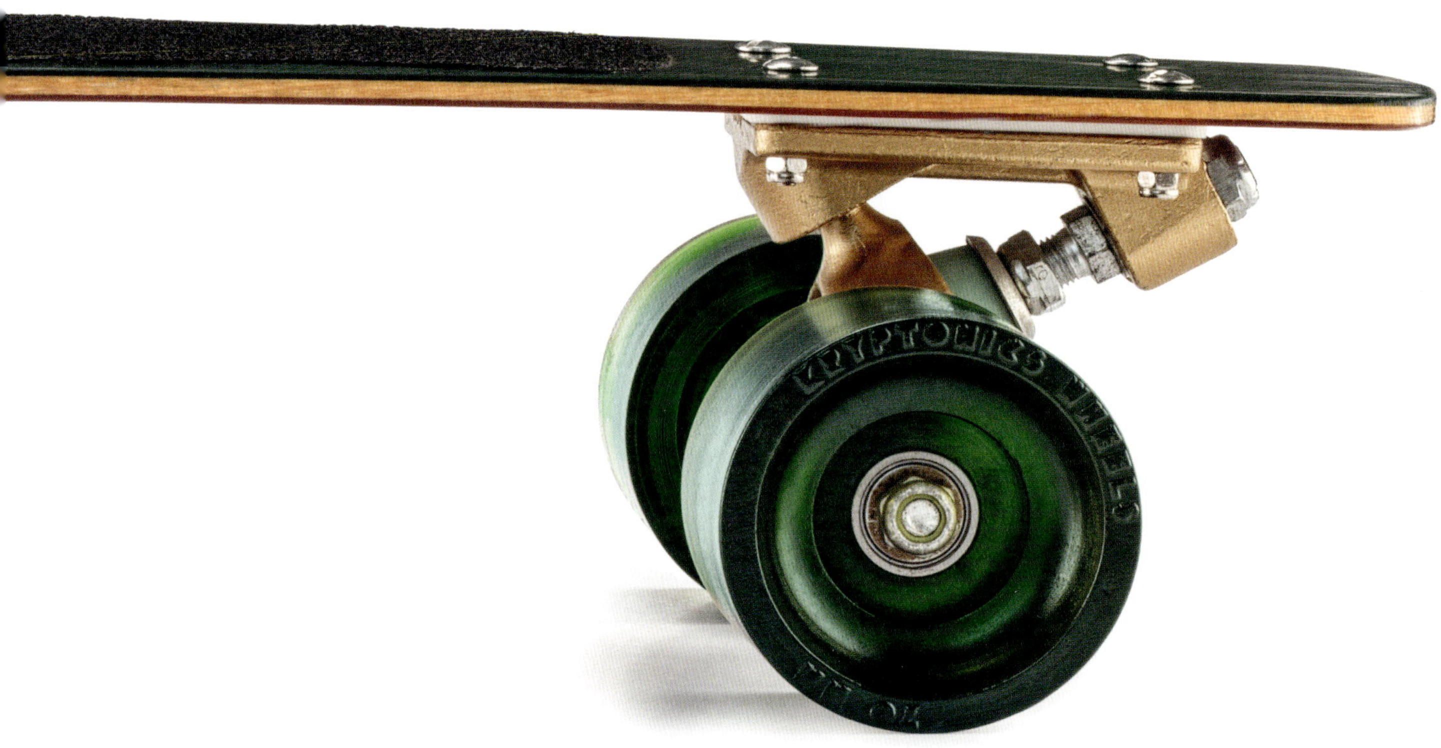

FibreFlex's first signature model, it was designed for one of slalom's true megastars, Henry Hester. Launched late 1976, it was the fourth slalom deck in the FibreFlex lineup after the Pro Slalom, 24" Slalom, and Cut Out. It subsequently became the industry template for signature models. Early Hesters were single ply, but later transitioned to a triple ply. This one has golden first-generation Gullwing Split Axle trucks and green first gen Kryptonic wheels.

Provenance

The NOS Henry Hester Slalom deck and NOS Kryptonic wheels were acquired from an online collector. The board was originally purchased in the UK in 1976. The NOS Gullwing Split Axle trucks were acquired from a Swiss collector.

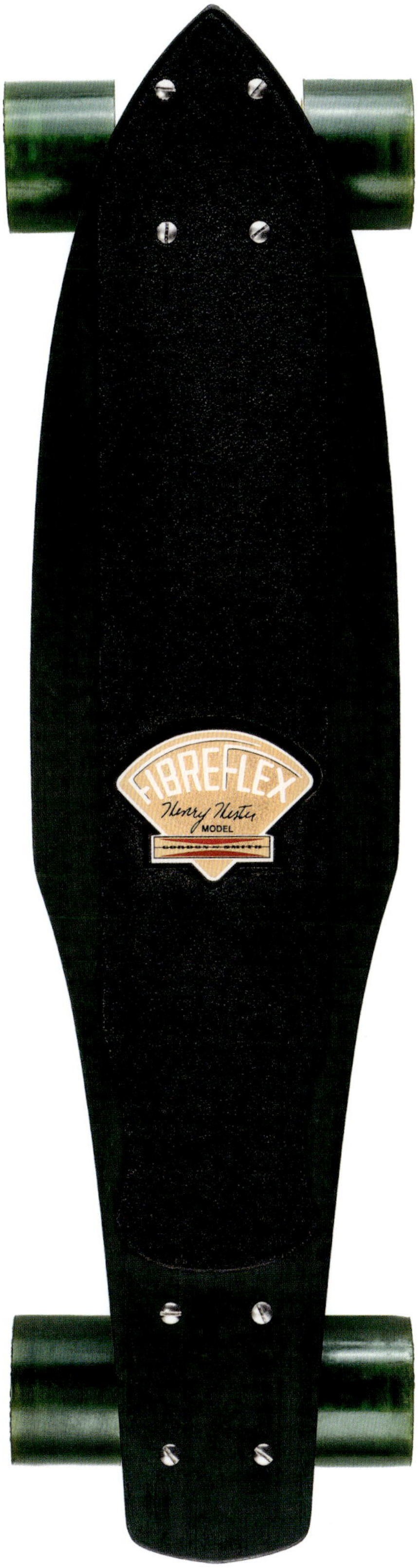

1976 Henry Hester Specs

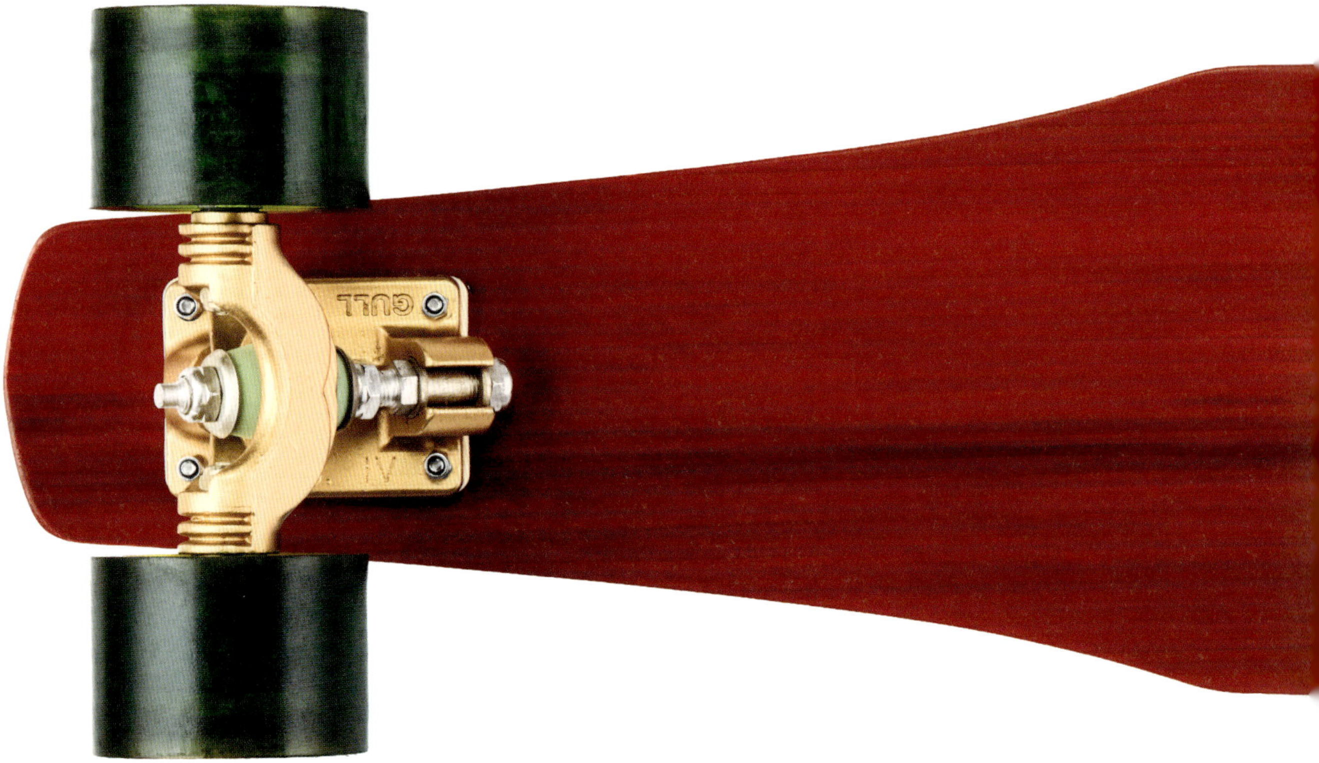

Deck

- NOS Henry Hester Slalom deck
- Single ply between two layers of Bo-Tuff
- Length: 28" (71cm)
- Width: 6 ½" (16cm)
- Thickness: ¼" (6.35mm)
- 3M rubber model-specific design grip tape

Trucks

- NOS first-generation Gullwing Split Axle (gold)
- Thin rubber pads between truck and deck

Wheels

- NOS first-generation green Kryptonics
- Diameter: 2.75" (70mm)
- Durometer: 85A
- Sealed SKF Bearings

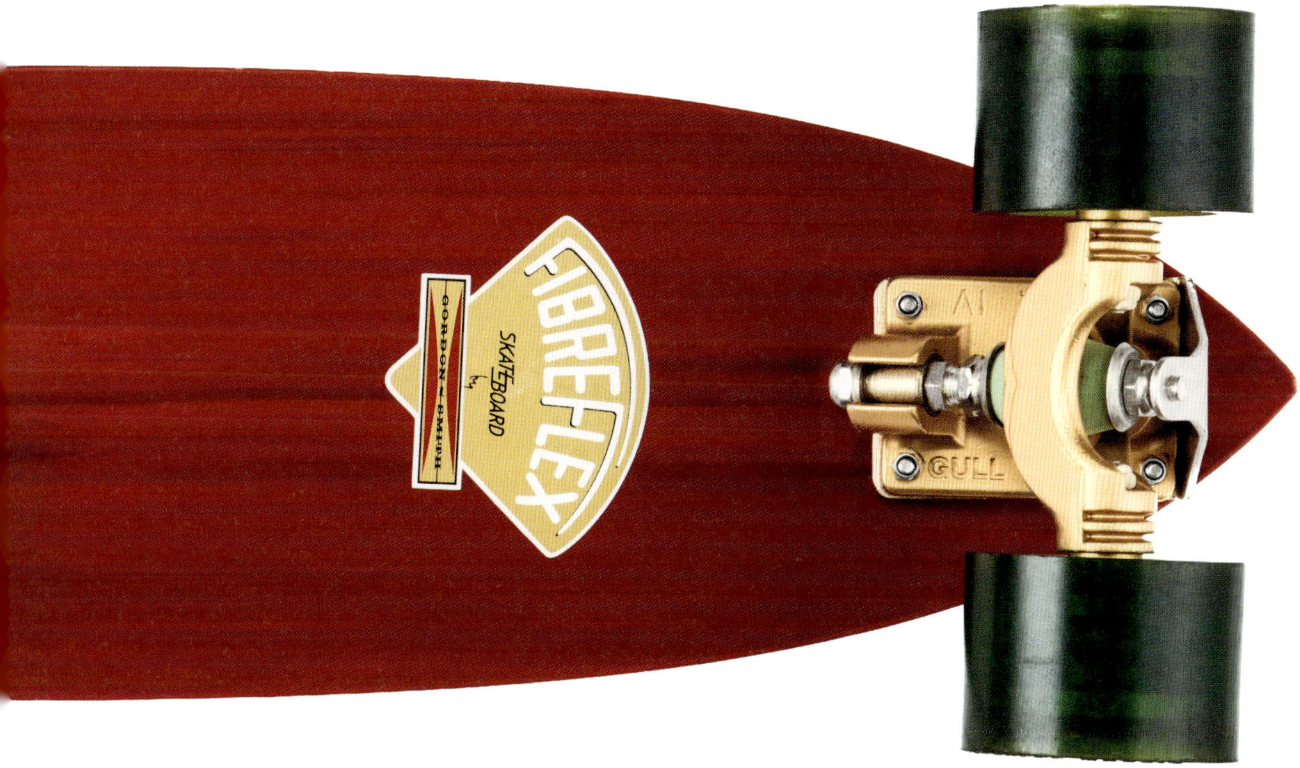

1977

Kicktail

"Year of '77"

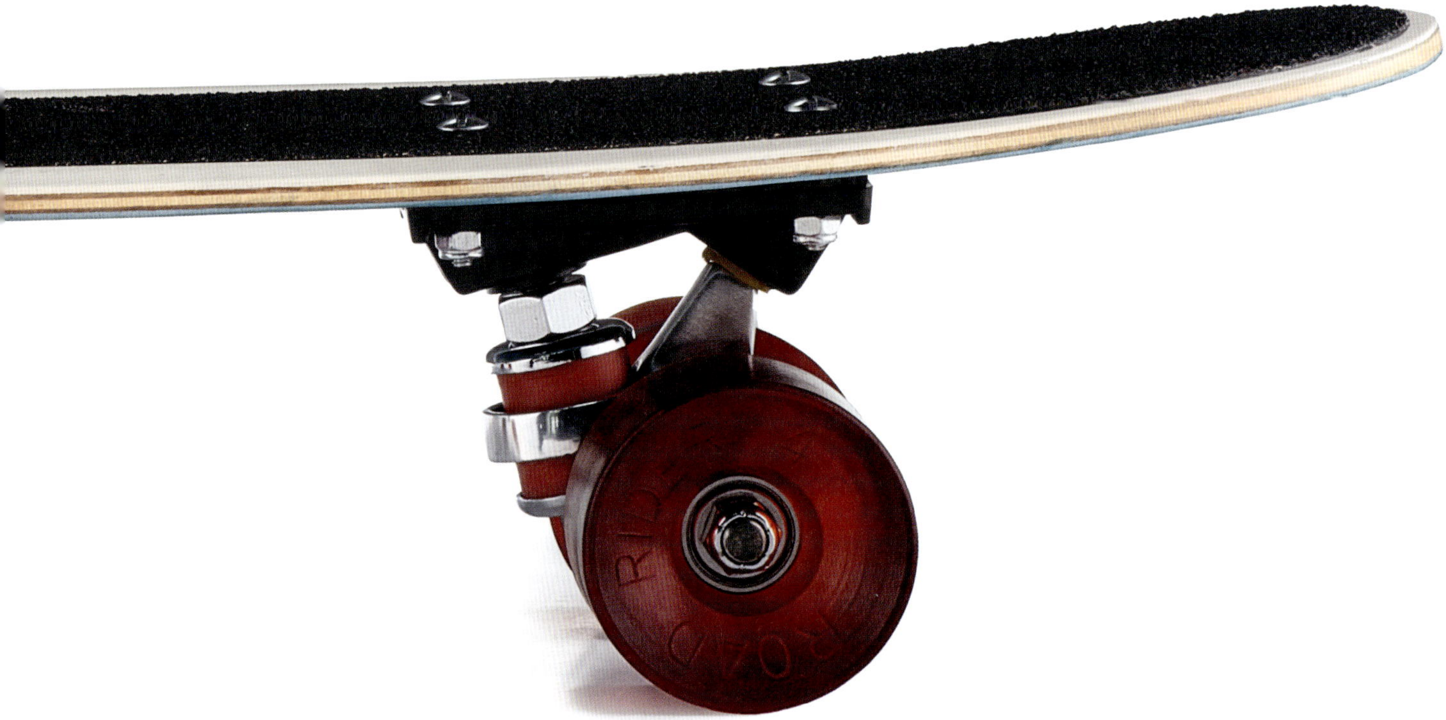

This next-generation Kicktail was launched in early 1977, and visually echoes the iconic Bowlrider. The Kicktail gained half an inch in width, moving to a three-ply maple core sandwiched between layers of Bo-Tuff. It was a relatively flexible board, aimed at freestyle riders who still wanted "life" and bounce in their decks. This example is an OG deck, refurbished, fitted with OG Bennett Hijackers and NOS Road Rider 4 wheels. The model came in two lengths: 25" (63cm) and 27" (69cm). This is the 25".

Provenance

This deck, acquired from a collector in Australia, has been refurbished by English restorer Mark Mayers. It is known as a "streaker," one of a rare number of FibreFlex decks with very distinct tone-on-tone striping. The NOS Road Rider 4 wheels were sourced from a UK collector.

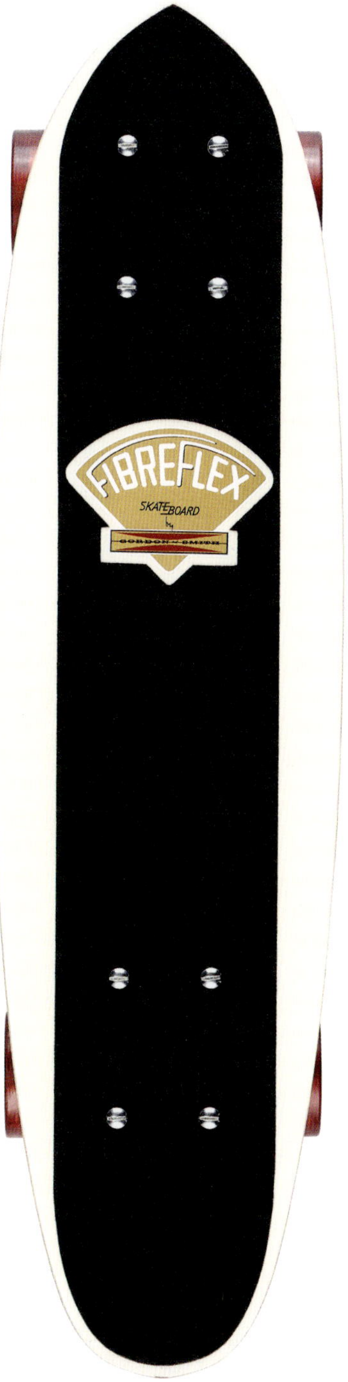

1977 Kicktail Specs

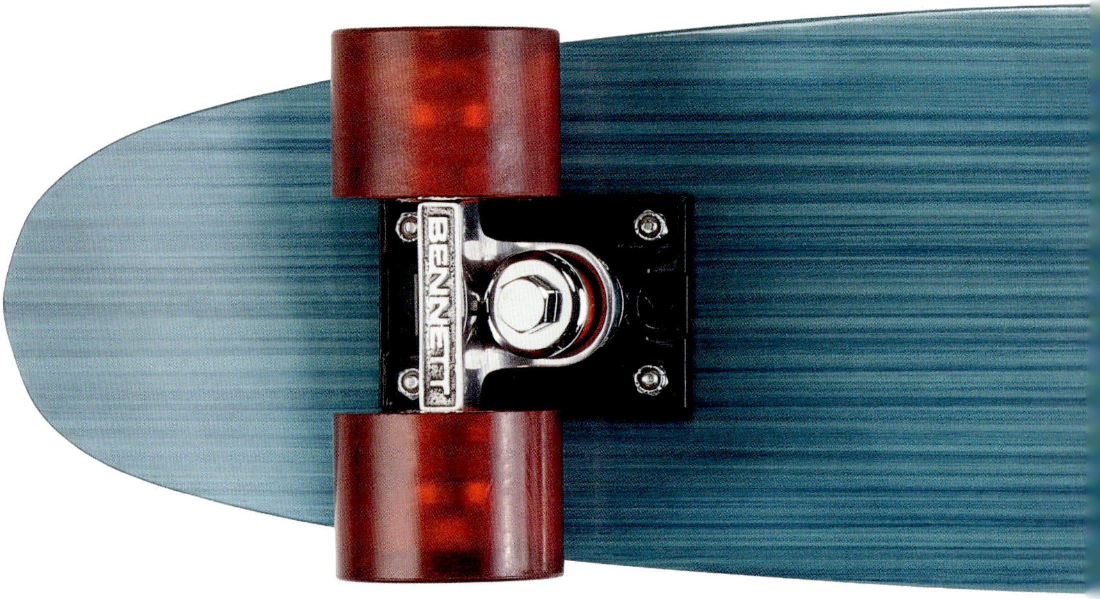

Deck

- OG refurbished Kicktail freestyle deck
- Triple-ply maple core with Bo-Tuff on both sides
- Length: 25" (63cm)
- Width: 6½" (16cm)
- Thickness: ¼" (6.35mm)
- 3M rubber grip tape

Trucks

- NOS Bennett Hijackers
- No risers

Wheels

- NOS Road Rider 4s
- Diameter: 2.36" (60mm)
- Durometer: 78-82A
- Sealed SKF Bearings

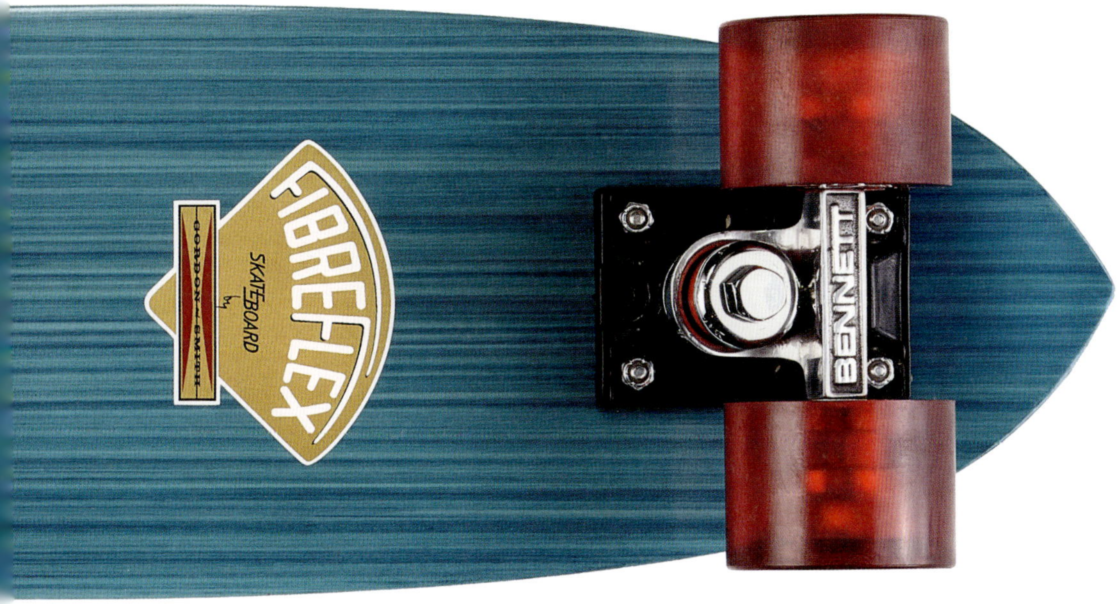

1977

Freestyle

"The Mother Ship"

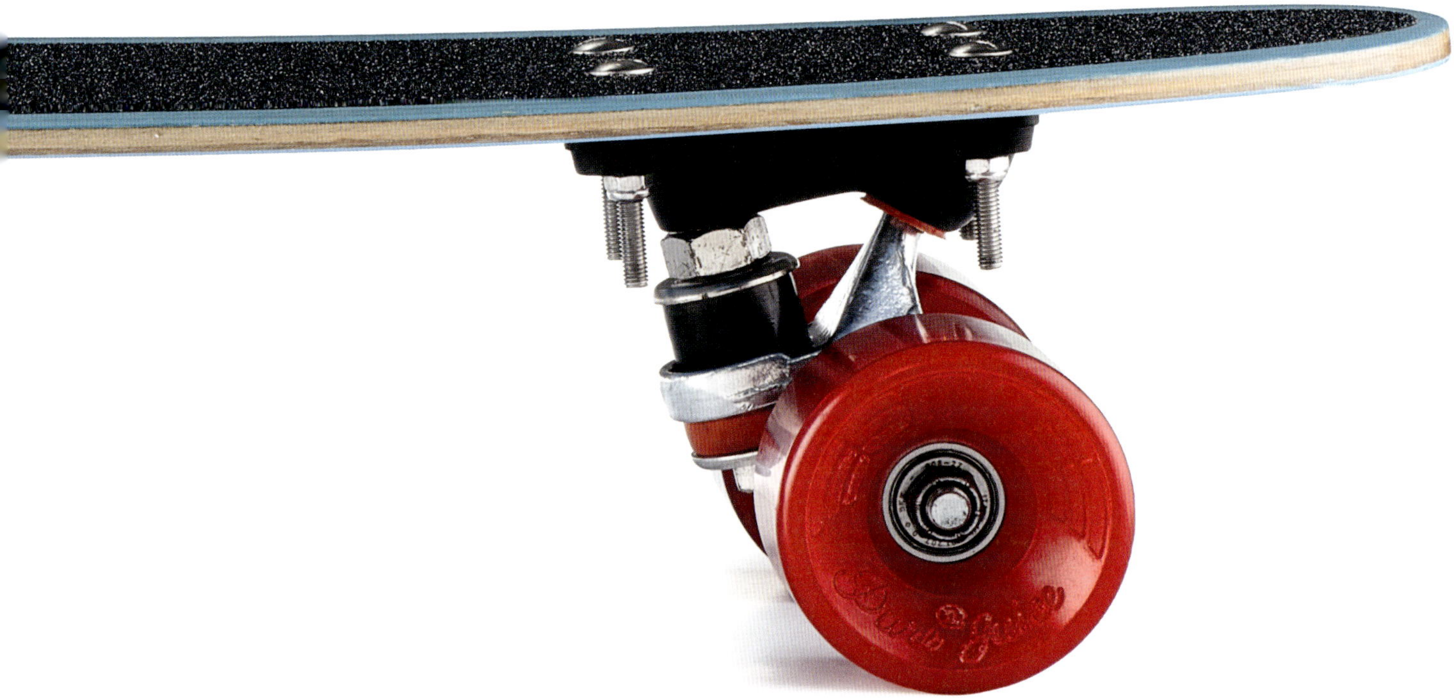

This Freestyle is the next generation of flat FibreFlex freestyle decks without a kicktail. It has a gentle rocker along the length, and dates from late 1977, when FibreFlex updated their grip tape approach—moving from the narrow 3M rubber strip to a more conventional mineral sparkle grip with a fuller coverage pattern. This model uses a triple-ply maple core with Bo-Tuff top and bottom, and at ¼" is still thin and flexible. The setup features NOS ACS 500 trucks and NOS Sims Pure Juice wheels.

Provenance

This is the board that re-ignited my passion. I found it in a “leftover” pile at a secondhand store and instantly felt like my 13-year-old self had woken up. I grabbed it and brought it home. It became my first refurbishment project and the first board in my complete original FibreFlex collection. The NOS Sims Pure Juice came from Pacific Coast Vintage in Paris, and the NOS ACS 500 trucks were found on eBay in the US.

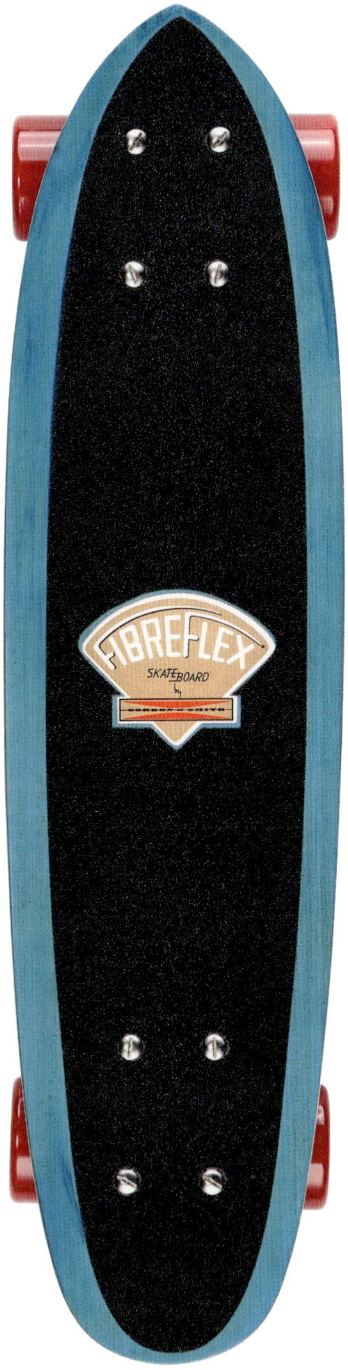

1977 Freestyle Specs

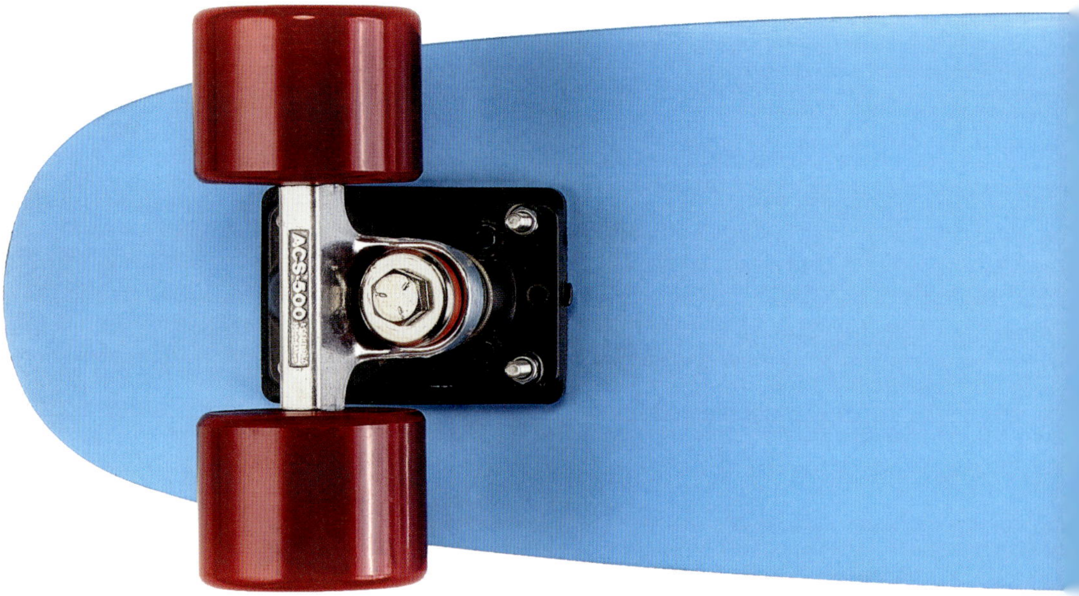

Deck

- OG refurbished Freestyle deck
- Triple-ply core with Bo-Tuff on both sides
- Length: 25" (63cm)
- Width: 6½" (16cm)
- Thickness: ¼" (6.35mm)
- Mineral sparkle grip tape

Trucks

- NOS ACS 500
- White rubber risers

Wheels

- NOS Sims Pure Juice
- Diameter: 2.44" (62mm)
- Durometer: High 70s
- Sealed SKF Bearings

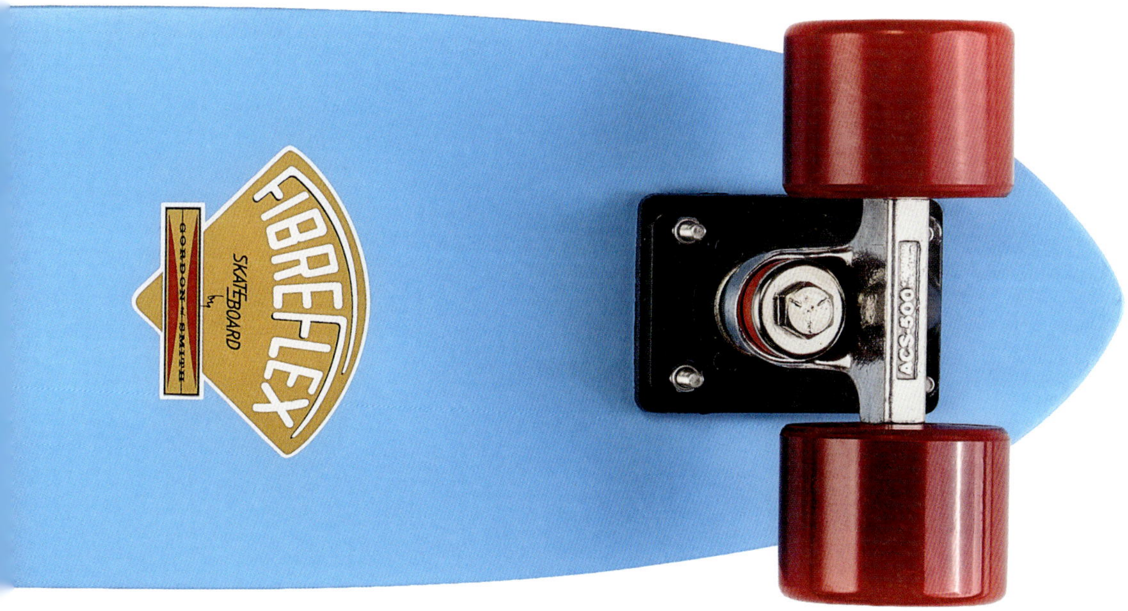

1977 Bowlrider

"The Hen's Teeth"

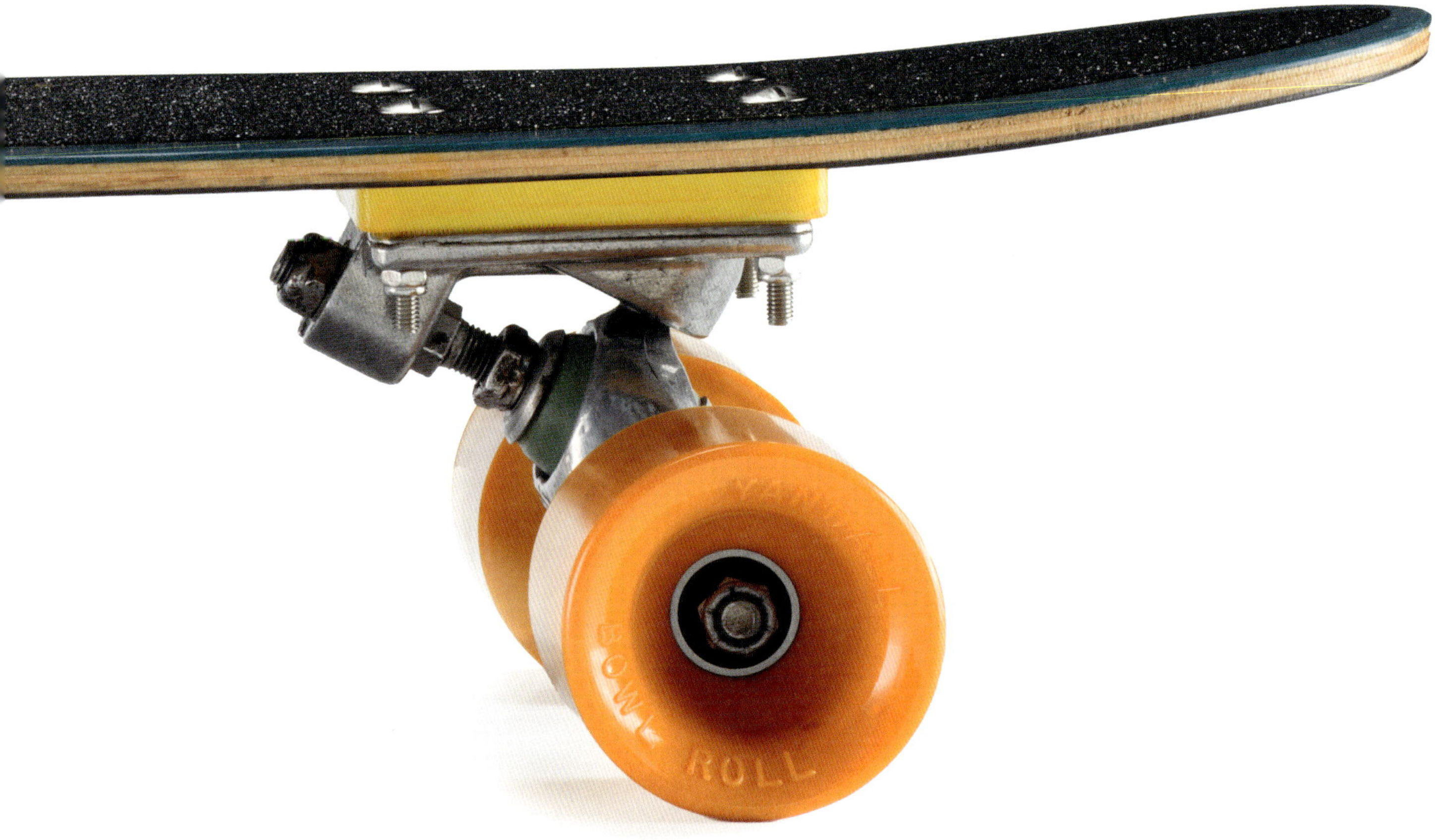

The Bowlrider is FibreFlex's breakthrough vertical board and one of the brand's most successful models. This example is a second-generation 1977 model. The first-generation versions still used the 3M rubber strip; this one has mineral sparkle grip. Vert skaters wanted stiffer decks, so the Bowlrider was introduced with the thicker and stiffer "Stifflex" triple ply with Bo-Tuff. This setup features NOS Gullwing Phoenix trucks and NOS Yandall Bowl Roll wheels.

Provenance

The deck, which is NOS and probably second grade, was acquired from an online UK vendor. The NOS Gullwing Phoenix trucks, developed for "grinding" (i.e. sliding along a surface on the trucks themselves) concrete pools, came from a French collector. The NOS Yandall Bowl Roll wheels were purchased from an Australian seller.

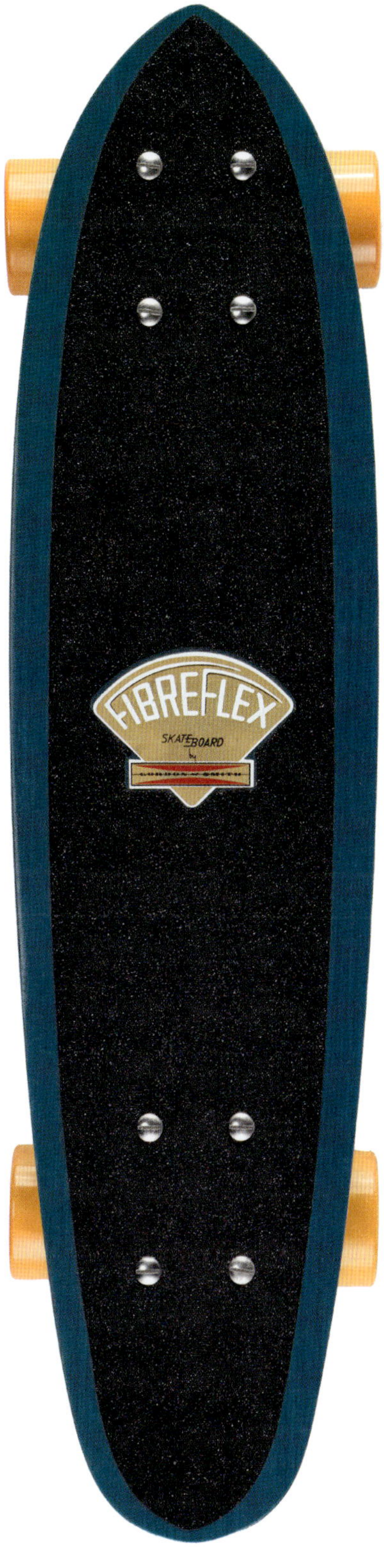

1977 Bowl Rider Specs

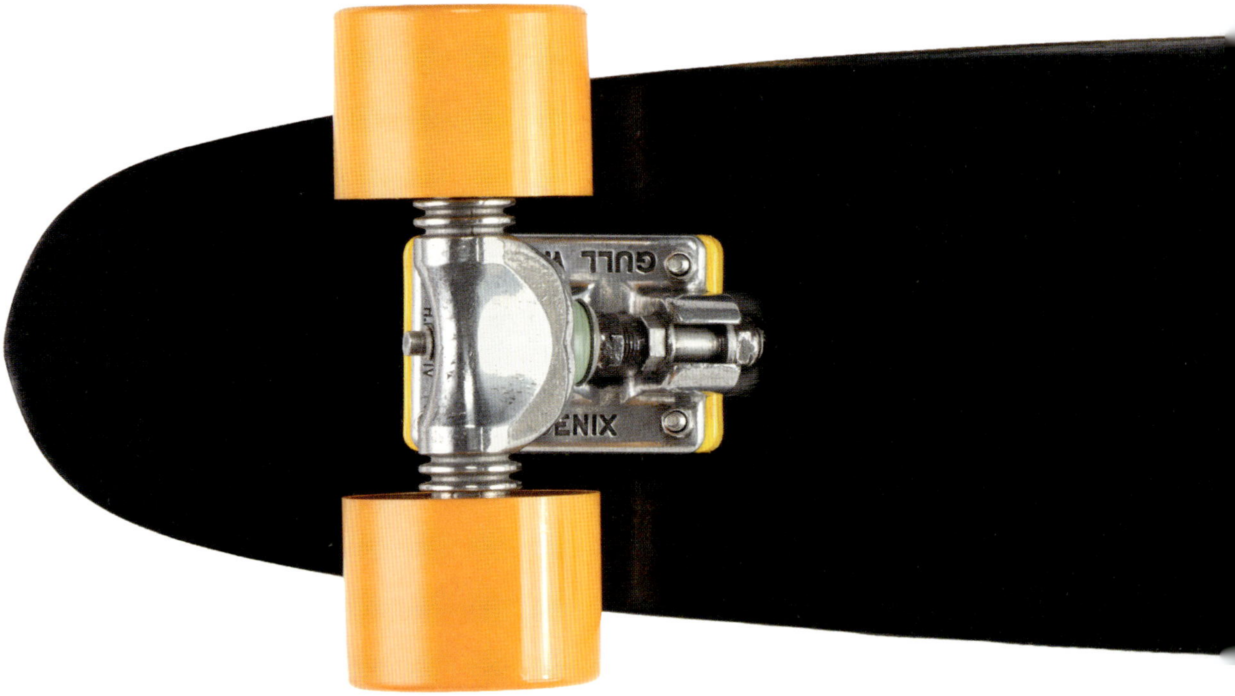

Deck

- OG refurbished Bowlrider deck
- Triple ply "Stifflex" core with Bo-Tuff on both sides
- Length: 27"(69cm)
- Width: 6½" (16cm)
- Thickness: ⁵⁄₁₆" (7.94mm)
- Mineral sparkle grip tape

Trucks

- NOS Gullwing Phoenix
- Urethane risers

Wheels

- NOS Yandall Bowl Rolls
- Diameter: 2.5" (64mm)
- Durometer: 88A
- SKF Sealed Bearings

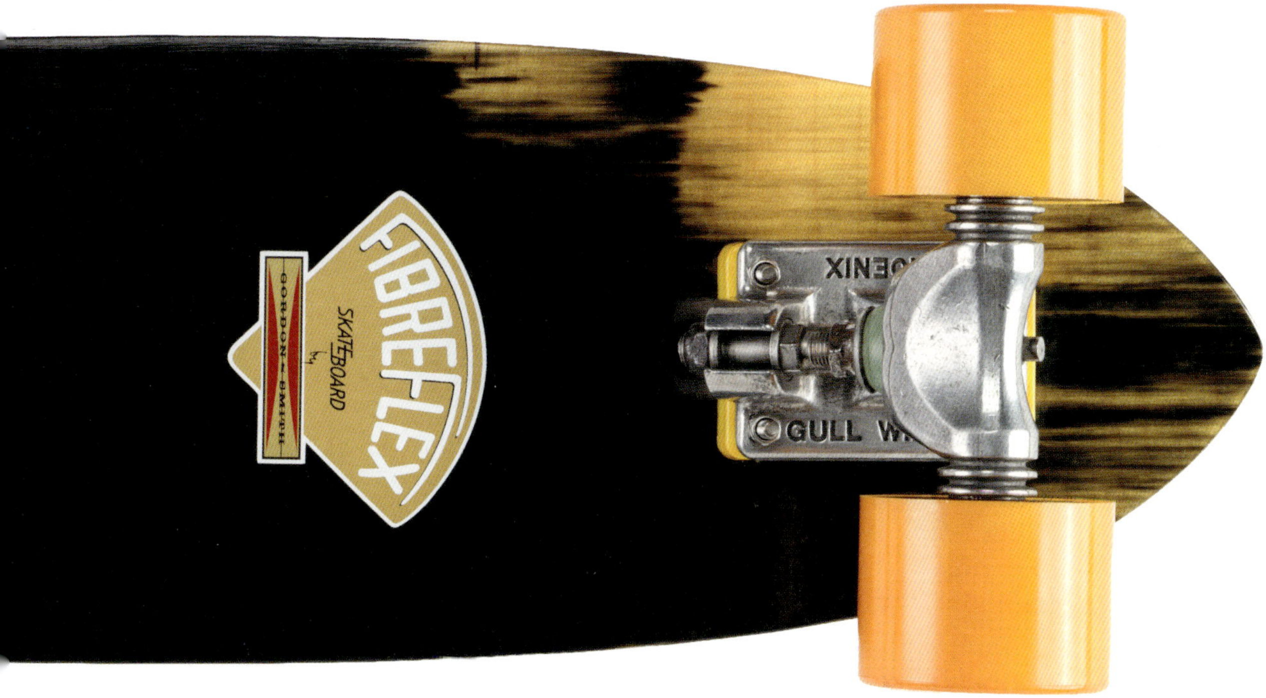

1977 Cut Out

"Pure Racing"

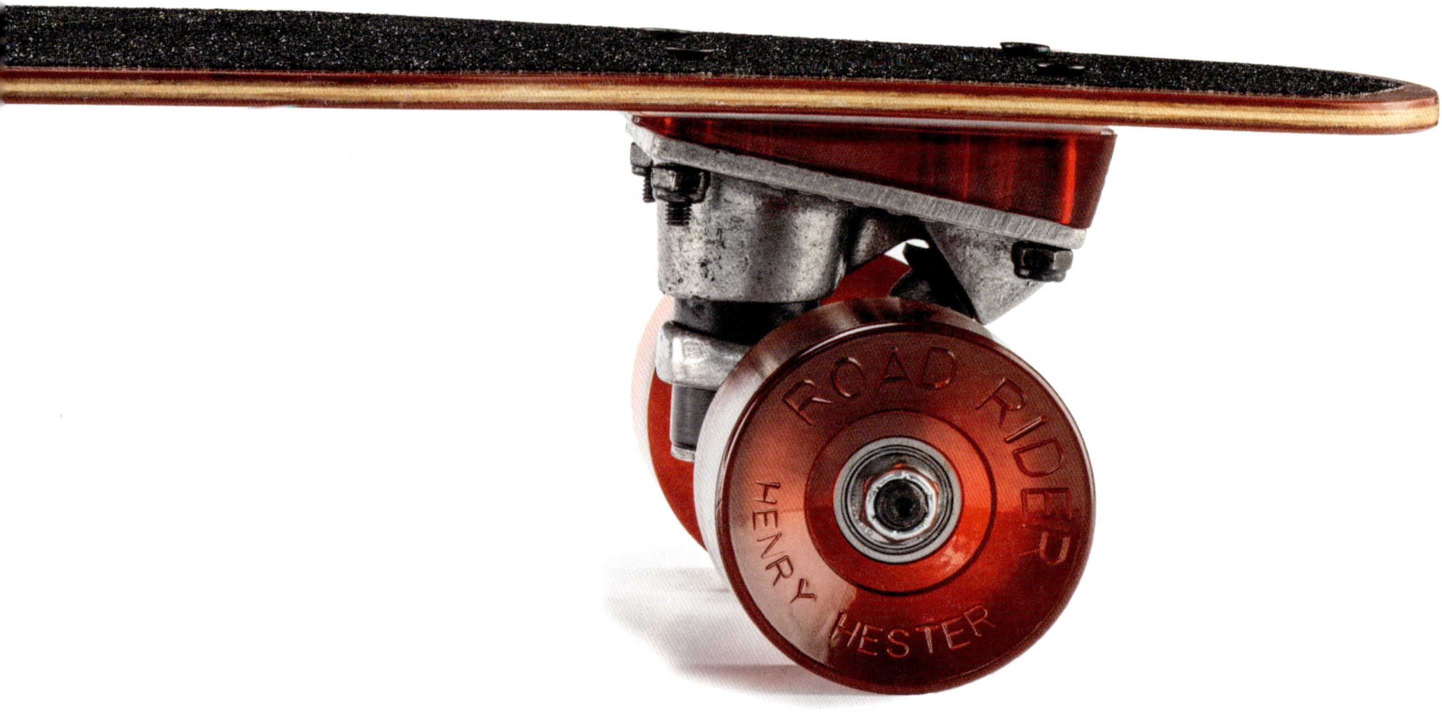

The Cut Out slalom deck first appeared in dealer price lists in September 1976, and was offered in single- and dual-ply versions with 3M rubber grip. This late 1977 example is a triple-ply, 26" (66cm) version with a rare mineral sparkle grip cut to match the outline of the board. The setup is performance-oriented. It features NOS Tracker Mid trucks, wedge risers, and NOS Road Rider Henry Hester signature wheels, which were the staple of slalom riders in the late 1970s. The larger team rider-specific bottom sticker is worth mentioning.

Provenance

The deck was purchased from Pacific Coast Vintage in Paris. The donor NOS Tracker Mid trucks were gifted by my cousin in Sweden. The NOS Road Rider Henry Hester wheels and SKF bearings were acquired as part of a complete board purchased from a UK collector.

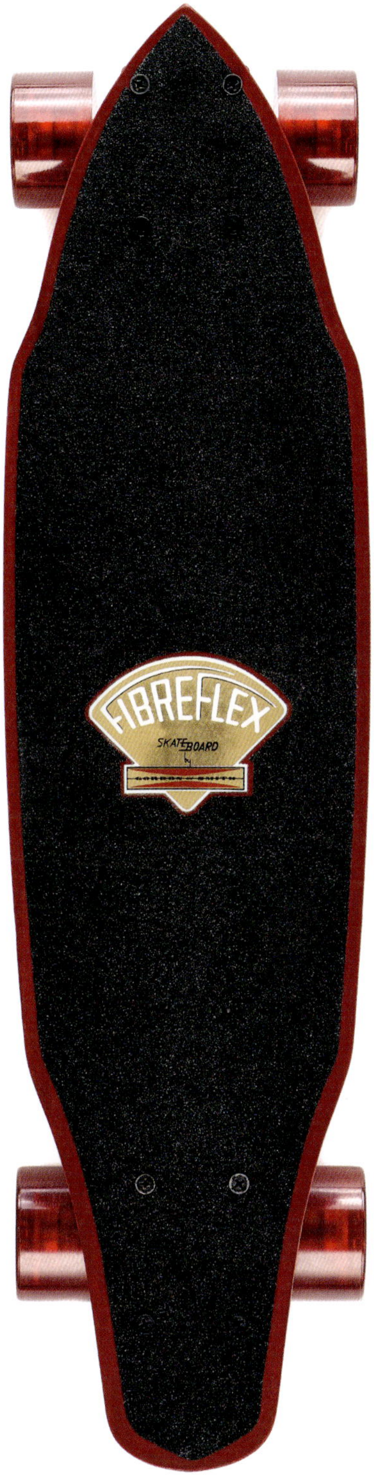

1977 Cut Out Specs

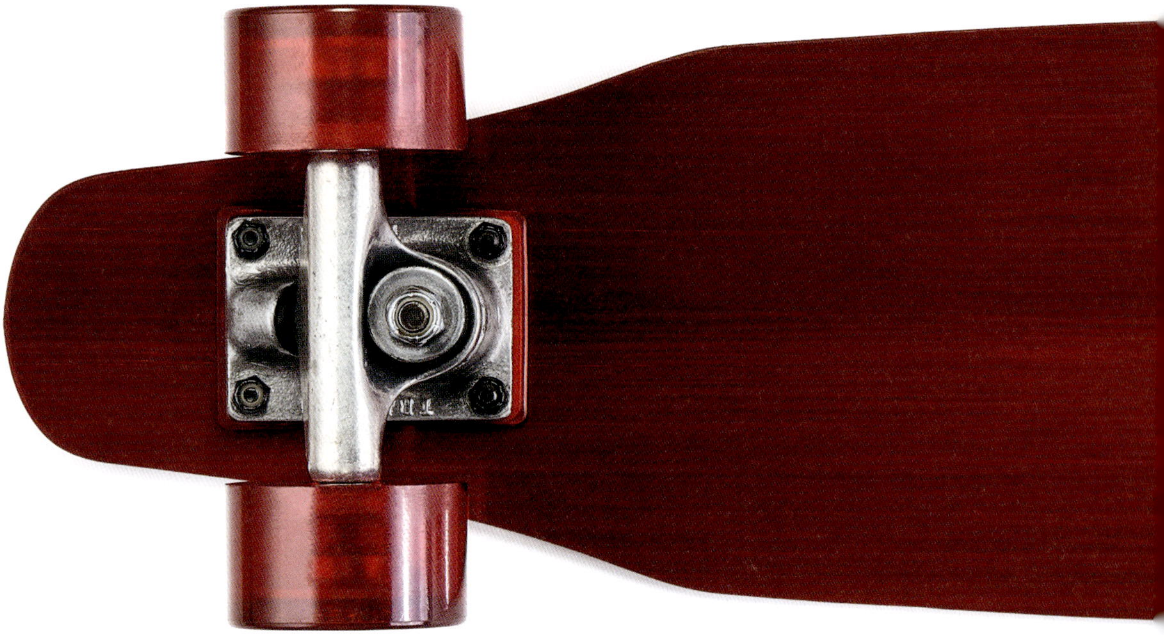

Deck

- NOS Cut Out (slalom)
- Triple ply core with Bo-Tuff on both sides
- Length: 26" (66cm)
- Width: 6½" (16cm)
- Thickness: ¼" (6.35mm)
- Mineral sparkle grip tape following the outline

Trucks

- NOS Tracker Mid trucks
- Urethane wedge risers

Wheels

- NOS Road Rider Henry Hester signature wheels
- Diameter: 2.48" (63mm)
- Durometer: 78-82A
- SKF Sealed Bearings

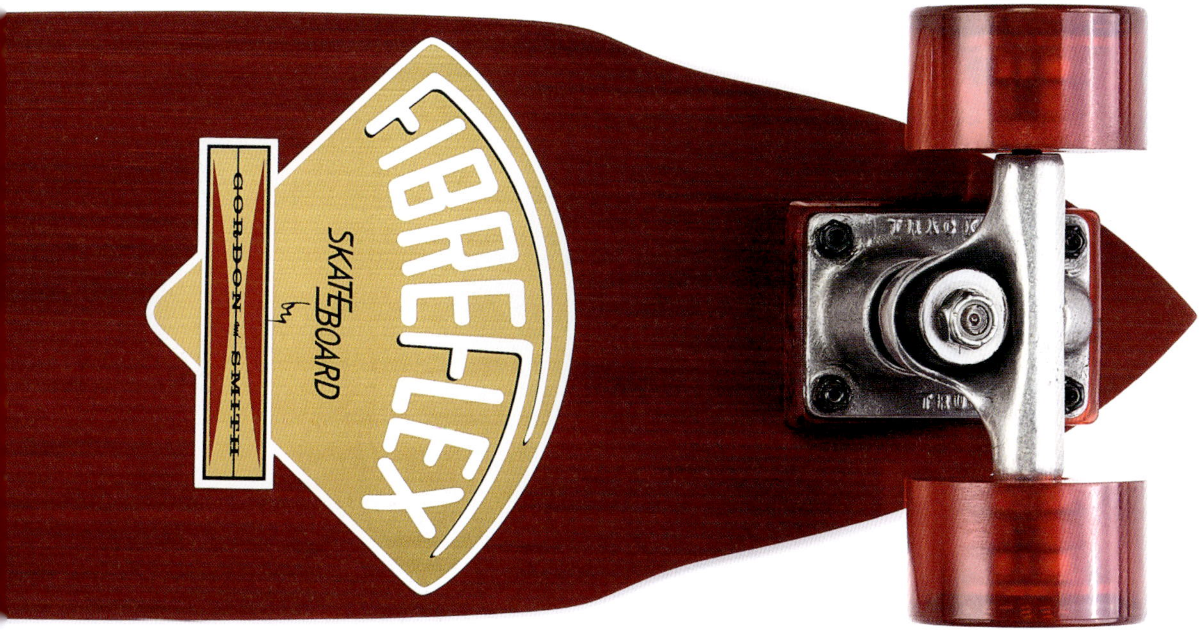

1977 Steve Cathey

"FibreFlex Yellow"

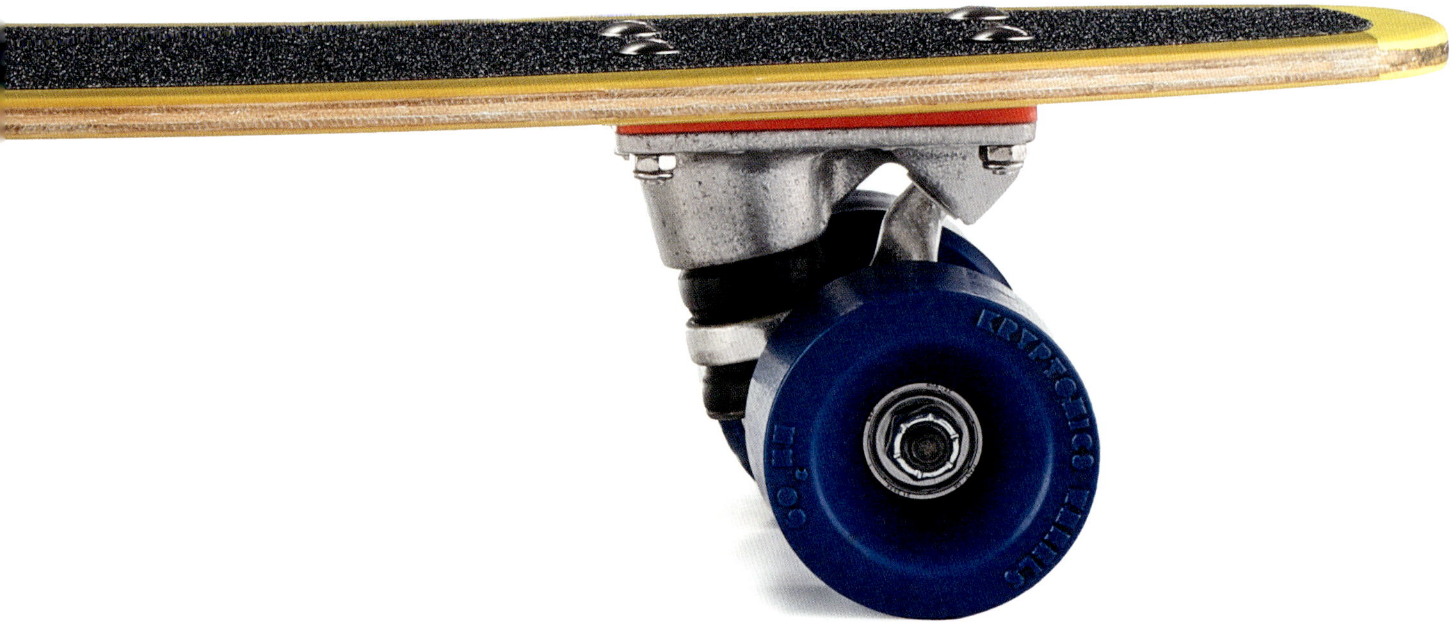

This Steve Cathey signature board marked the arrival of FibreFlex's second pro model. Essentially a stiffened version of the standard Freestyle deck, it used the thicker triple-ply "Stifflex" construction first introduced on the Bowlrider. This particular example is a late 1977 version with mineral sparkle grip in a distinctive droplet-shaped layout. The board is equipped with Tracker Haf trucks and NOS first-generation 60mm Kryptonics.

Provenance

This OG deck, which I refurbished, was bought online from a US seller. The OG Tracker Haf trucks were acquired from a donor setup, and the NOS 60mm Kryptonics were purchased from a UK collector.

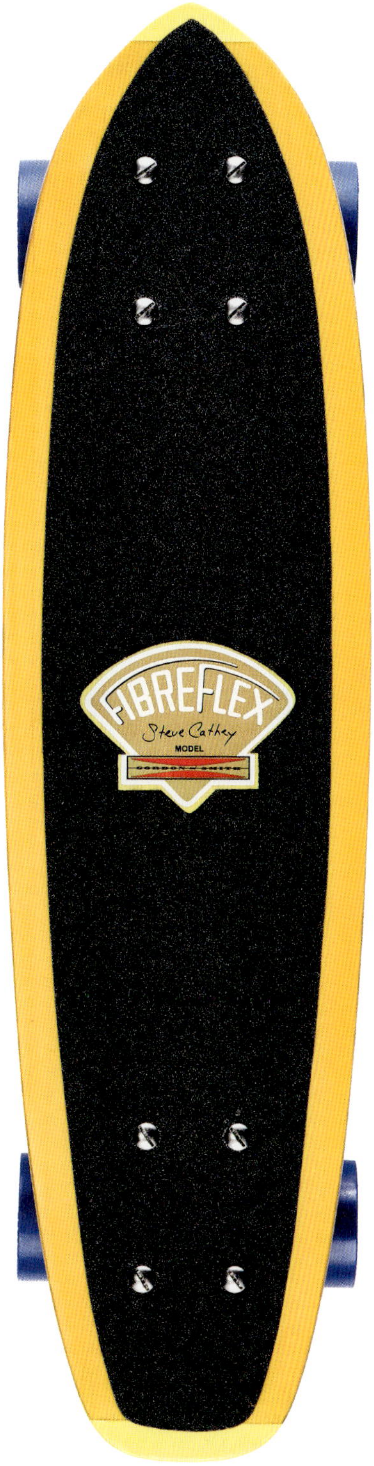

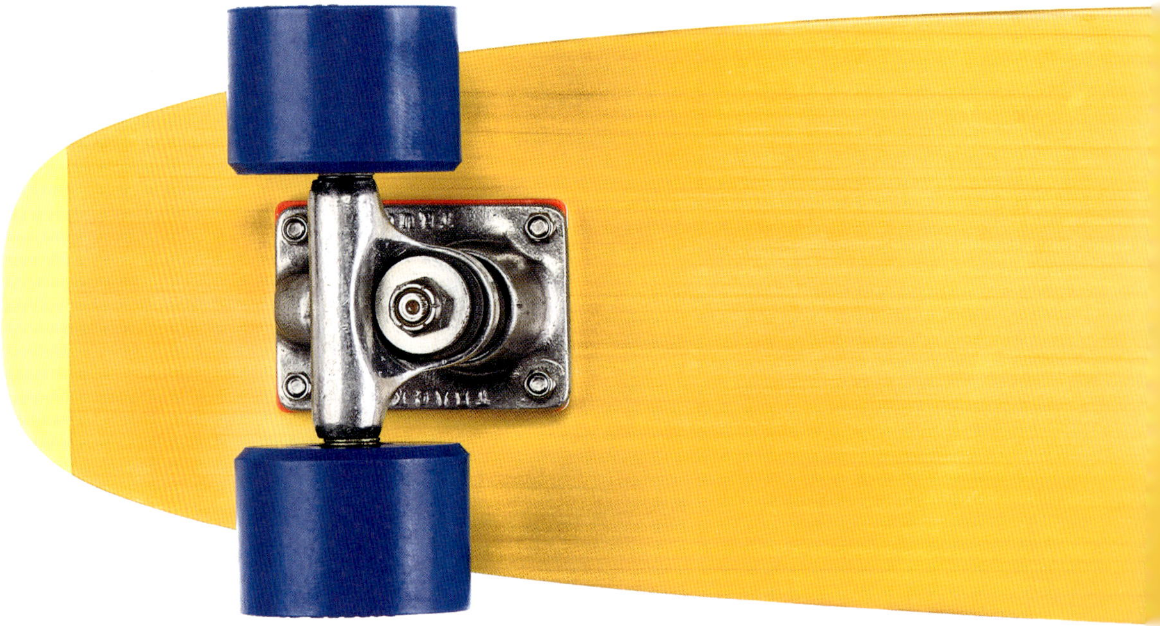

Deck

- OG refurbished Steve Cathey Signature freestyle deck
- Triple-ply maple core between two layers of Bo-Tuff
- Length: 26” (66cm)
- Width: 6½” (16cm)
- Thickness: $\frac{5}{16}$” (7.94mm)
- Mineral sparkle grip tape following the outline

Trucks

- OG refurbished Tracker Haf trucks
- Rubber risers

Wheels

- NOS first-generation Kryptonics
- Diameter: 2.36” (60mm)
- Durometer: 80A
- SKF Sealed Bearings

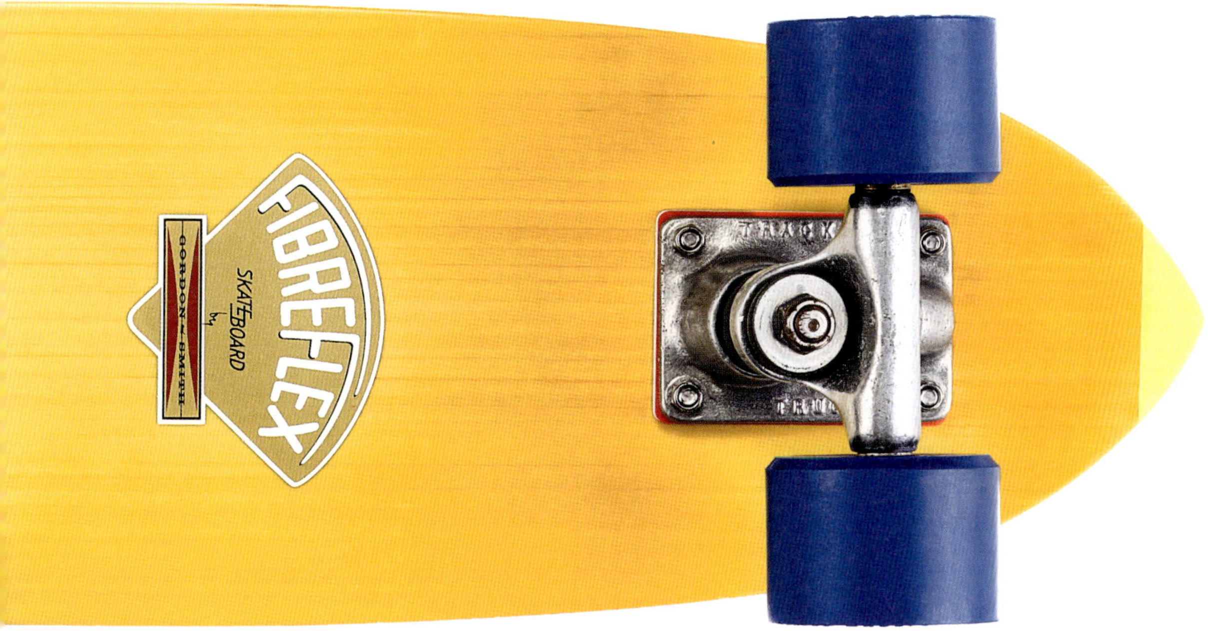

1977–78

Cut Out / Cut Away / Pro Slalom

"The Workhorse"

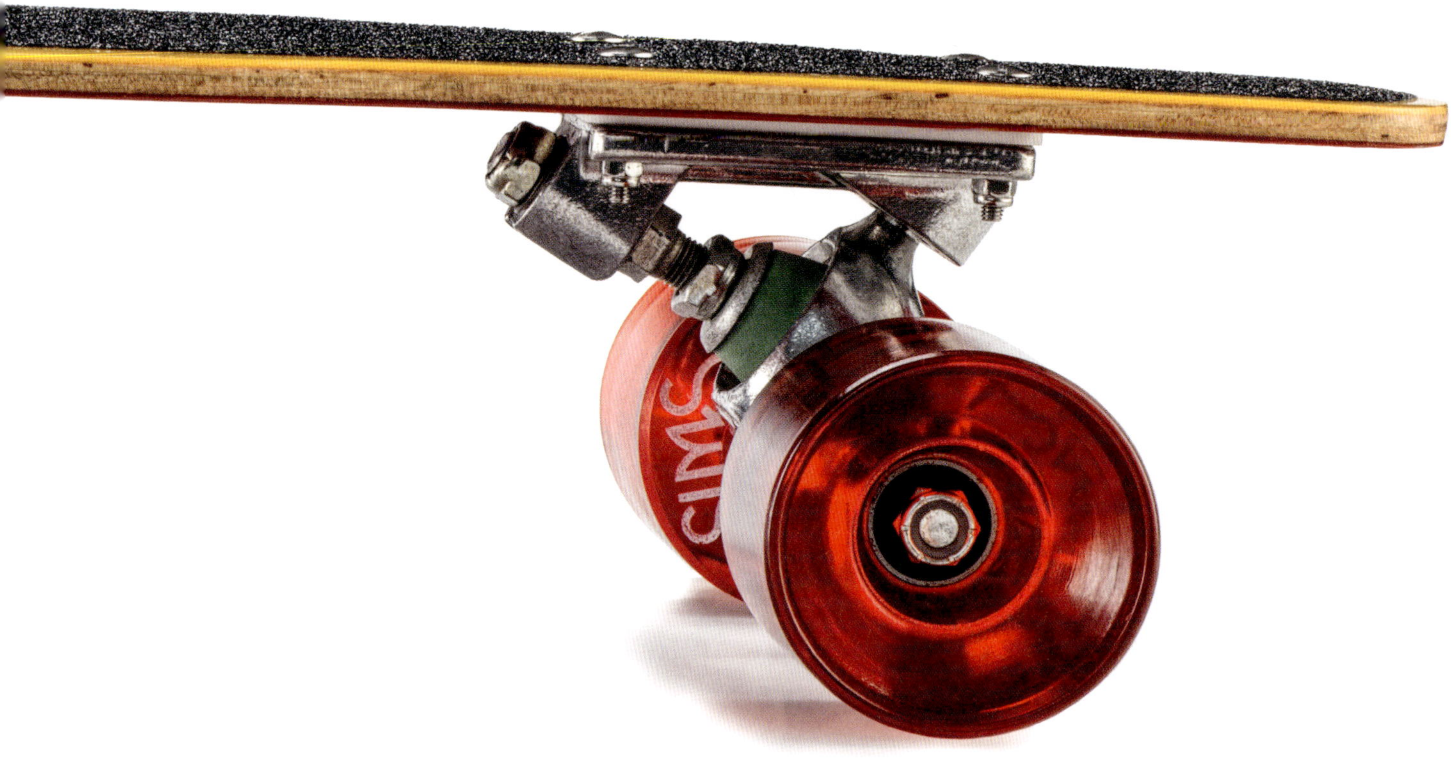

One of the most popular slalom boards of its era, this deck is related to the Cut Out slalom, which was introduced in 1976. By late 1977, the board evolved into a thicker, stiffer plywood construction, much like the Stifflex approach used for the Bowlrider and Steve Cathey models—a move away from the ultra-flexible earlier versions featuring single, dual, and triple-ply cores. This one has NOS Gullwing Split Axle trucks and Sims Competition wheels, and is designed for racing.

Provenance

The OG deck was acquired in France and restored to its original color scheme by the English refurbisher Mark Mayers. The NOS Gullwing Split Axle trucks were purchased from a Swiss collector, and the NOS Sims Competition wheels were bought at auction in Canada.

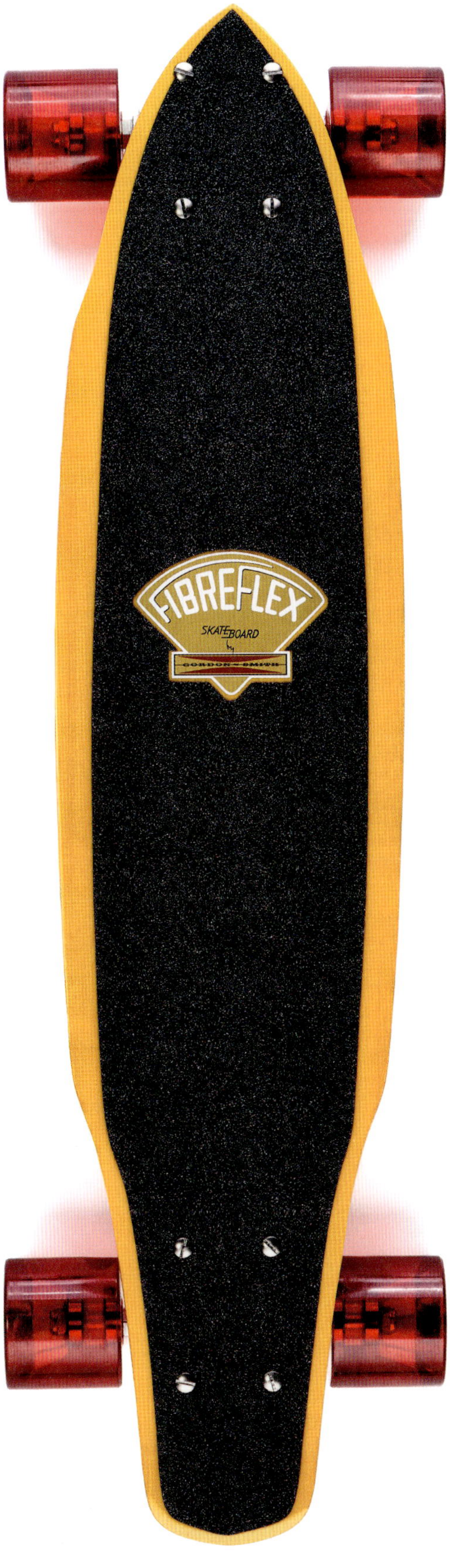

1977–78 Cut Out Specs

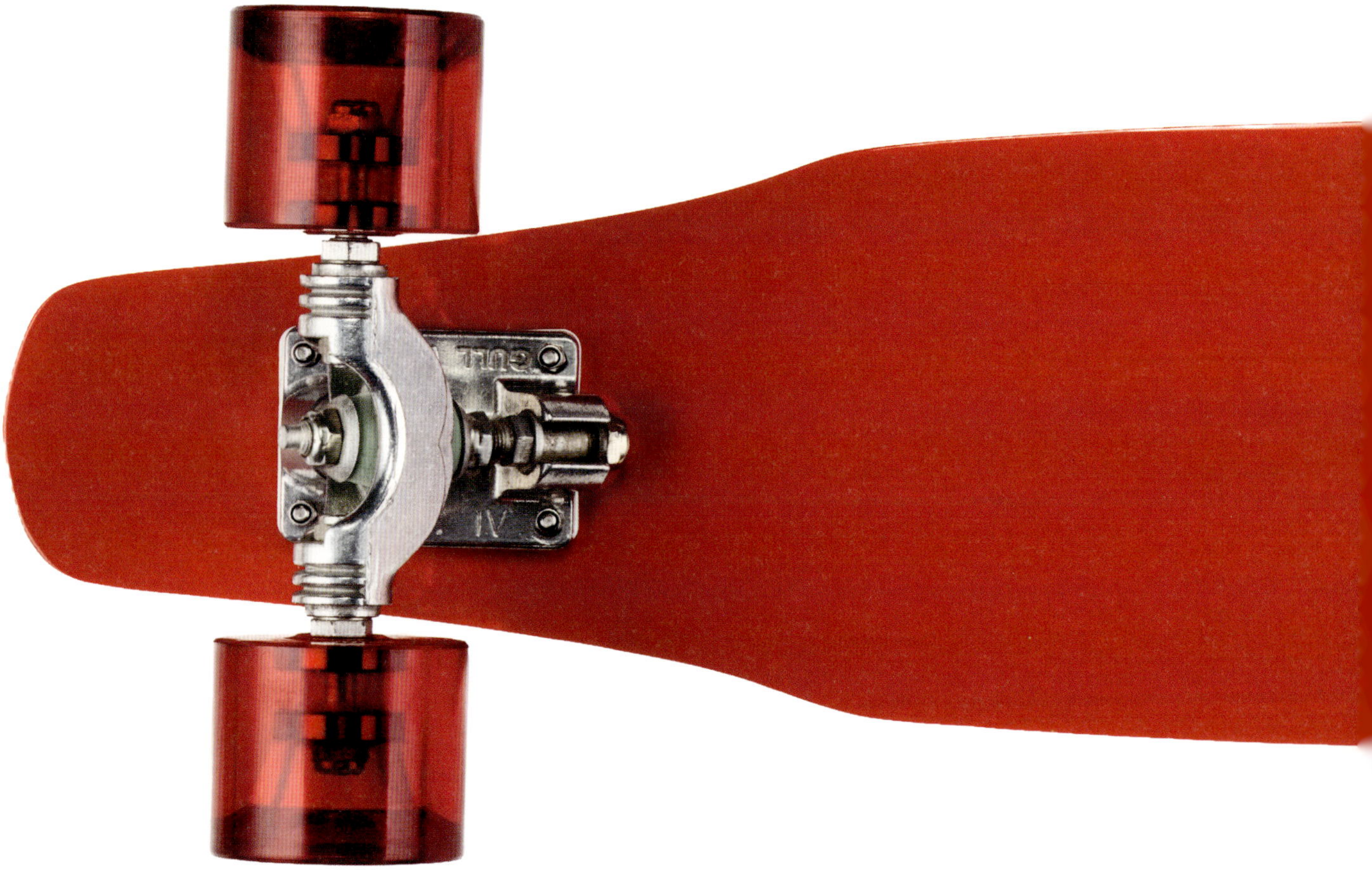

Deck

- Refurbished 1978 Cut Out triple-ply core between two layers of Bo-Tuff
- Length: 29" (74cm)
- Width: 6½" (16cm)
- Thickness: 5⁄16" (7.94mm)
- Mineral sparkle grip tape following the outline

Trucks

- NOS Gullwing Split Axle
- Thin rubber risers

Wheels

- NOS Sims Competition
- Diameter: 2.5" (64mm)
- Durometer: High 70s
- Sealed SKF Bearings

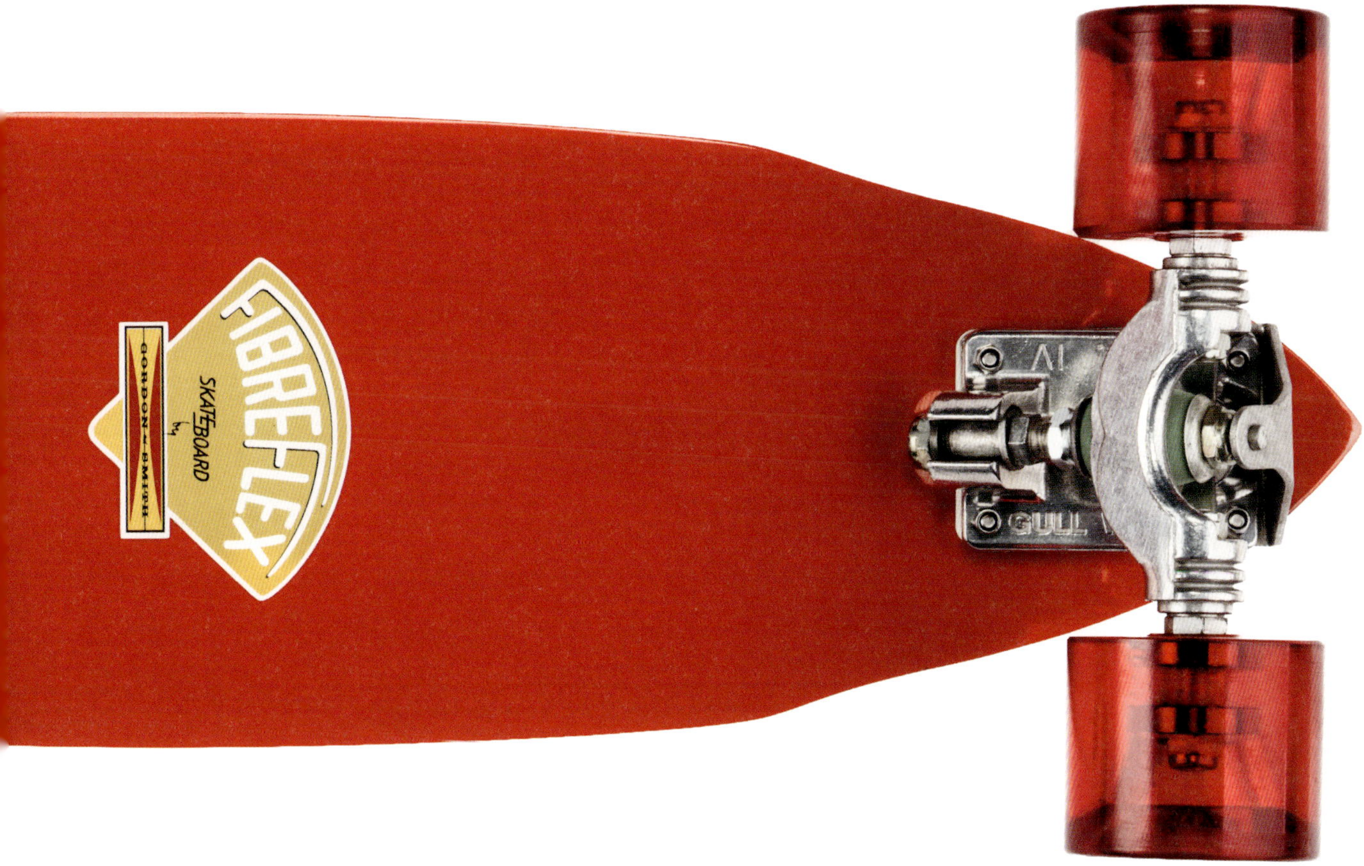

1978 Freestyle 26”

“The 26” Freestyle”

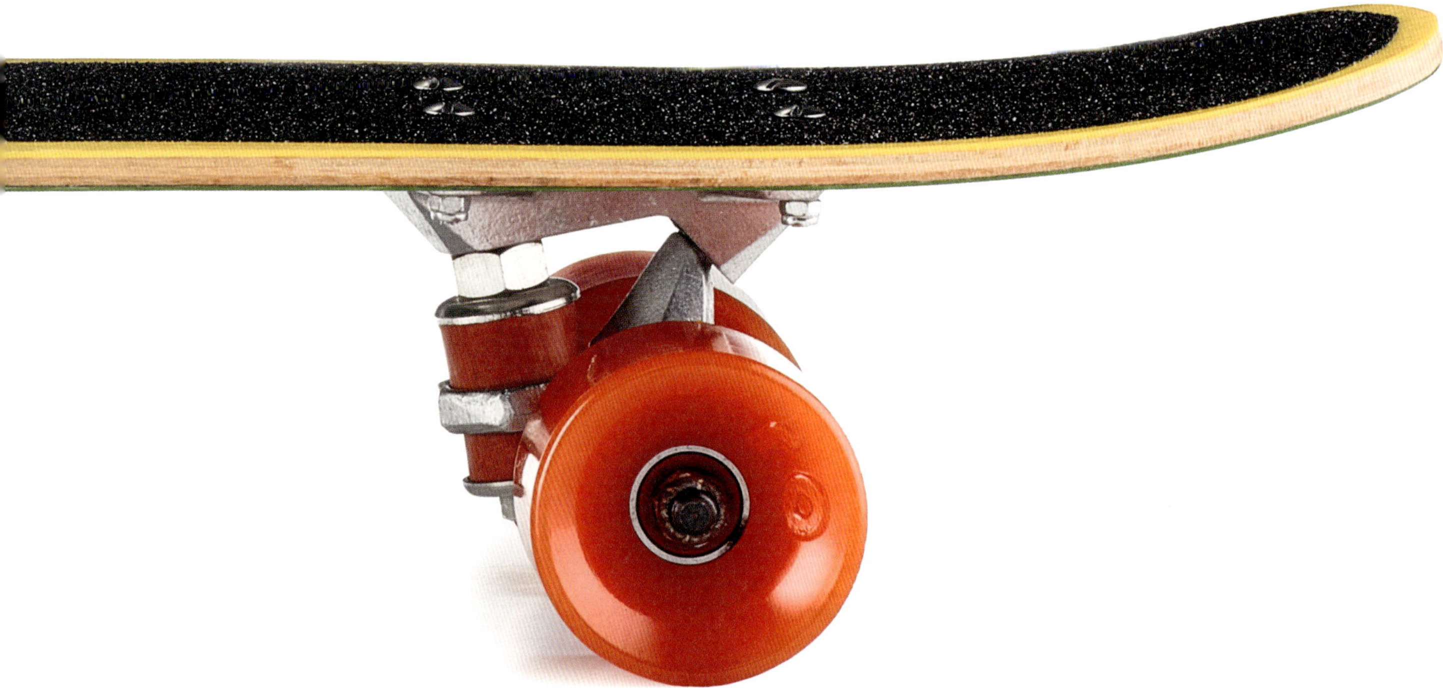

This NOS 1978 26” Freestyle remains true to the FibreFlex “flex-deck” heritage. It is a medium thin, triple-ply board with an updated outline—slightly wider and squarer than earlier freestyle models. By 1978, slalom and vertical decks were stiff, whereas the Freestyle was—aside from its slalom decks—notable for combining flexibility with a degree of rigidity. This one is equipped with NOS Lazer Freestyle trucks and NOS OJ Hot Juice wheels.

Provenance

The NOS 1978 Freestyle 26" deck was purchased – in its original plastic bag – from a Swiss collector. The Lazer Freestyle trucks were bought from Pacific Coast Vintage in Paris, and the OJ Hot Juice wheels were acquired from a private sale.

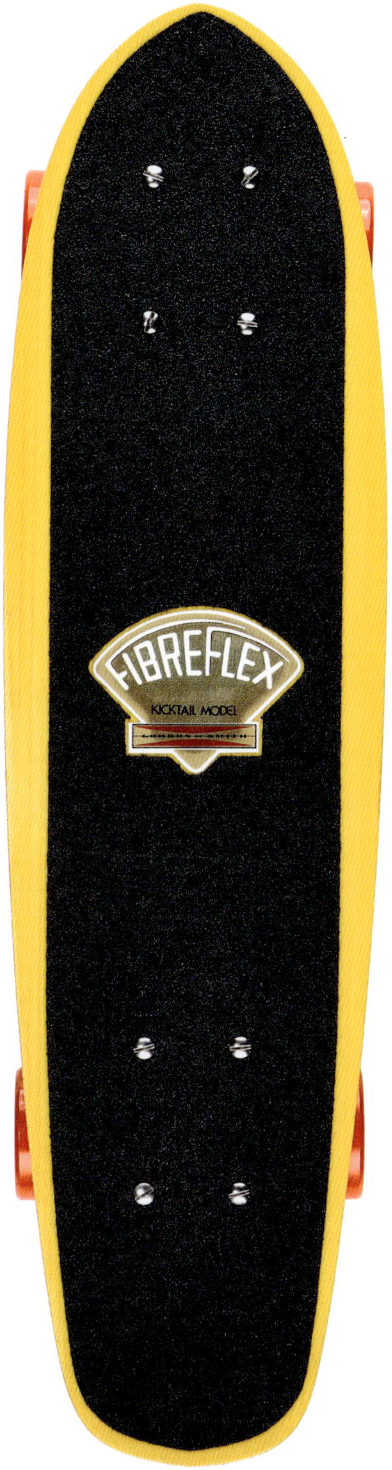

1978 Freestyle 26" Specs

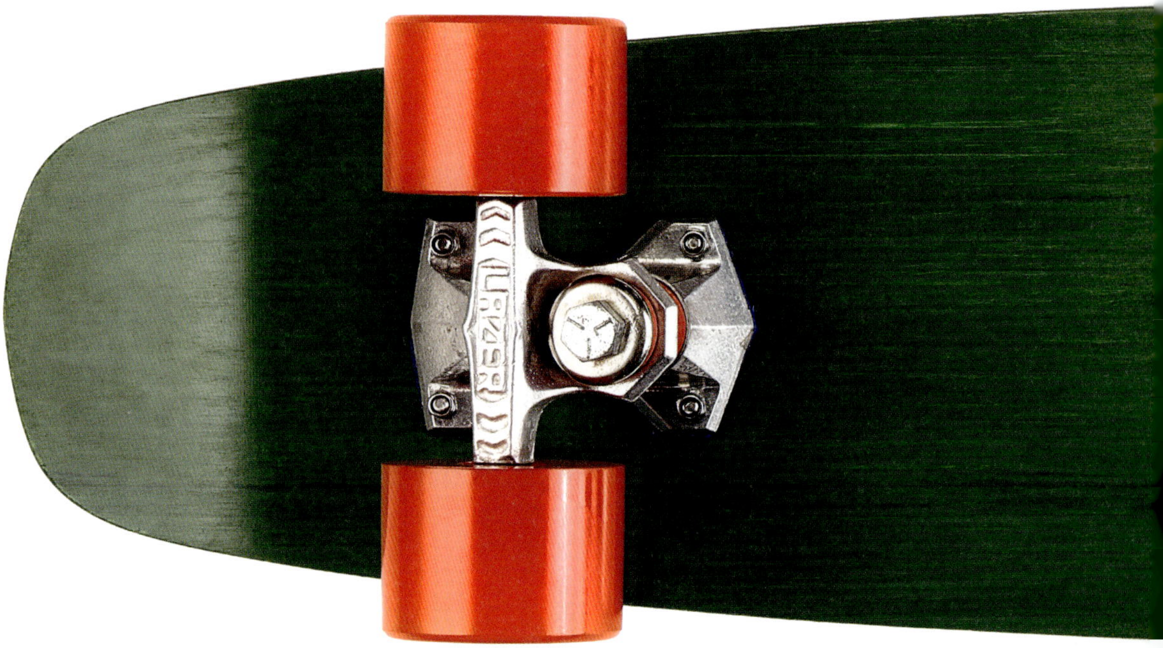

Deck

- NOS Freestyle 26”
- Triple-ply core with Bo-Tuff on both sides
- Length: 26” (66cm)
- Width: 6.6” (17cm)
- Thickness: $\frac{5}{16}$” (7.94mm)
- Solid black grip tape

Trucks

- Lazer Freestyle trucks
- Lazer risers

Wheels

- NOS OJ Hot Juice
- Diameter: 2.36” (60mm)
- Durometer: assumed 78A
- Sealed SKF Bearings

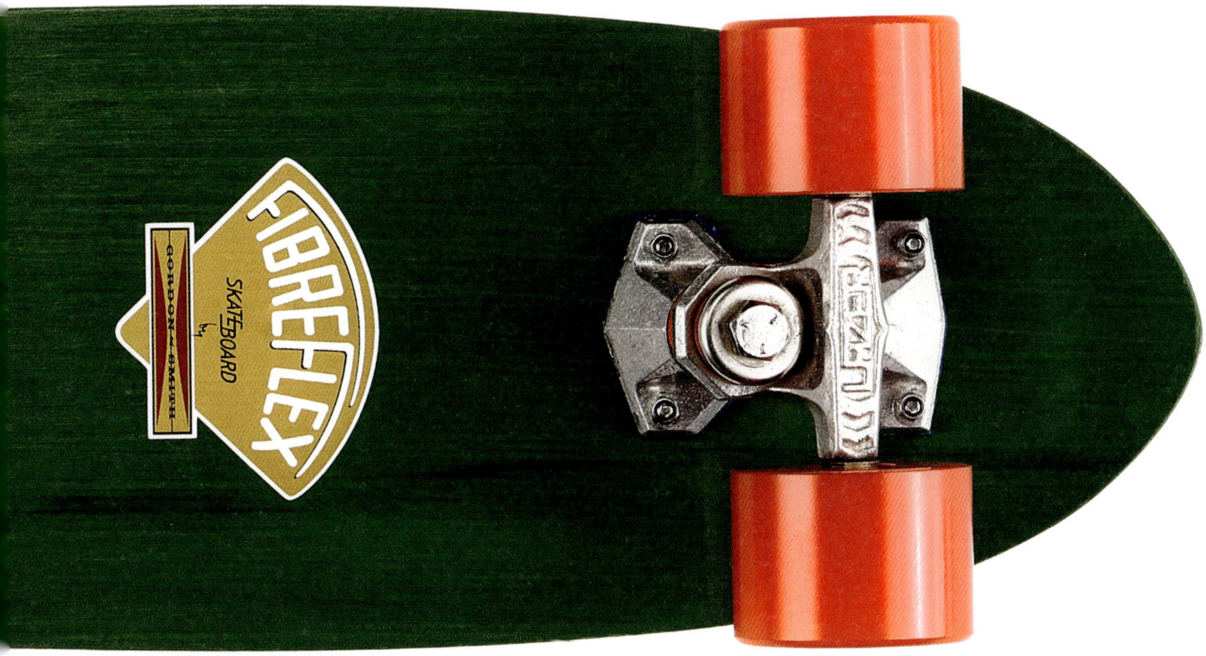

1978 Freestyle 28”

“The Taller Bro”

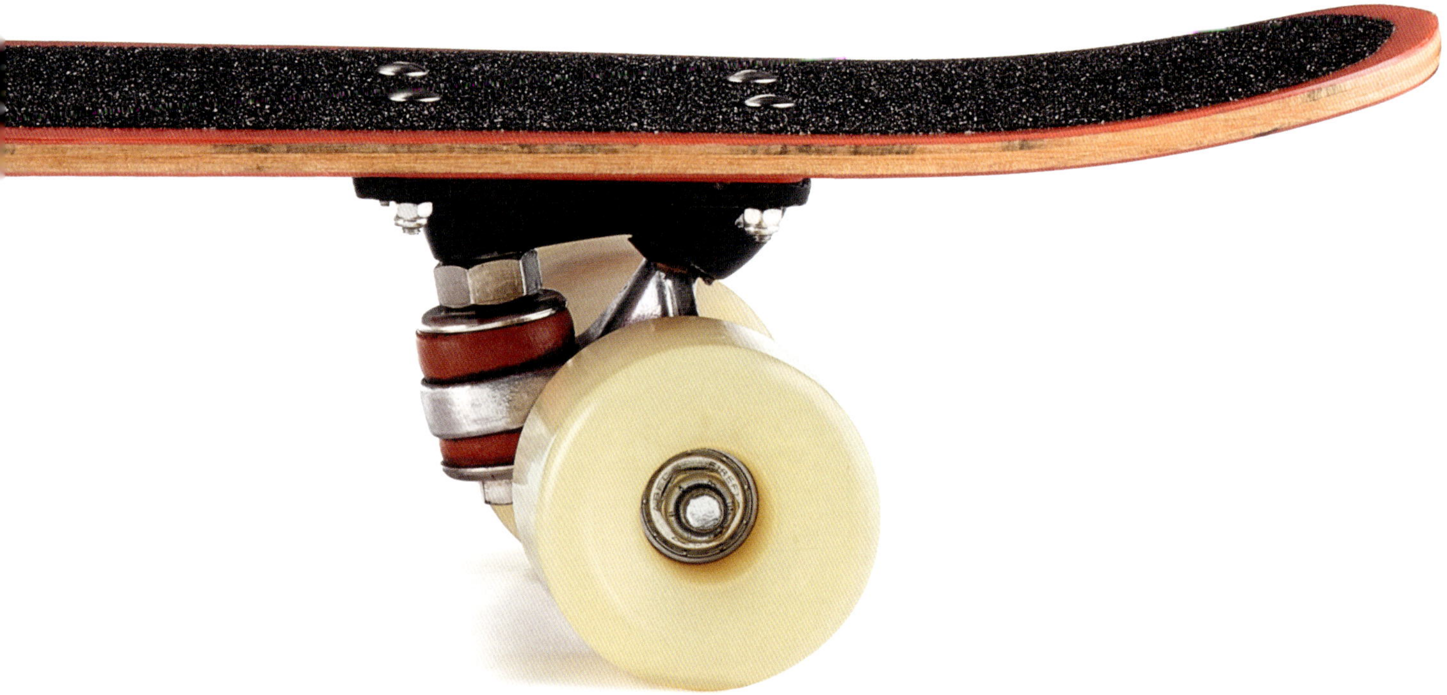

A thin, triple-ply, “flexy” board with the wider, squarer 1978 outline, the Freestyle 28” is the longer sibling of the 26” model. Again, in an era racing toward stiffness, while the Freestyle line was thicker and more rigid, it was still equipped with Stifflex. This meant that, though it was still stiffer than earlier FibreFlex models, it was one of the last “flexy” boards before decks became rigid as standard. As such, it exemplifies the company’s original philosophy. This board is set up with OG ACS 650 trucks and NOS white G&S YoYo wheels.

Provenance

This NOS deck was purchased with the Freestyle 26” from the same Swiss collector. The OG ACS 650 trucks were bought from a U.S. collector. The NOS white G&S YoYo wheels were bought from Pacific Coast Vintage in Paris.

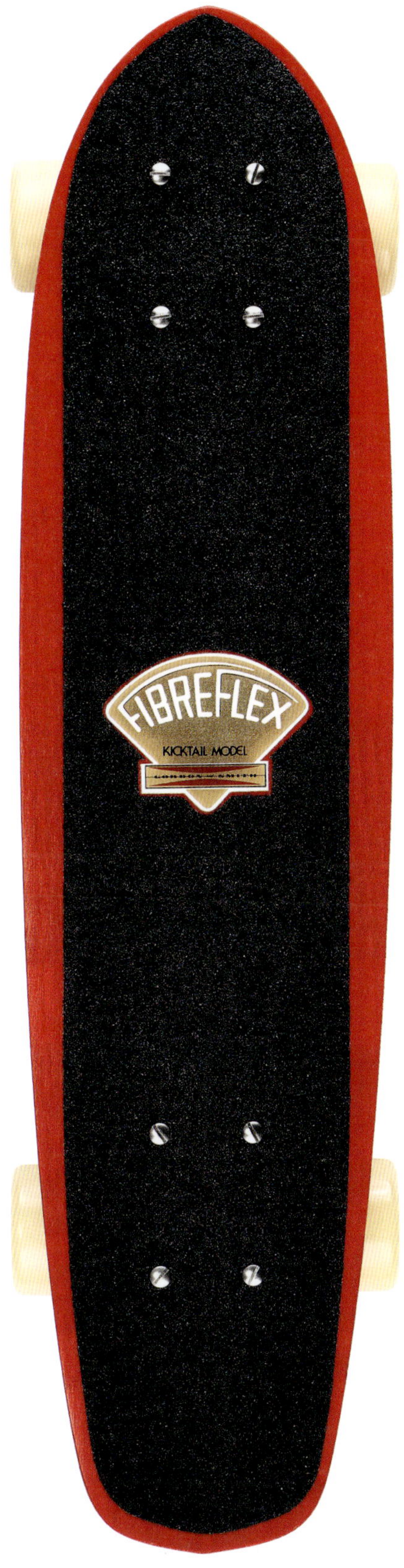

1978 Freestyle 28” Specs

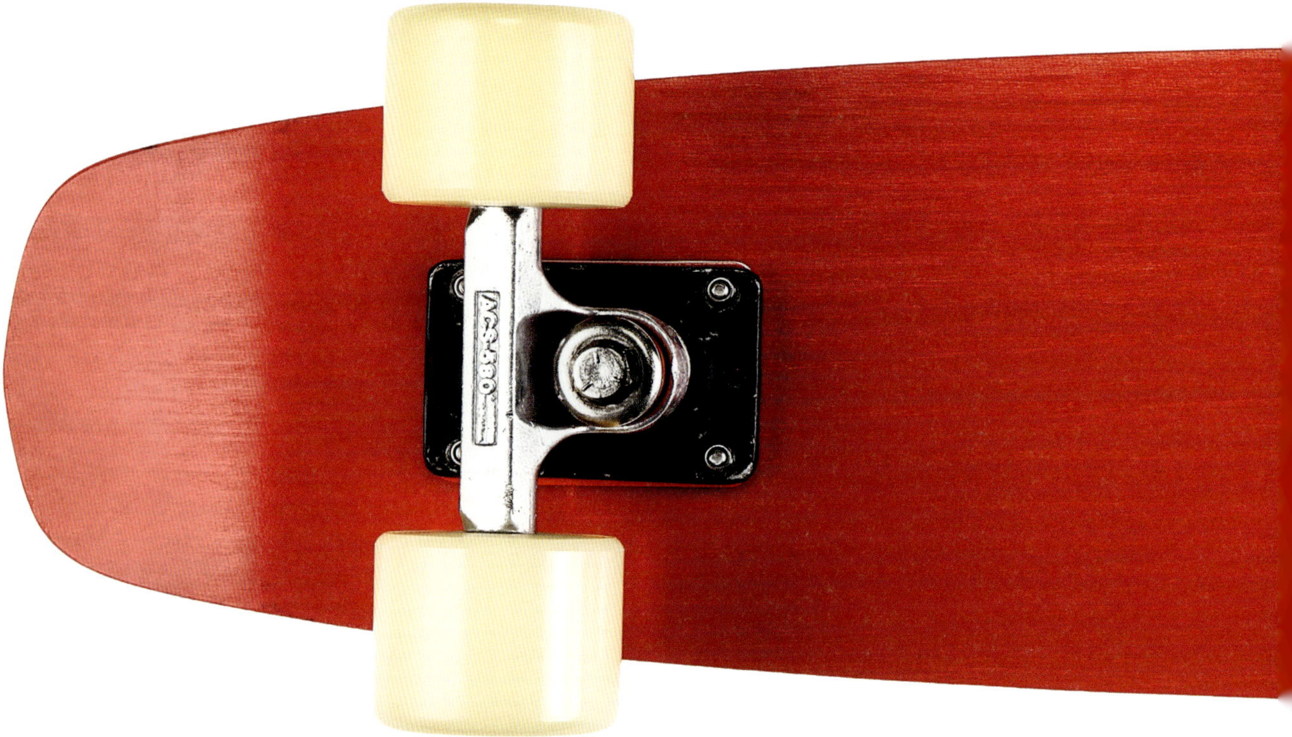

Deck

- NOS Freestyle
- 3-ply core with Bo-Tuff on both sides
- Length: 28” (71cm)
- Width: 6.6” (17cm)
- Thickness: $\frac{5}{16}$” (7.94mm)
- Solid black grip tape

Trucks

- OG ACS 650
- Cell Block Risers

Wheels

- NOS White G&S YoYos
- Diameter: 2.4” (61mm)
- Durometer: 83A
- Sealed SKF bearings

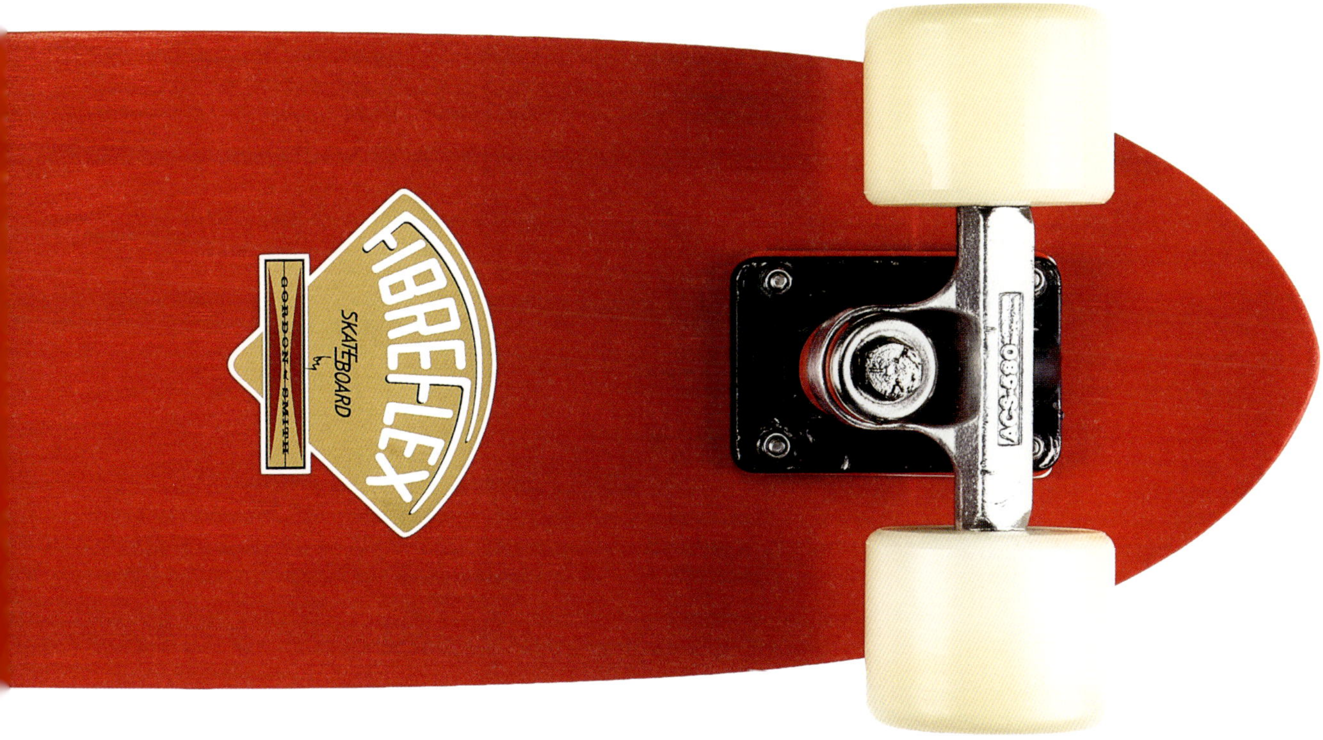

1978 Bowlrider

"Fading Canary"

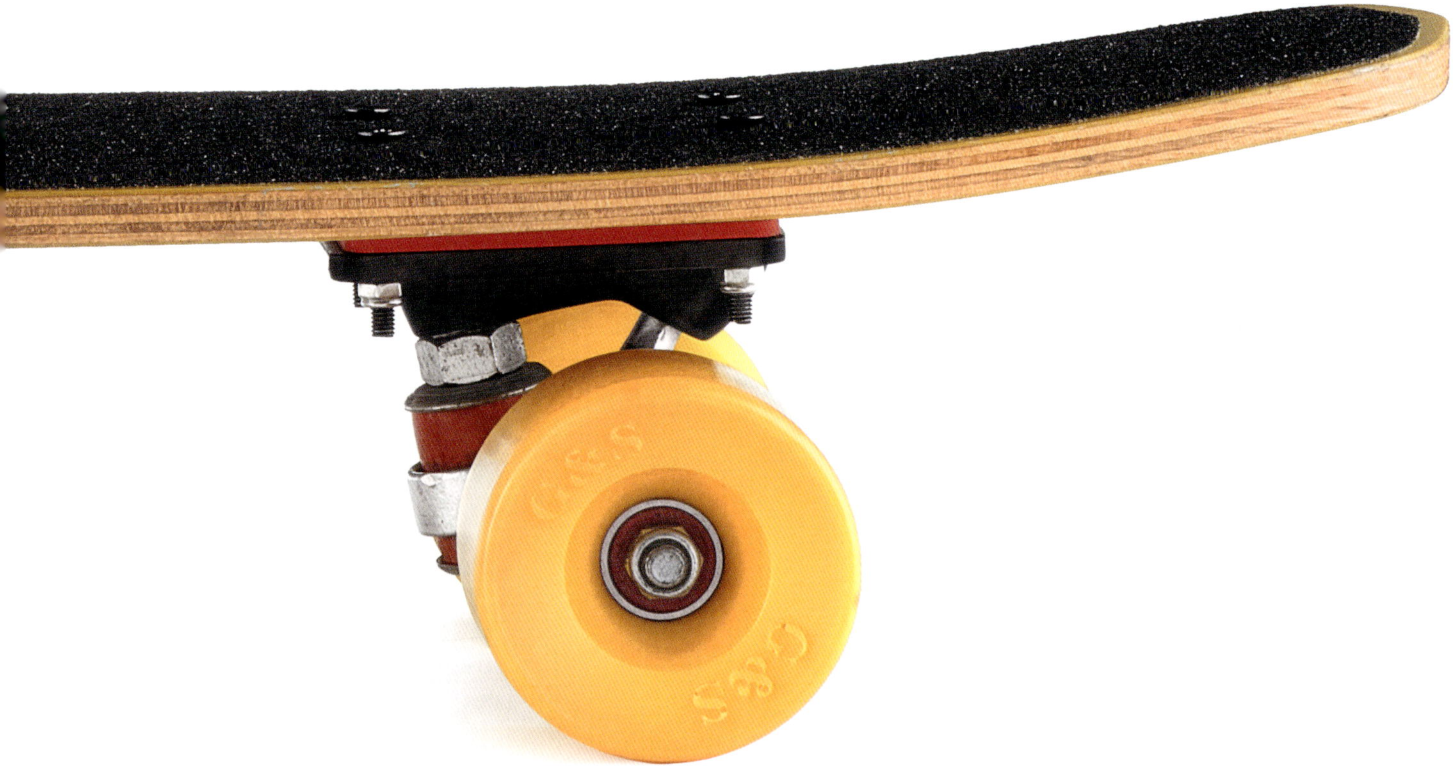

This NOS second-and-a-half-generation Bowlrider continues the evolution of FibreFlex's most successful vertical board. While the 1977 model used a triple-ply Stifflex construction, this one, which features five-ply with exterior layers of Bo-Tuff, is completely stiff. It is wide, for ramp skating, has a slight rocker, and features the larger FibreFlex team sticker on the bottom. This setup has broad ACS 651 trucks and NOS G&S Wonkers wheels with SKF bearings.

Provenance

This slightly faded but completely NOS 1978 Bowlrider was acquired from a collector in England. The NOS ACS 651 trucks and the NOS G&S Wonkers were purchased from Swedish and British collectors.

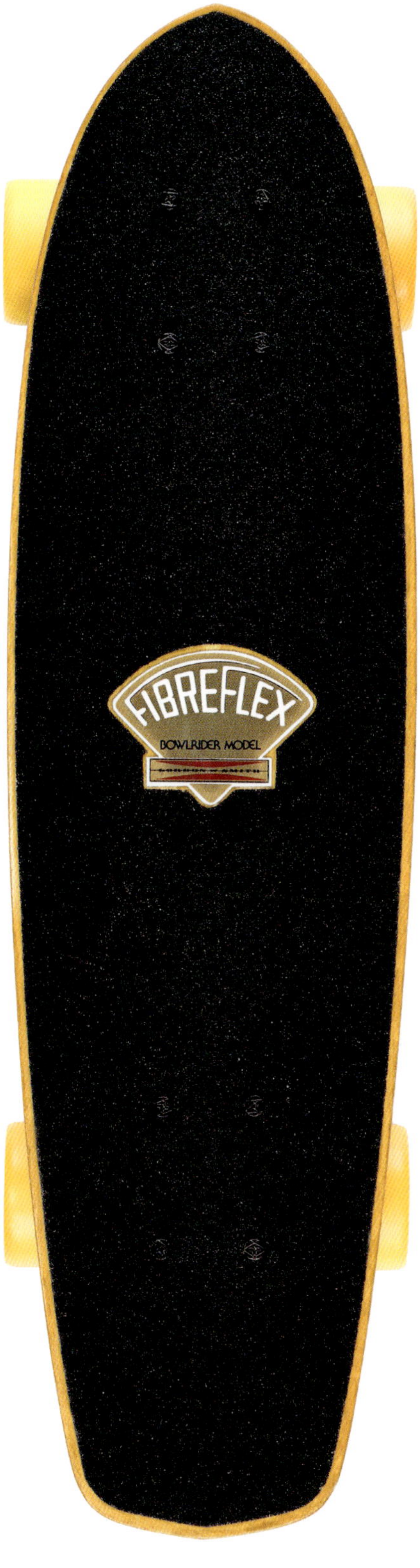

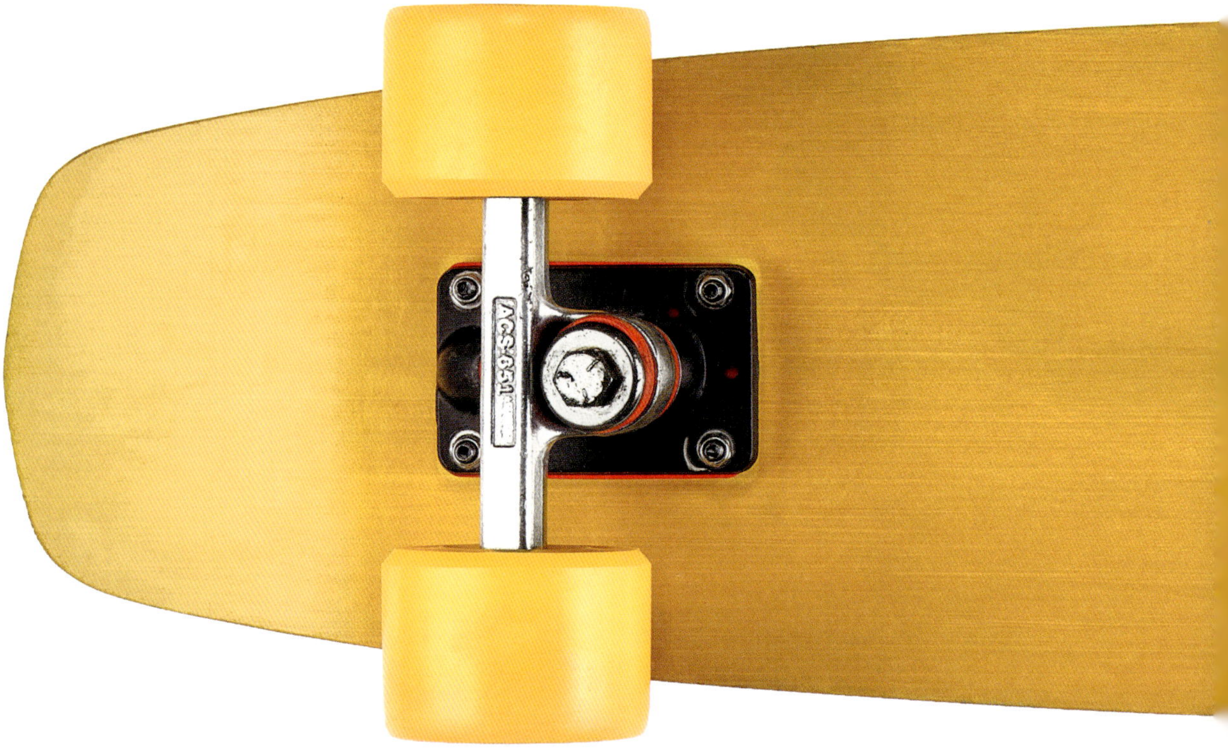

Deck

- NOS Bowlrider
- Rigid five-ply core with Bo-Tuff on both sides
- Length: 27" (69cm)
- Width: 7¼" (18cm)
- Thickness: 5⁄16" (7.94mm)
- Solid black grip tape

Trucks

- NOS ACS 651
- Rubber risers and Cell Blocs

Wheels

- NOS G&S Wonkers
- Diameter: 2.68" (68mm)
- Durometer: 92A
- Sealed SKF Bearings

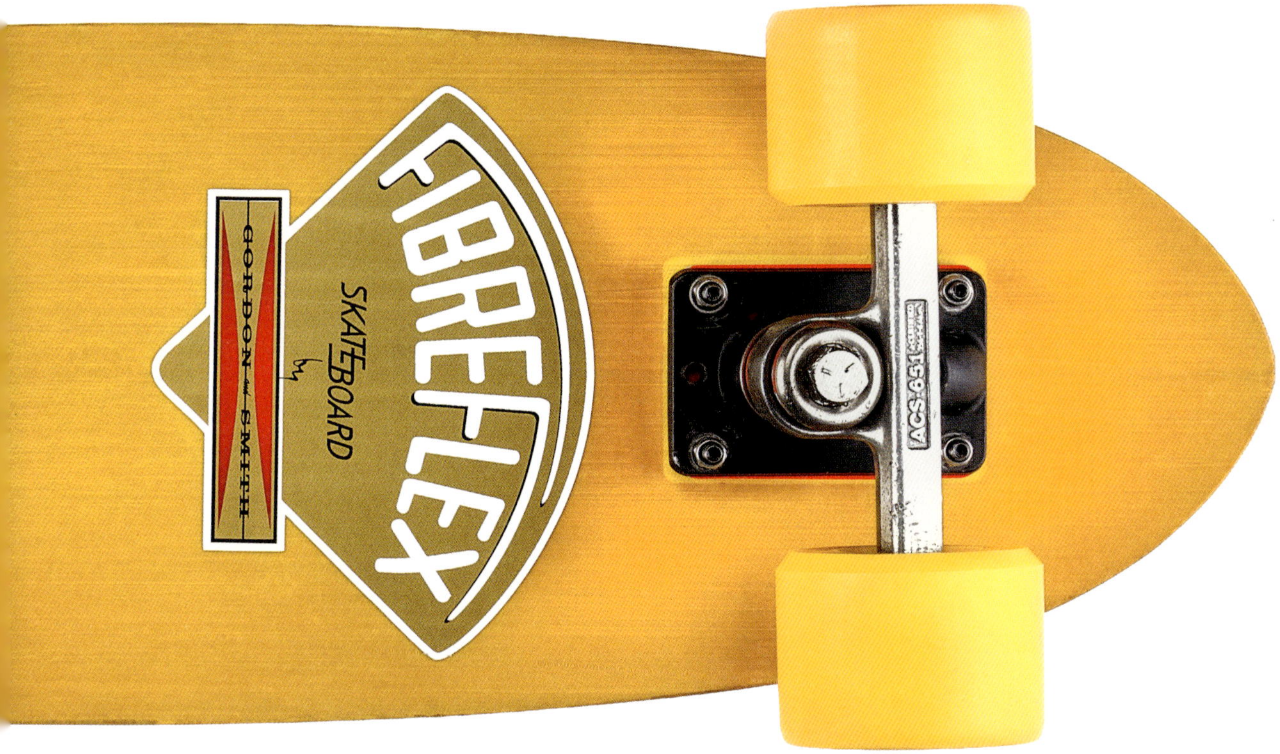

1978 Teamrider

"New Era"

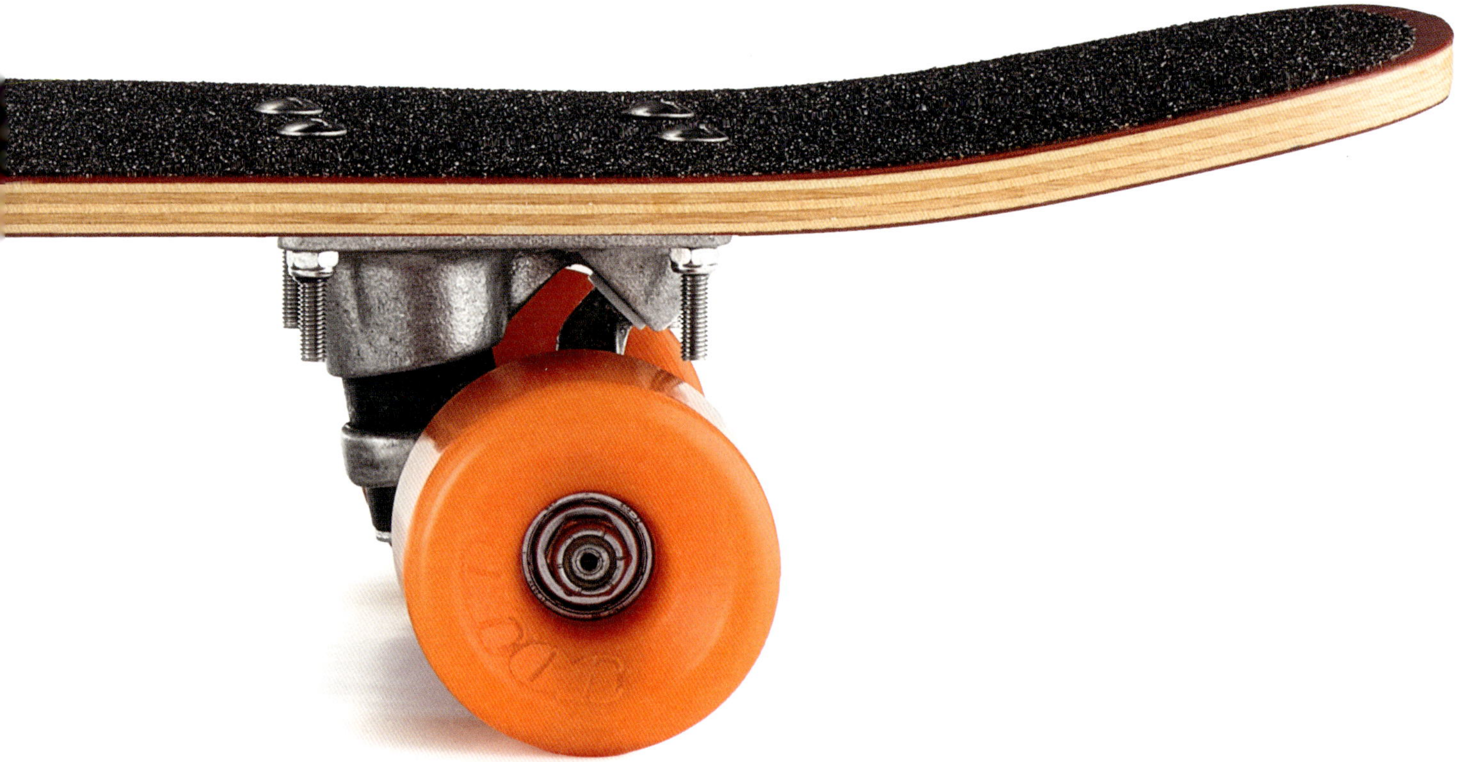

The Teamrider, launched in 1978, was a very successful model that bridged two styles of skateboarding. The project was a collaboration between the FibreFlex team riders, Doug Saladino and Dennis Martinez. One inch wider than its FibreFlex ancestors, it was used by both freestyle and vert ramp riders. Structurally, it is a fully solid deck with a five-ply wood core and Bo-Tuff top and bottom. This specimen is finished with OG Tracker Ful trucks and NOS orange G&S YoYo wheels. Designed by Steve Cathey and released in fall 1978, these wheels were also popular with both freestyle and vert riders alike.

Provenance

The NOS Teamrider deck was bought from a UK collector. The Tracker Ful trucks are assembled from OG components from several sources. The NOS orange G&S YoYo wheels were purchased from an English collector.

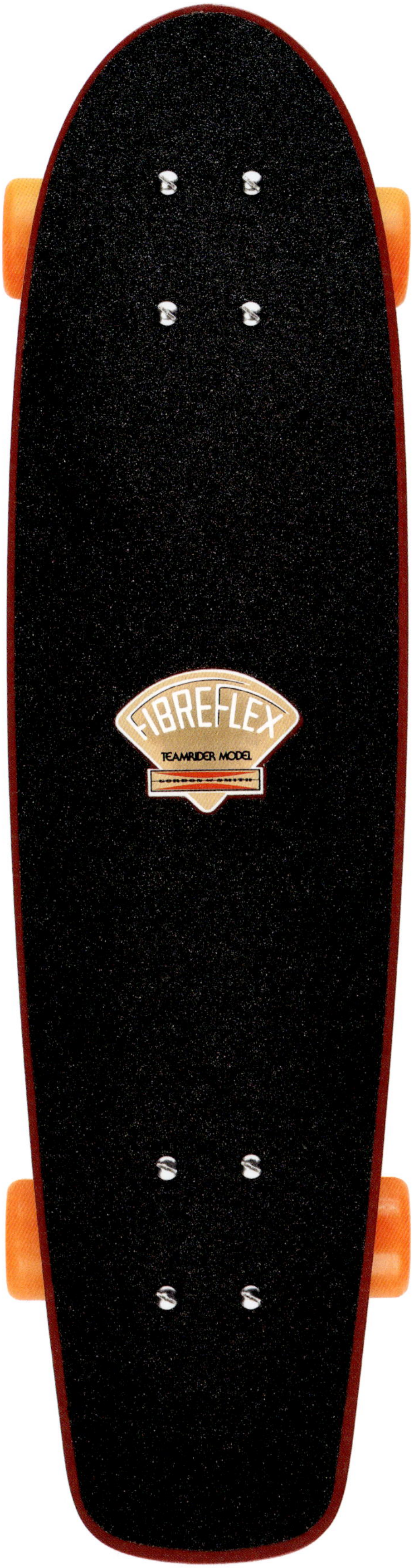

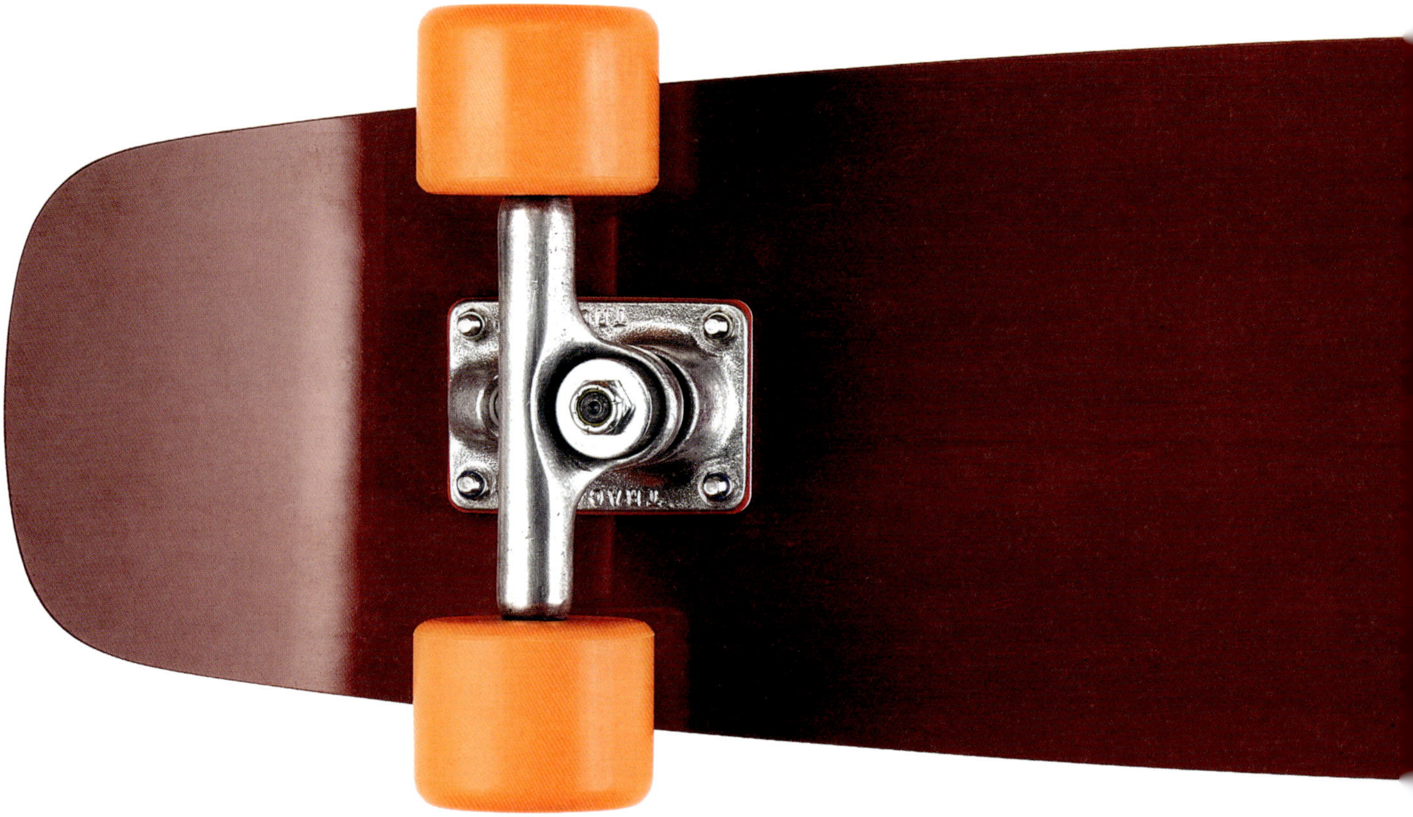

Deck

- NOS Teamrider
- Rigid five-ply core with Bo-Tuff on both sides
- Length: 30" (76cm)
- Width: 7¾" (20cm)
- Thickness: 5/16" (7.94mm)
- Solid black grip tape

Trucks

- OG Tracker Ful trucks
- Risers double Cell Blocks

Wheels

- NOS Orange G&S YoYos
- Diameter: 2.4" (61mm)
- Durometer: 94A
- Sealed SKF Bearings

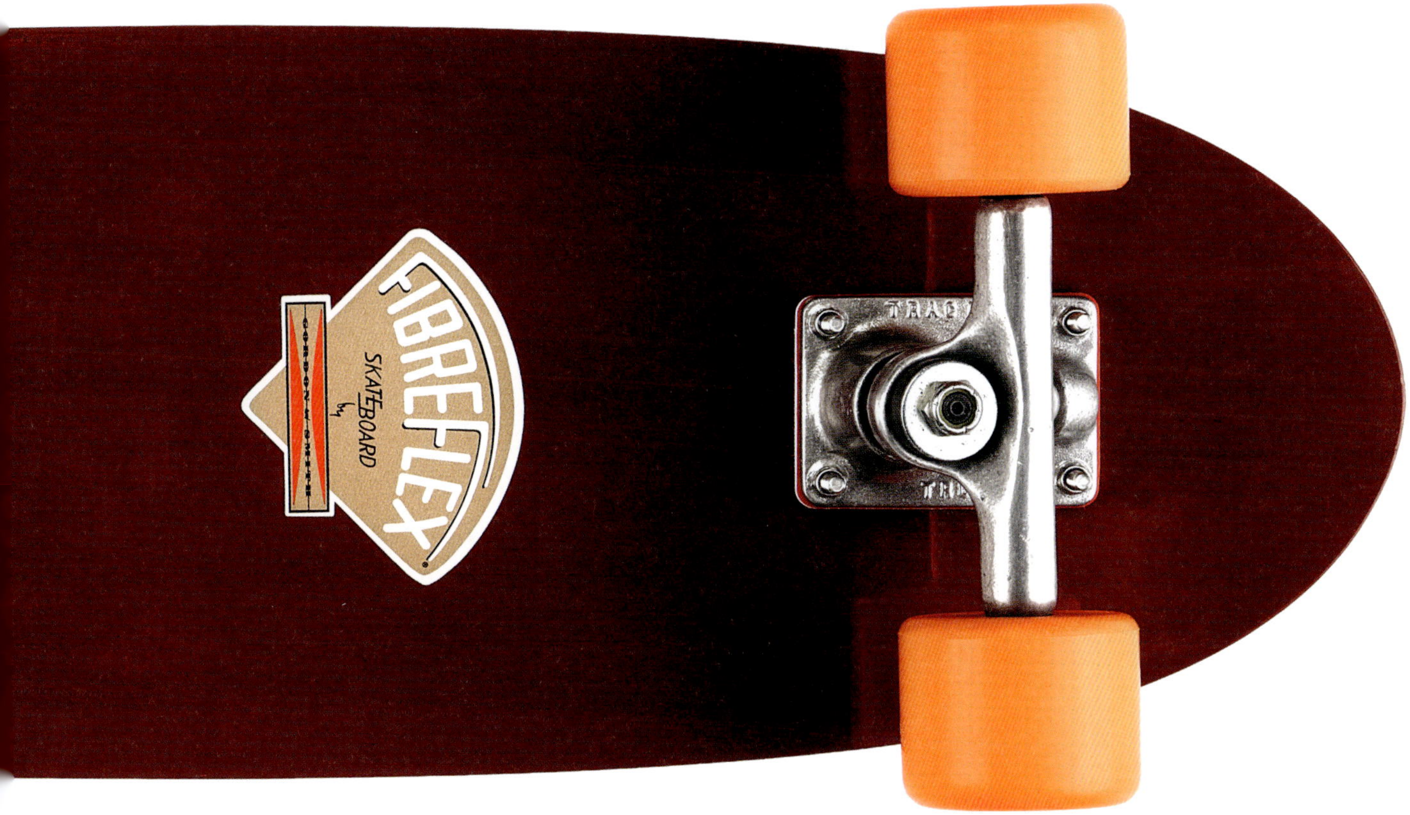

1978

Greg Taie

"The Gem"

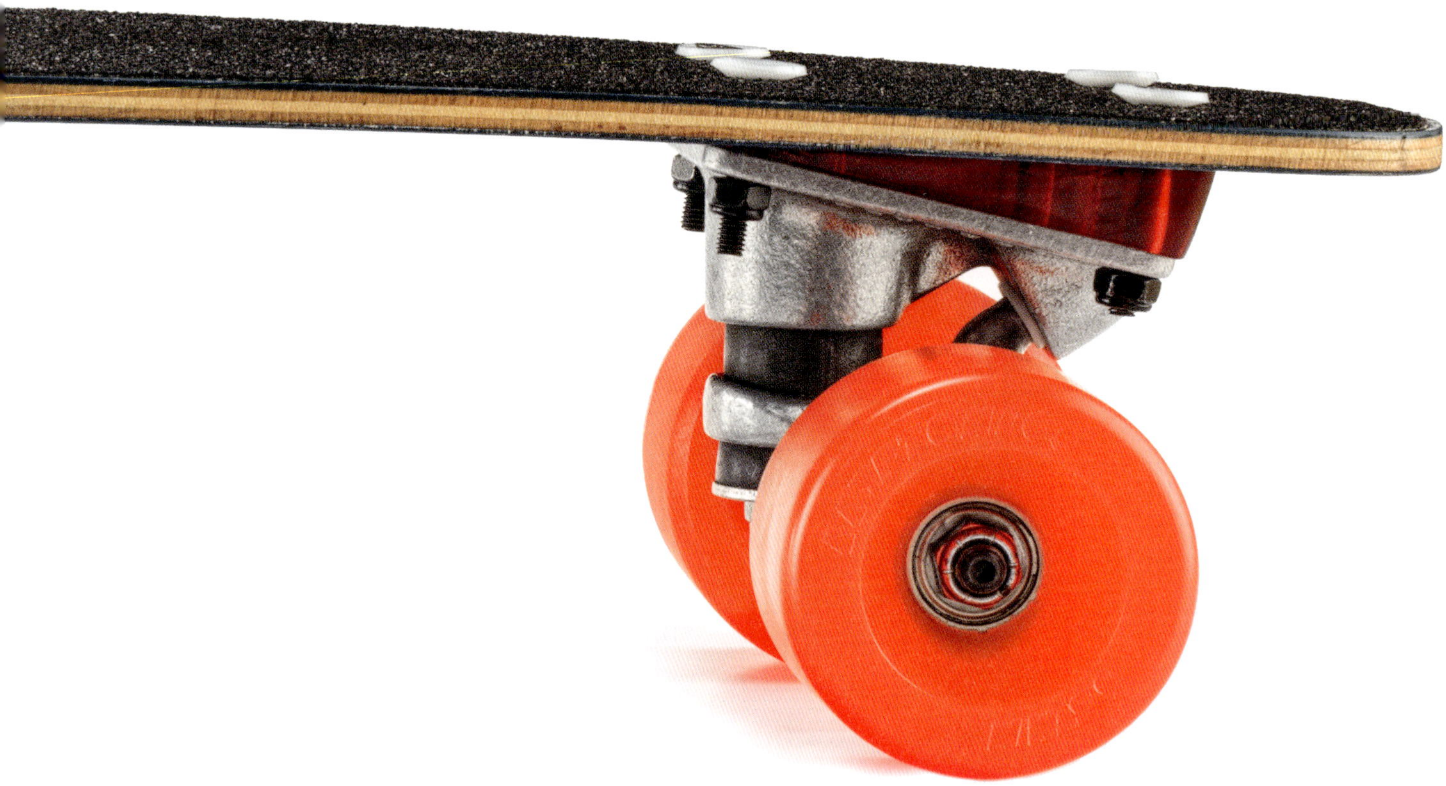

This rare NOS signature Greg Taie Slalom deck is the last 1970s model produced by FibreFlex before the brand stopped producing slalom boards. Launched in late 1978, it represents the final chapter of the brand's original race- and slalom-oriented story. This skateboard is built with NOS Tracker Mid trucks, a rubber Rad Pad slalom wedge front and a urethane wedge riser at the back, and a mix of OG second-generation and reissued Kryptonics wheels in red (at the front, for grip) and green (at the rear, for speed). It's a setup ideal for slaloming on slippery concrete.

Provenance

This NOS Greg Taie Slalom deck was a gift from my colleagues at CAKE, who purchased it from Pacific Coast Vintage in Paris, France. The trucks are NOS Tracker Mids from my cousin, who bought them approximately 50 years ago. The red rear wheels are NOS second-generation Kryptonics, acquired from a private vendor, and green front wheels are reissues purchased directly from Kryptonics.

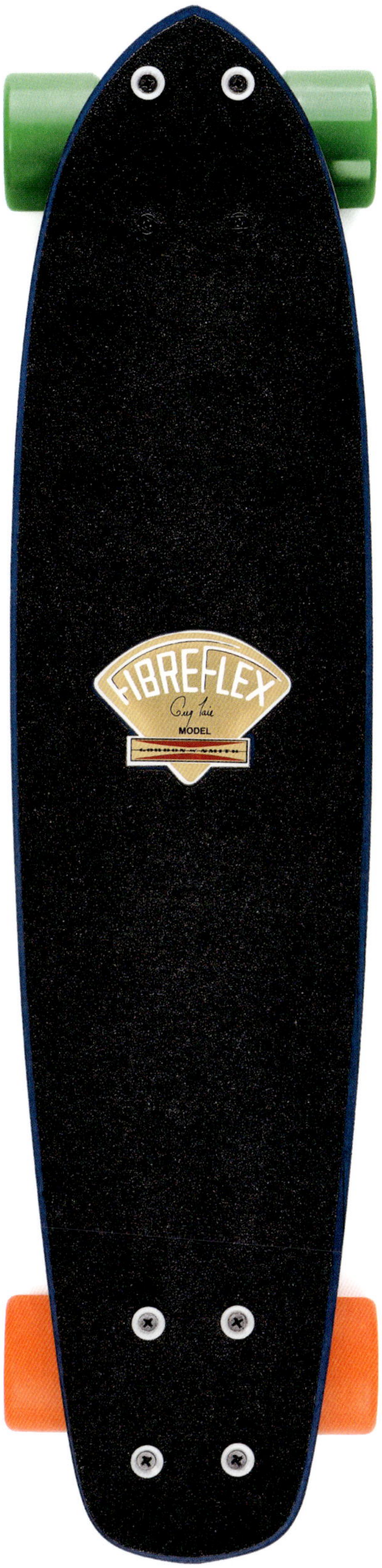

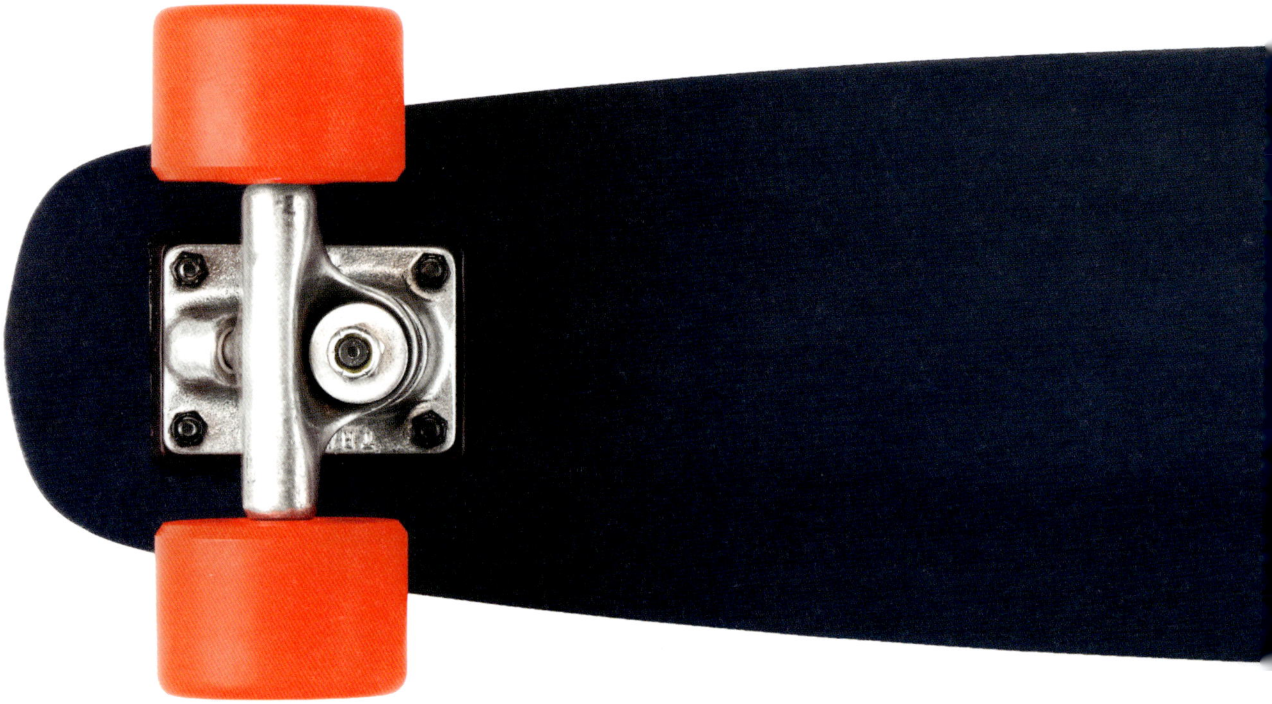

Deck

- NOS Greg Taie Slalom
- 3-ply core Bo-Tuff on both sides
- Length 28" (71cm)
- Width 6.5" (16.5cm)
- Thickness $^{5}/_{16}$" (7.94mm)
- Full black grip tape

Trucks

- NOS Tracker Mid trucks
- Rad Pad Slalom Wedge risers (front) and Rad Pad Urethane risers (rear)

Wheels

- NOS second-generation red Kryptonics (rear) and reissued green Kryptonics (front)
- Diameter: 2.56" (65mm)
- Durometer: 78A (red); 91A (green)
- Sealed SKF bearings

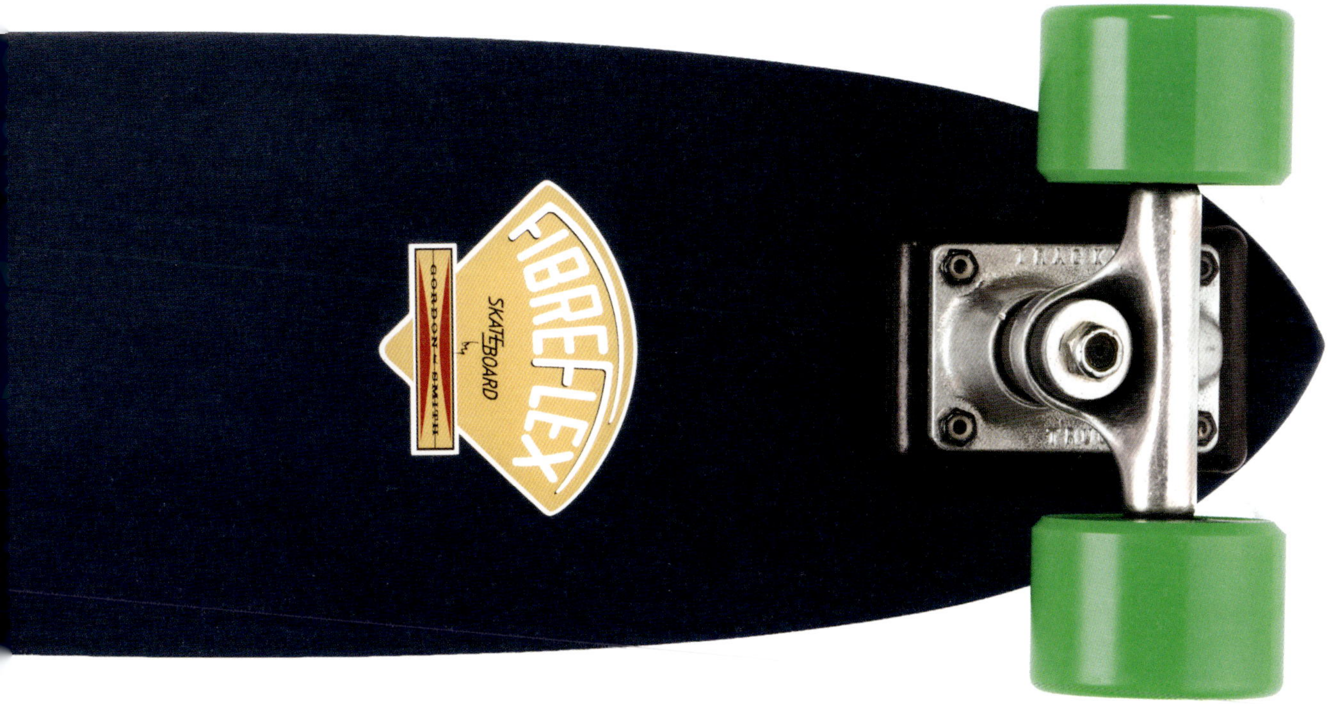

1979 Dennis Martinez Flying Ace

"The End"

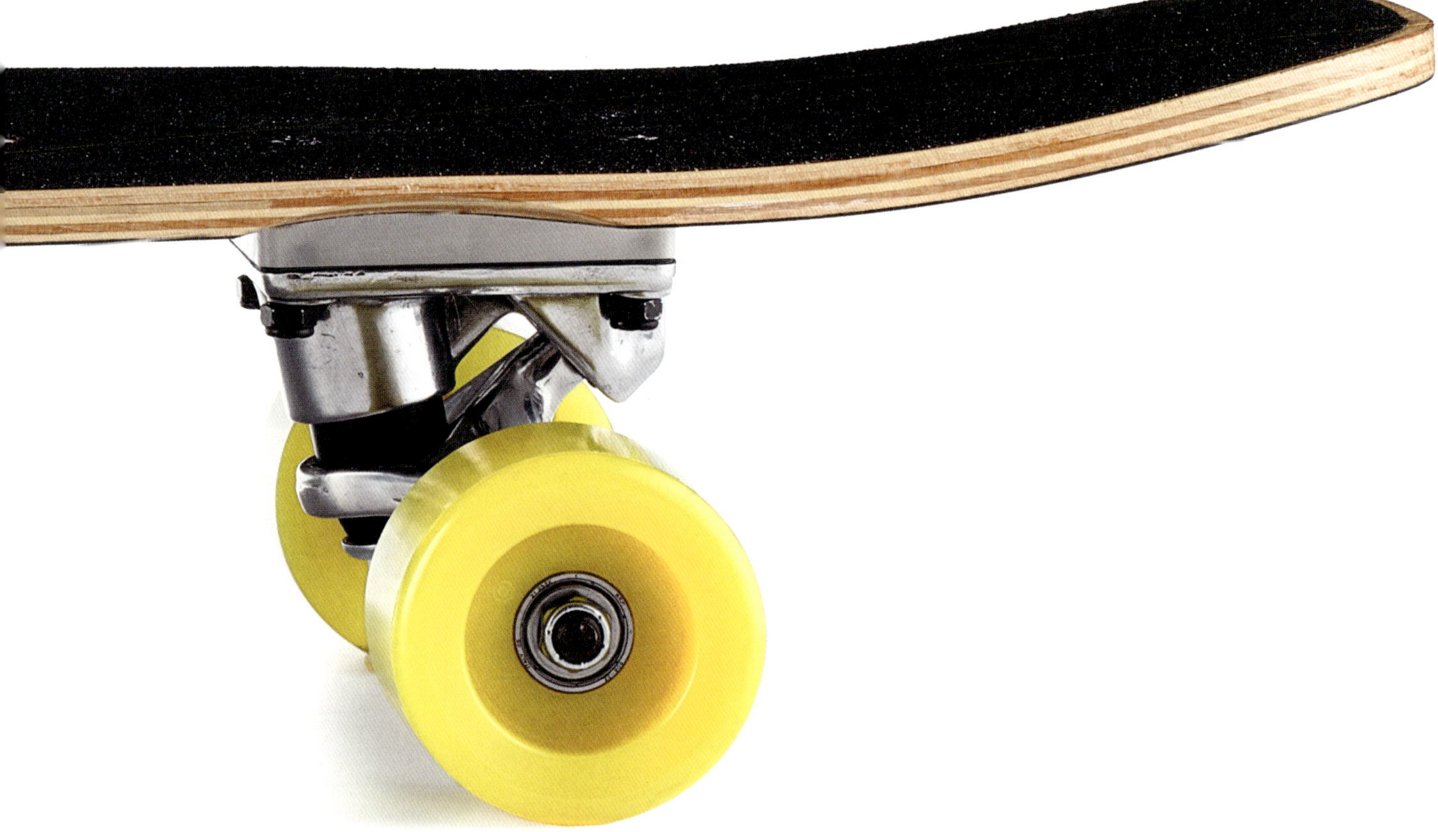

The NOS Flying Ace, a Dennis Martinez signature model, was the last FibreFlex deck of the 1970s. Ten inches wide, it was designed for pools and vert ramps, and its pig-like shape was a gesture of what was to come in the 1980s. A stiff, five-ply construction, it only had Bo-Tuff on its bottom layer. This deck is fitted with OG Gullwing Super Pro 9.0 trucks and NOS Bennett Supergator wheels. The wheels are designed to be slightly conical, with less urethane touching the ground. This design is ideal for straight-line speed, while still offering ample surface area and grip for turning.

Provenance

By far my most expensive purchase, this deck came in its original waxed bag from a collector in Spain. The OG Gullwing Super Pro 9.0 trucks and the NOS Bennet Supergator wheels were bought from collectors in the US and the UK, respectively.

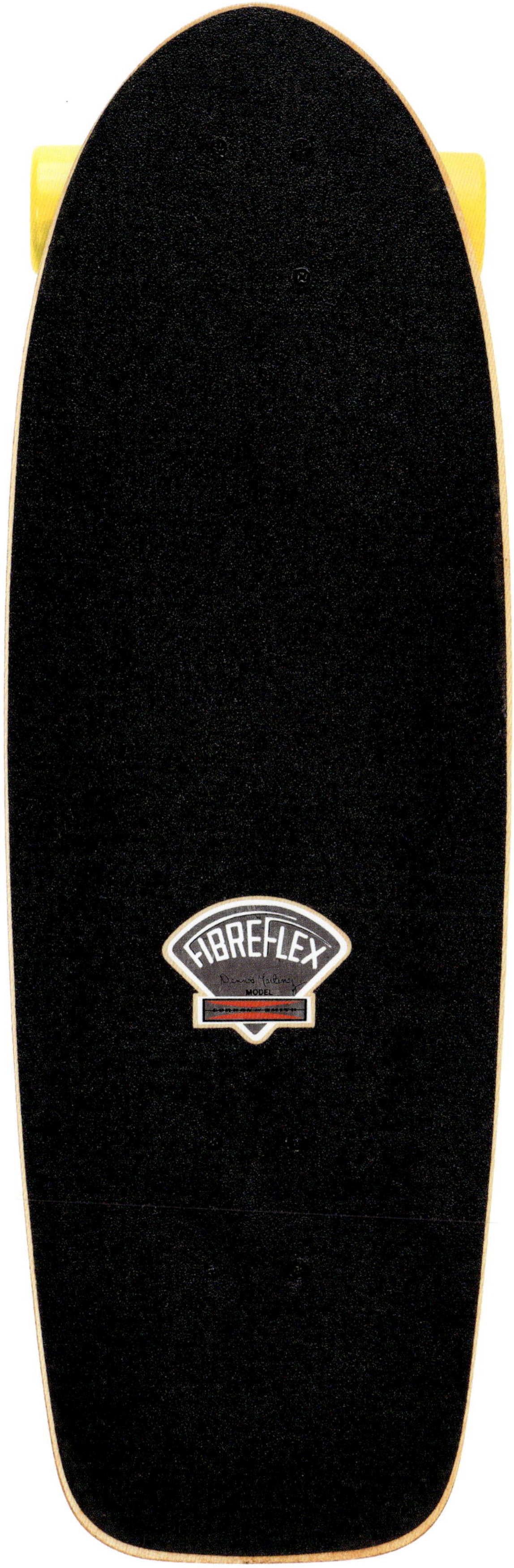

1979 Flying Ace Specs

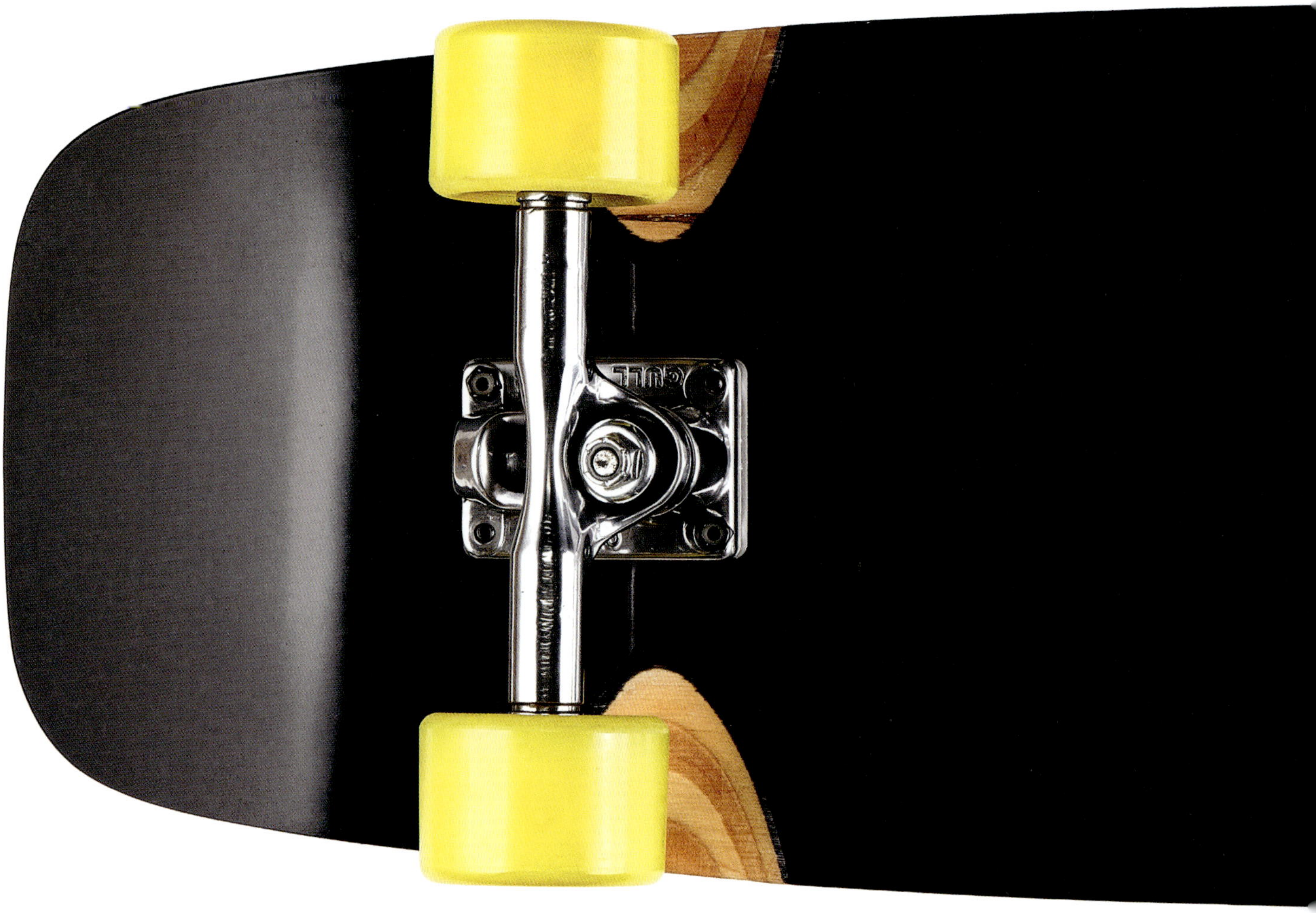

Deck

- NOS Dennis Martinez Flying Ace
- Five-ply core with a single Bo-Tuff layer on the bottom
- Length: 30½" (77cm)
- Width: 10" (25cm)
- Thickness: 5⁄16" (7.94mm)
- Full black grip tape

Trucks

- OG Gullwing Super Pro 9.0"
- Tracker risers

Wheels

- Bennett Supergators
- Diameter: 2.6" (66mm)
- Durometer: mid 80s
- Sealed SKF Bearings

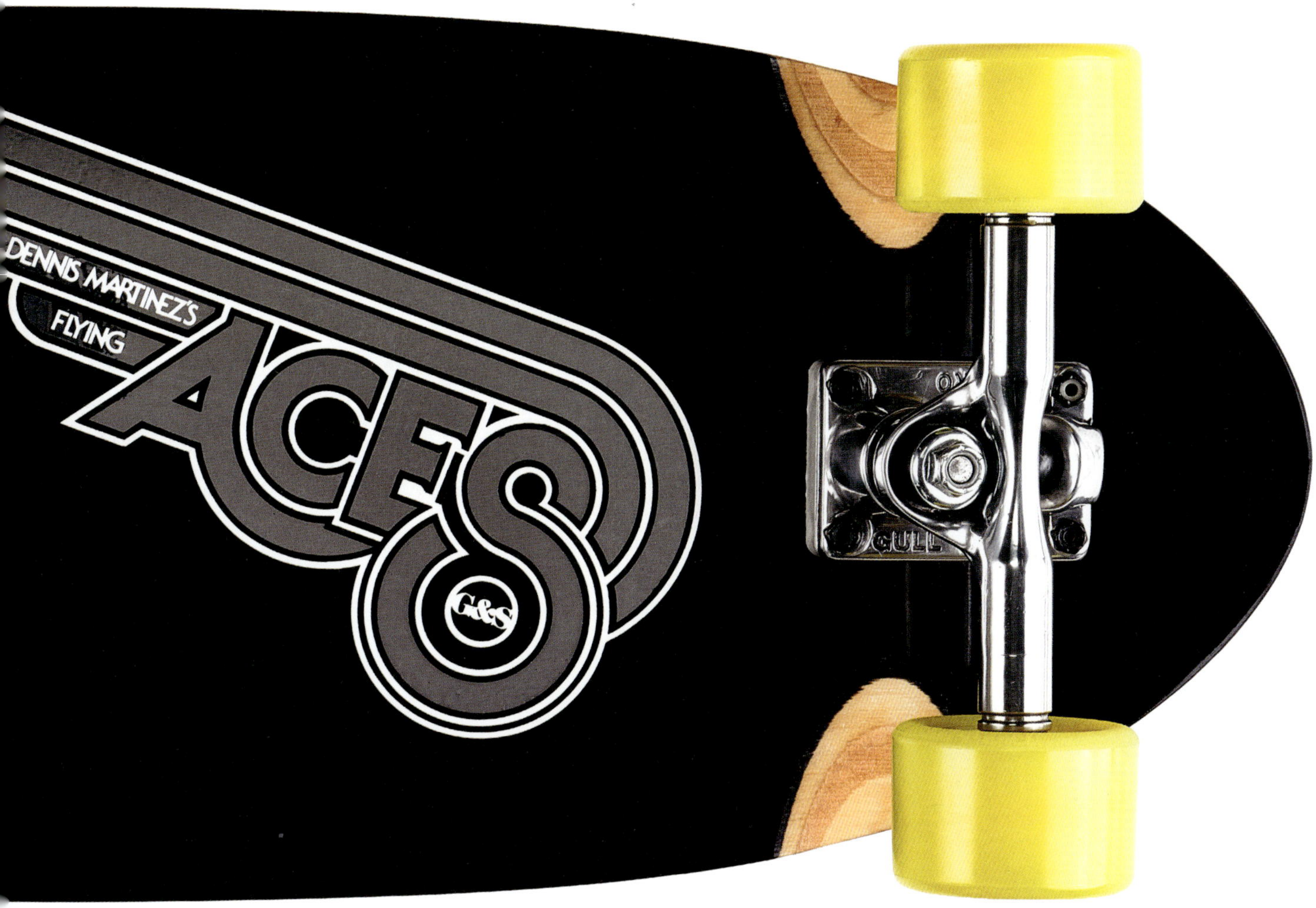

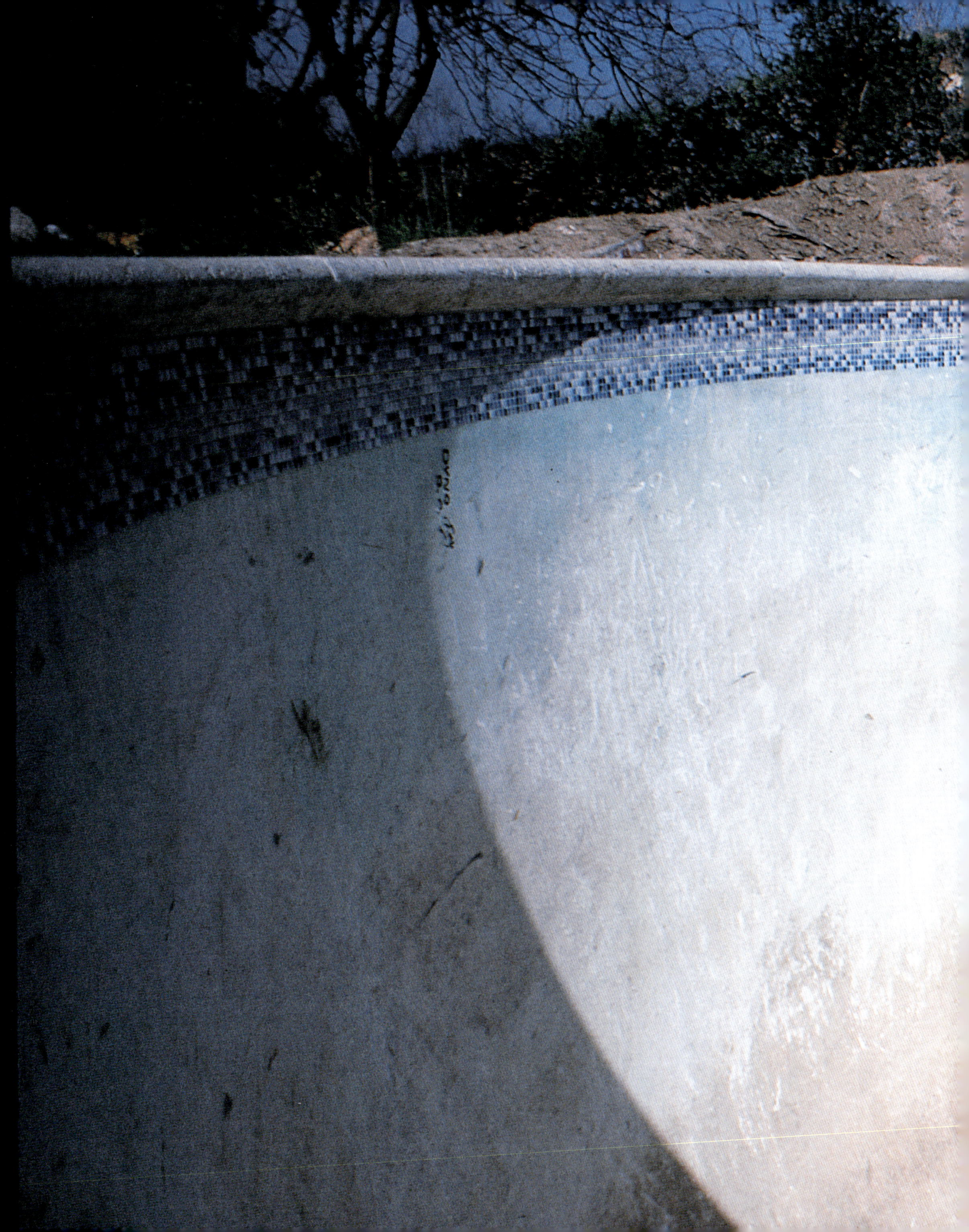

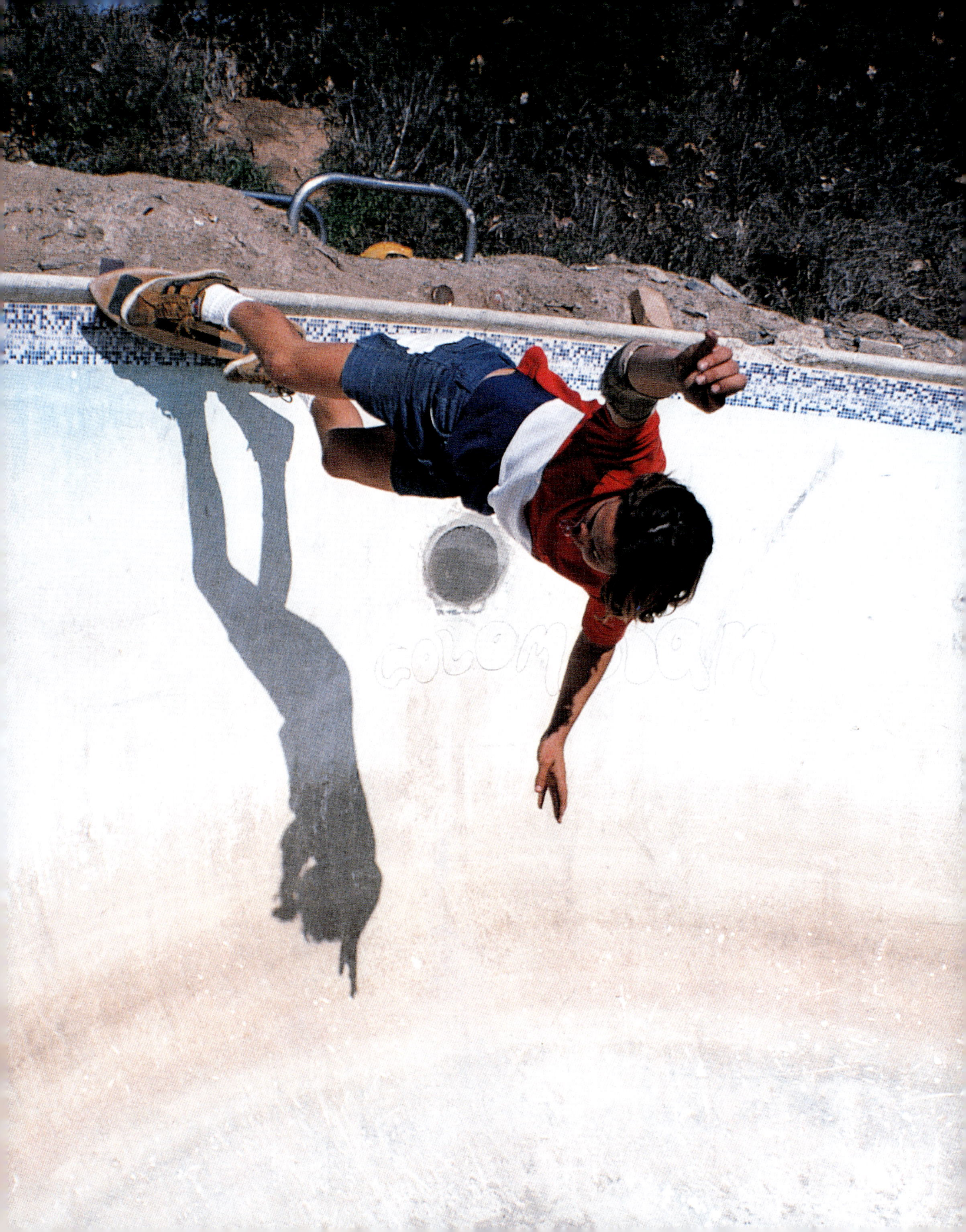

SkateBoarder Magazine

For skateboarding enthusiasts, *SkateBoarder* magazine didn't just document the sport—it made it. Featuring profiles of skaters, photos of "sessions" at ramps, bowls, hillsides, and other locations in California, and publishing news on the latest technology, it helped produce the mythology surrounding skateboarding's golden era in the late 1970s. Today, its back issues are both a valuable resource for collectors and a link to the past.

When I think about my collection of FibreFlex skateboards from 1975–79, I automatically think of *SkateBoarder* magazine. Started in 1964 and relaunched in 1975, just as skateboarding entered one of its most innovative periods, it was more than a magazine. A cultural engine and dream-machine, it became the collective memory of skateboarding's most innovative period.

Today, my collection – which I've pieced together via back issues – would not exist without it. But while old copies are an invaluable resource for modern collectors, *SkateBoarder* was a holy text for skaters of the era. In the 1960s, skateboarding had already enjoyed a first wave of popularity, which declined due to the hard, noisy, brittle wheels available by the early 1970s. This changed with the introduction of rubber-like urethane wheels. Suddenly, skateboards became smooth, fast, and controllable, and skaters were finally able to push the limits of what they could do.

SkateBoarder's return in the mid-1970s was perfectly timed. The cover of its relaunch was a photo taken by Warren Bolster – the Henri Cartier-Bresson of skateboard photography – of Greg Weaver carving around a drained concrete pool. At the time, a drought in California had drained thousands of backyard pools, and riders were exploring them. The moment demanded documentation, and *SkateBoarder* provided it.

What set the magazine apart was its instinct that skateboarding was a movement. Photography by Hugh Holland, Craig Stecyk, Art Brewer, James Cassimus, and Glen Friedman – all of Magnum quality – mythologized skate spots and skaters. In turn, pools, concrete ditches, and backyard ramps became places worthy of pilgrimages. These images shaped the era's emotional palette: silhouettes suspended on vertical walls, kids sitting at the top of ramps, waiting for something extraordinary to happen.

The writing carried the same spirit. It was informed yet youthful, giving voice to a generation. Through interviews, profiles, travelogues, equipment guides, and philosophical reflections, this prose processed what it all meant. It turned skateboarders into characters, and "sessions" – those long days skating – into legends. For its readers, each issue was a window into a world at once magical and accessible.

In a pre-Internet age, *SkateBoarder* was a font of information. Printed monthly, each issue was hotly anticipated. It documented the first aerial tricks performed off ramps, long before the X Games popularized them, along with the earliest skateparks, bowl sessions, the rise and fall of slalom, and the emergence of vertical riding. And by featuring era-defining skaters such as Tony Alva, Jay Adams, Ellen O'Neal, Henry Hester, Shogo Kubo, Stacy Peralta, Tom Sims, Steve Cathey, and Rodney Mullen, among others, it established a canon of skateboarding lore.

Indeed, this is why the years 1975–79 are pivotal for my collection. Through images and text, *SkateBoarder* also captured breakthroughs in equipment such as decks, trucks, and wheels – technology in which FibreFlex was one of the true forerunners. It also showed how quickly that technology could become obsolete. As skating grew more vertical and riders demanded stiffer, more responsive platforms, the flex that had defined FibreFlex gradually lost its edge. By the end of the decade, even FibreFlex itself had moved away from flexible decks, producing rigid boards while keeping the brand name. That arc, from innovation to obsolescence in barely four years, is part of what makes this period so compelling to me. As such, I tend to think of my collection not as an assembly of objects but as a time capsule of a technology in motion: boards that trace the full arc from breakthrough to eclipse and show just how fast the sport was evolving around them.

The boards in my collection are artifacts – physical evidence of a cultural explosion that *SkateBoarder* painstakingly recorded. The shapes, graphics, materials, and technologies of each board correspond almost directly to the stories told in the magazine. Without *SkateBoarder*, the meaning of these objects would be almost completely obscured. But with it, they form a tangible link to the past – a time capsule, if you will.

If, then, *SkateBoarder* defined skateboarding in the 1970s, my collection is a tribute to the shared language it created. FibreFlex was the skate brand I admired most as a teenager, and I still revere it today, but its significance now rests not only in the boards themselves, but also in the way the magazine helped frame and circulate their importance. To put it simply, without *SkateBoarder*, this era of skateboarding would have felt very different, and my collection would likely never have taken shape.

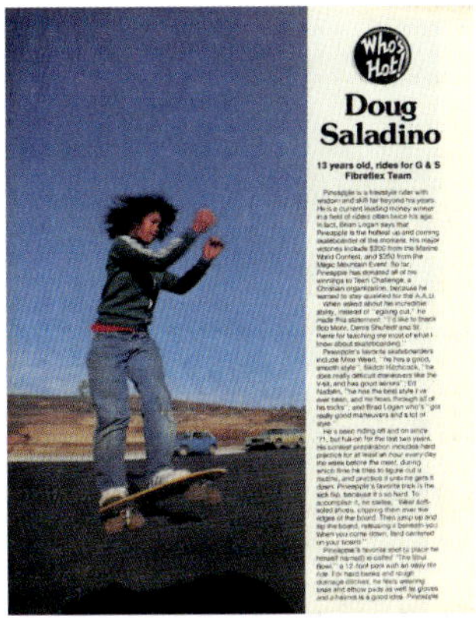
Who's Hot!
Doug Saladino
13 years old, rides for G & S Fibreflex Team

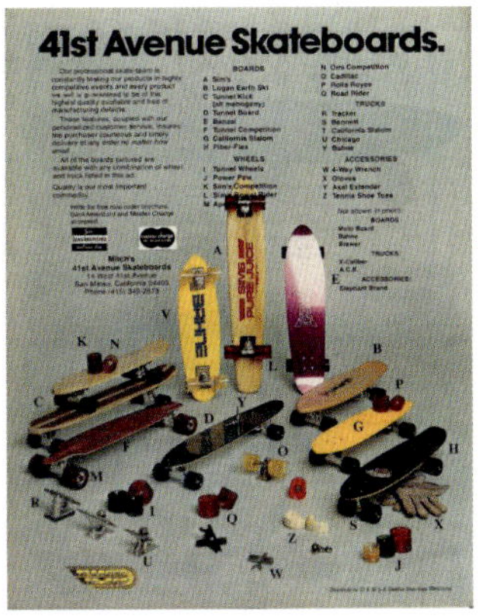
41st Avenue Skateboards.

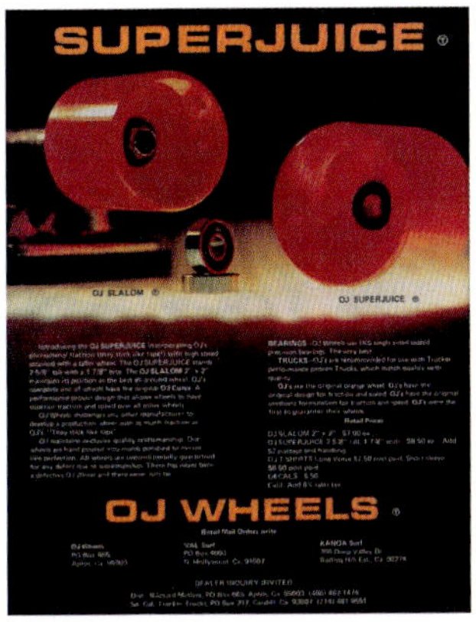
SUPERJUICE
OJ WHEELS

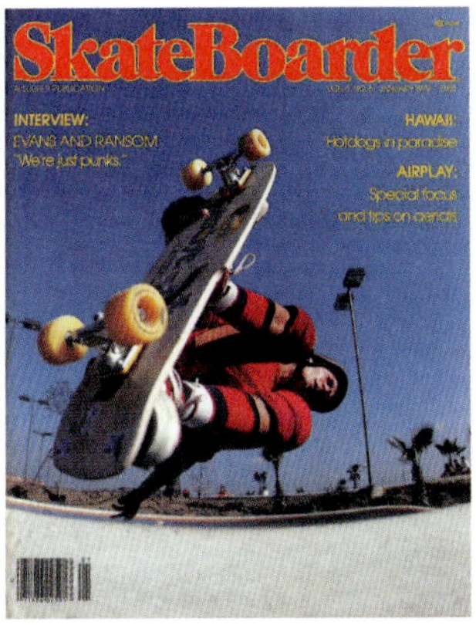
SkateBoarder
INTERVIEW:
EVANS AND RANSOM:
"We're just punks."
HAWAII:
Hotdogs in paradise
AIRPLAY:
Special focus
and tips on aerials

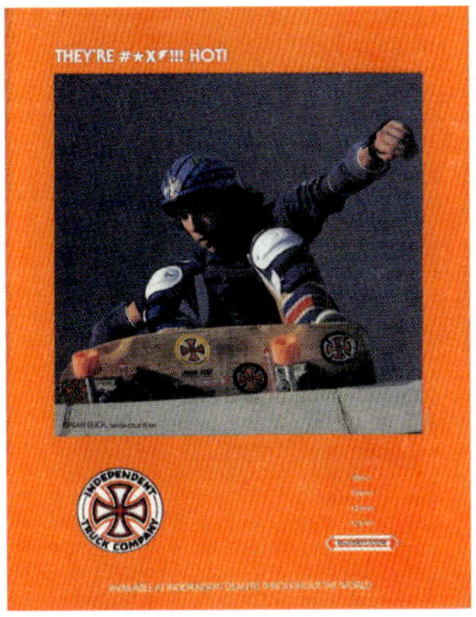
THEY'RE #★X❢!!! HOT!
INDEPENDENT TRUCK COMPANY

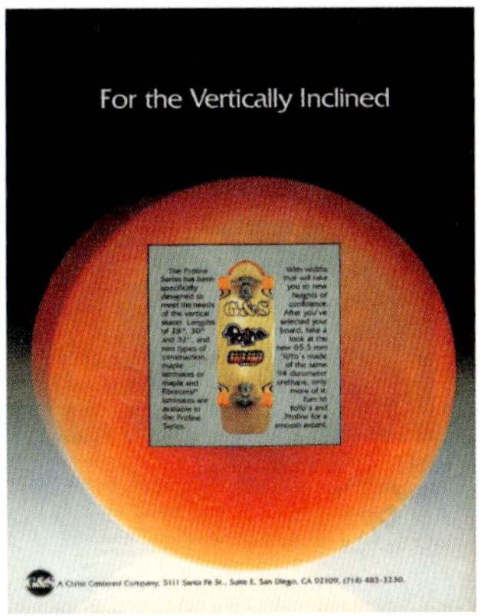
For the Vertically Inclined

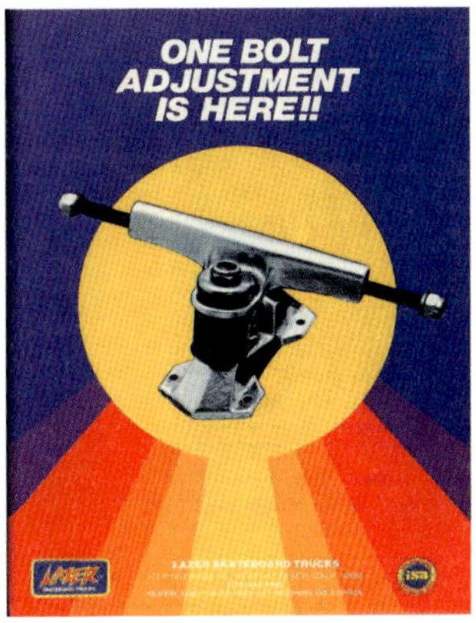
ONE BOLT
ADJUSTMENT
IS HERE!!

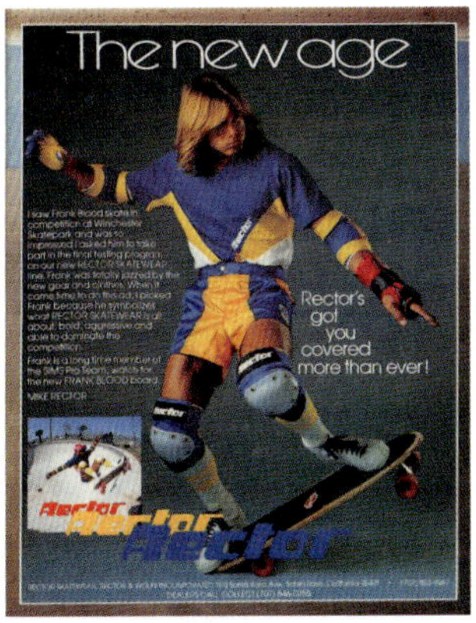
The new age
Rector's
got
you
covered
more than ever!
Rector

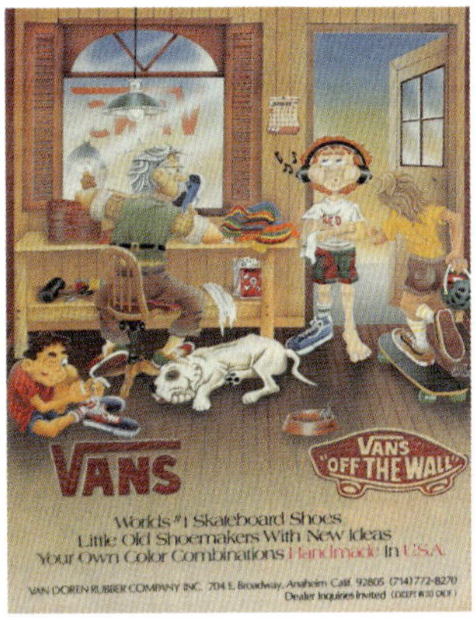
VANS
VANS "OFF THE WALL"
World's #1 Skateboard Shoes
Little Old Shoemakers With New Ideas
Your Own Color Combinations Handmade In U.S.A.

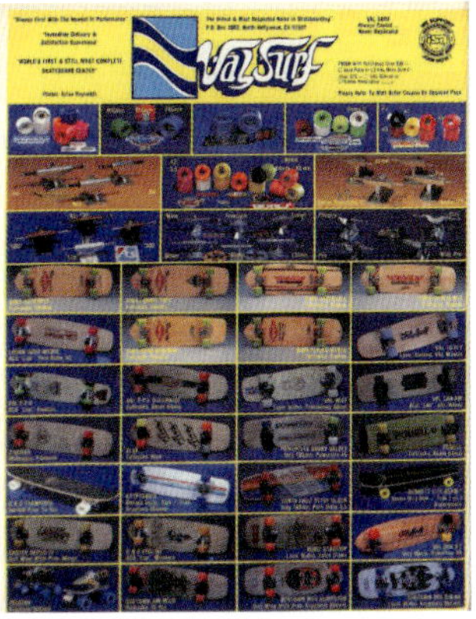
Val Surf

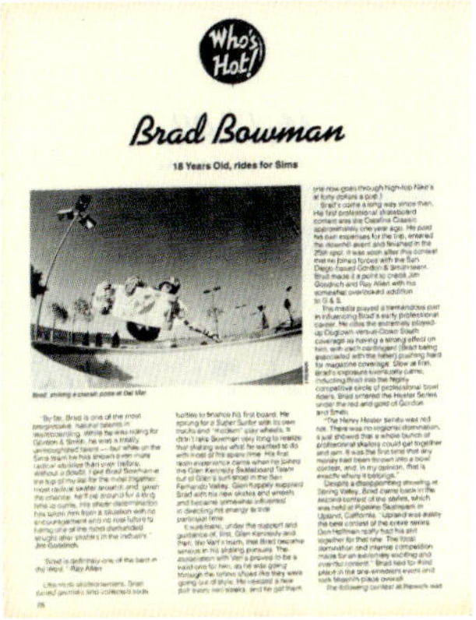
Who's Hot!
Brad Bowman
18 Years Old, rides for Sims

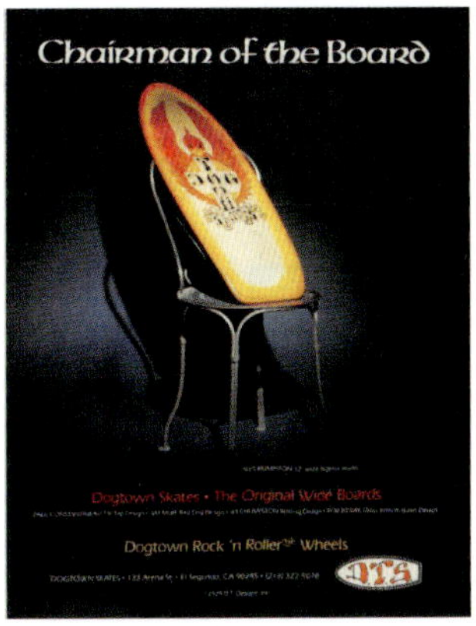
Chairman of the Board
Dogtown Skates • The Original Wide Boards
Dogtown Rock 'n Roller Wheels

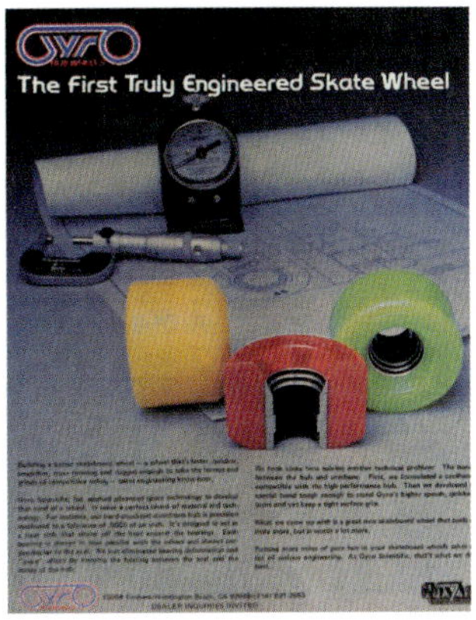
GYRO
The First Truly Engineered Skate Wheel

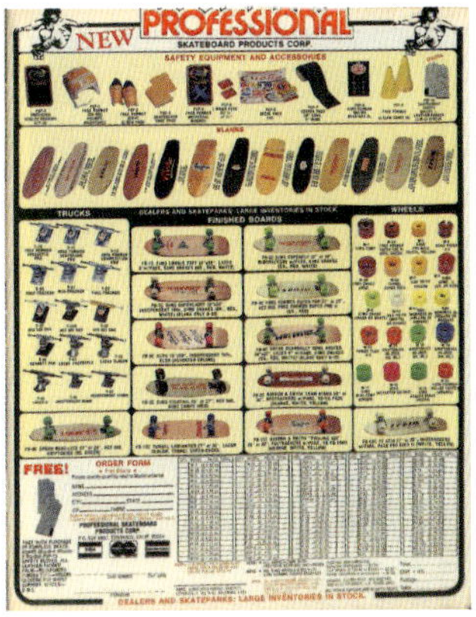
NEW PROFESSIONAL
SKATEBOARD PRODUCTS CORP.
FREE!

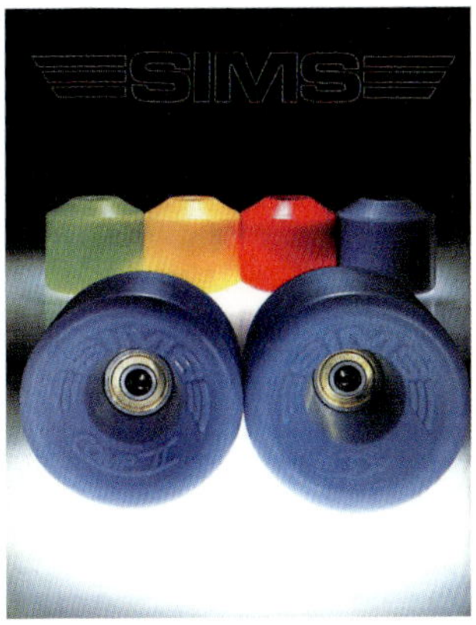
SIMS

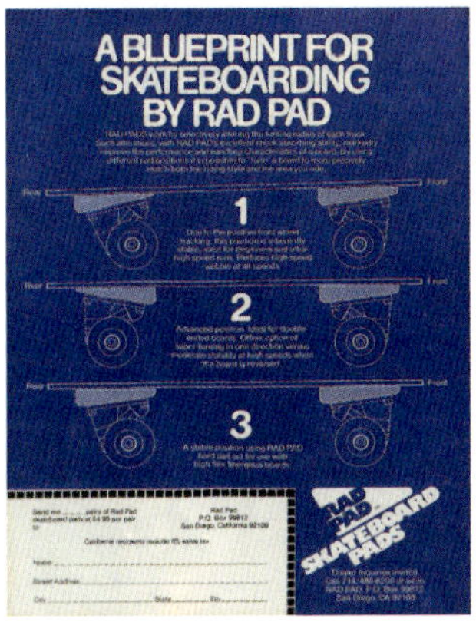
A BLUEPRINT FOR
SKATEBOARDING
BY RAD PAD
1
2
3
RAD PAD SKATEBOARD PADS

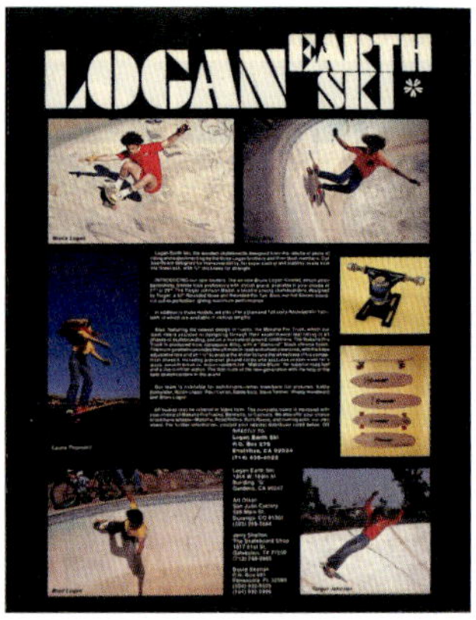
LOGAN EARTH SKI

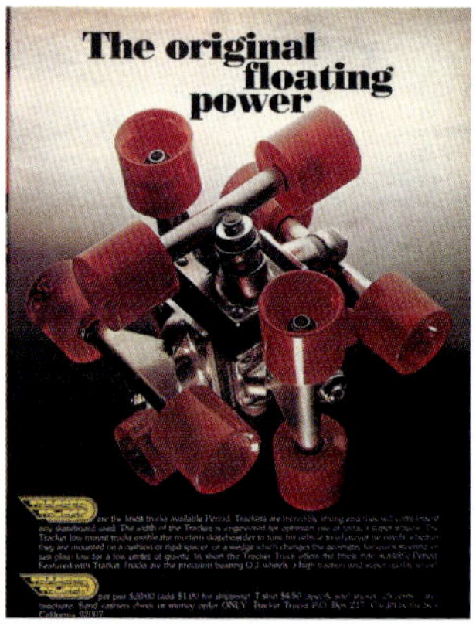
The original floating power

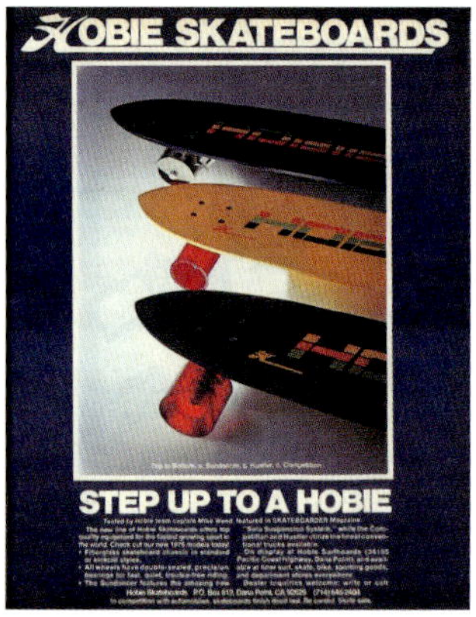
HOBIE SKATEBOARDS
STEP UP TO A HOBIE

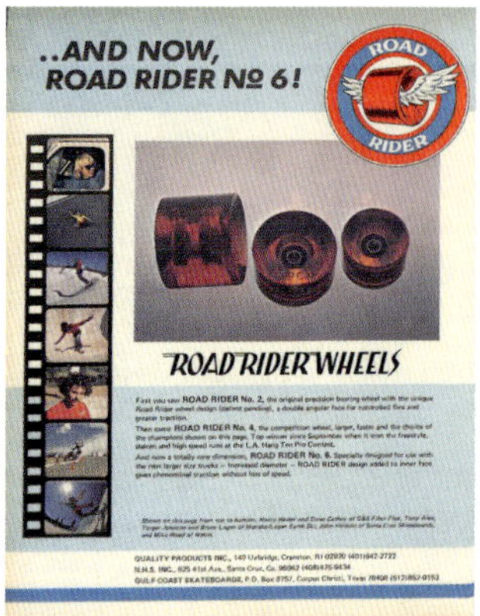
..AND NOW,
ROAD RIDER No 6!
ROAD RIDER
ROAD RIDER WHEELS

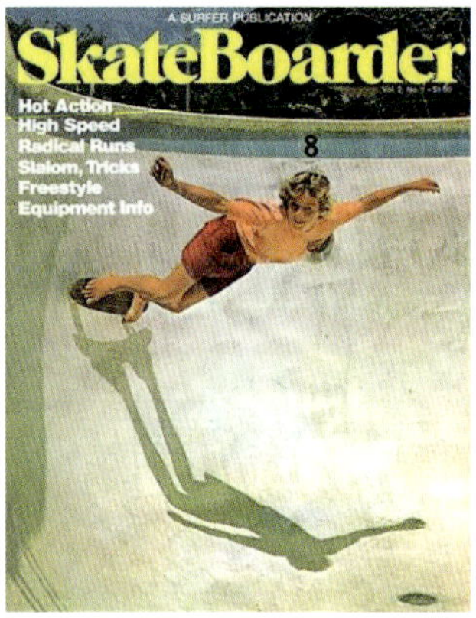
A SURFER PUBLICATION
SkateBoarder
Hot Action
High Speed
Radical Runs
Slalom, Tricks
Freestyle
Equipment Info

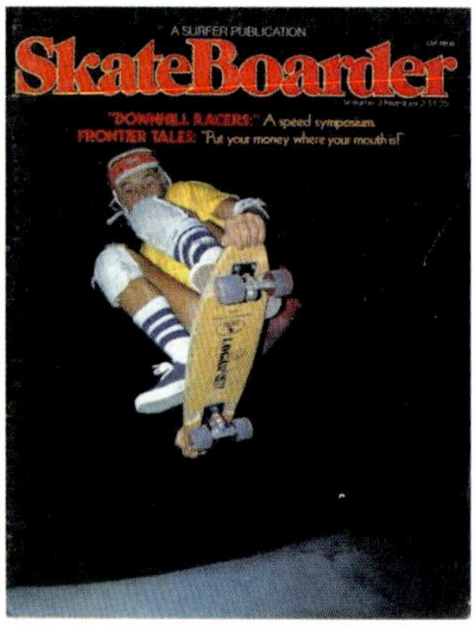
A SURFER PUBLICATION
SkateBoarder
"DOWNHILL RACERS:" A speed symposium.
FRONTIER TALES: "Put your money where your mouth is!"

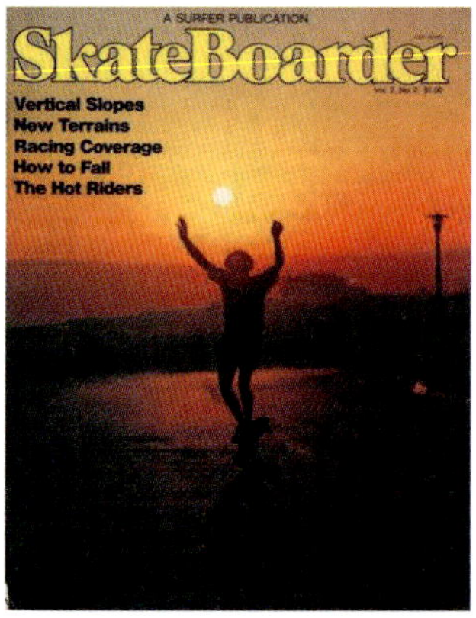
A SURFER PUBLICATION
SkateBoarder
Vertical Slopes
New Terrains
Racing Coverage
How to Fall
The Hot Riders

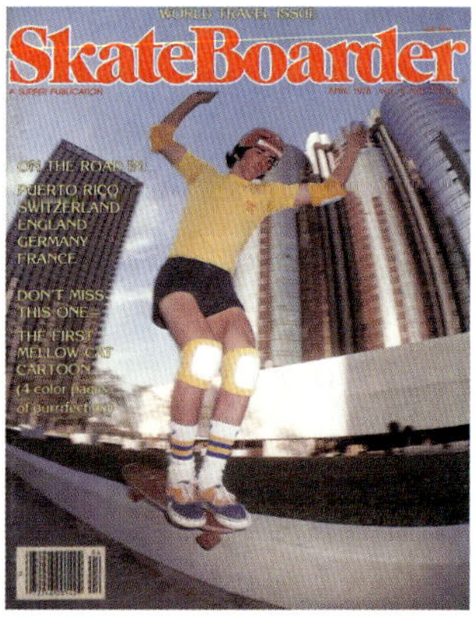
SkateBoarder
ON THE ROAD IN
PUERTO RICO
SWITZERLAND
ENGLAND
GERMANY
FRANCE
DON'T MISS THIS ONE
THE FIRST MELLOW CAT CARTOON

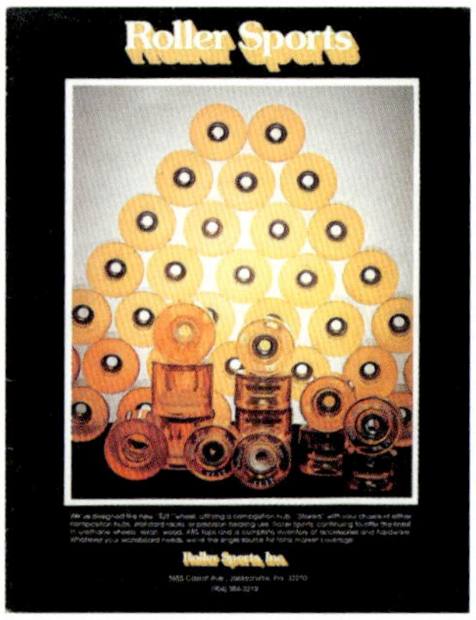
Roller Sports

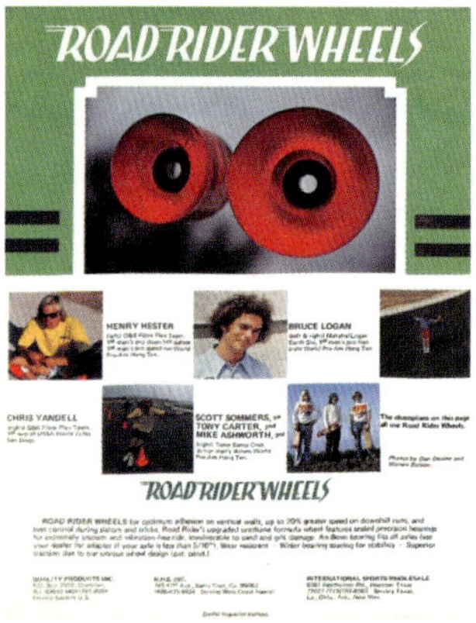
ROAD RIDER WHEELS
HENRY HESTER
BRUCE LOGAN
CHRIS YANDALL
ROAD RIDER WHEELS

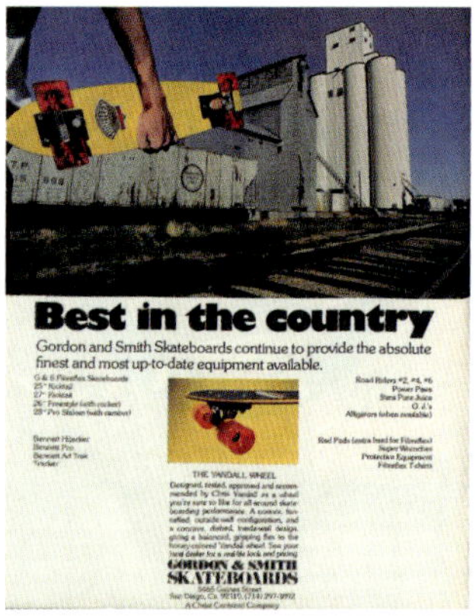
Best in the country
Gordon and Smith Skateboards continue to provide the absolute finest and most up-to-date equipment available.
GORDON & SMITH SKATEBOARDS

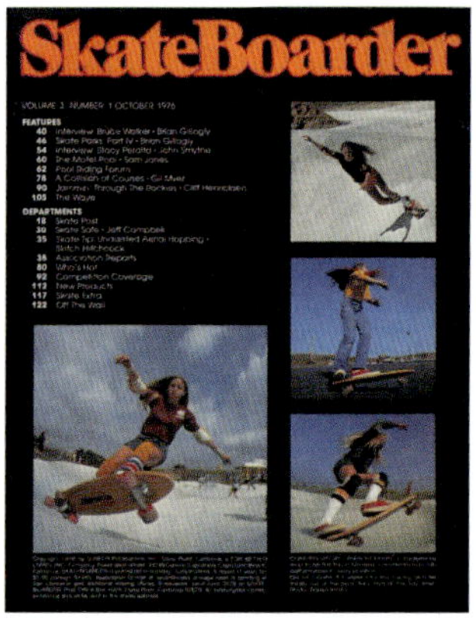
SkateBoarder

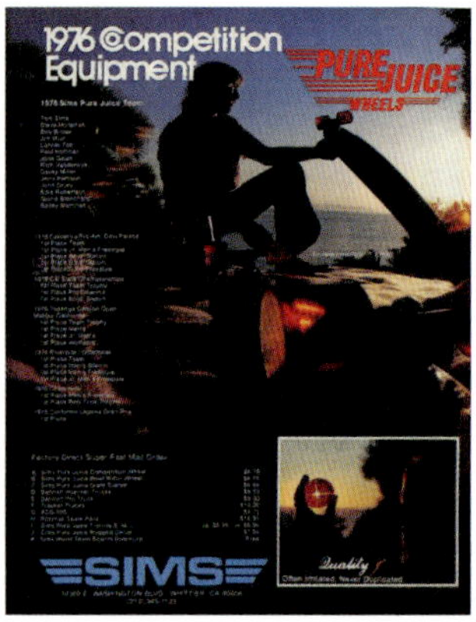
1976 Competition Equipment
PURE JUICE WHEELS
SIMS

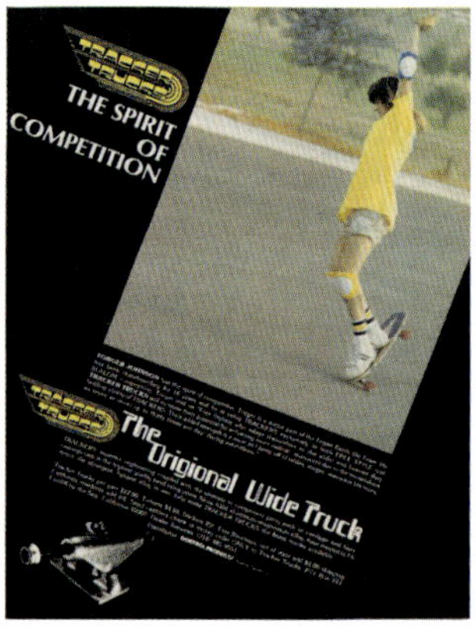
THE SPIRIT OF COMPETITION
The Original Wide Truck

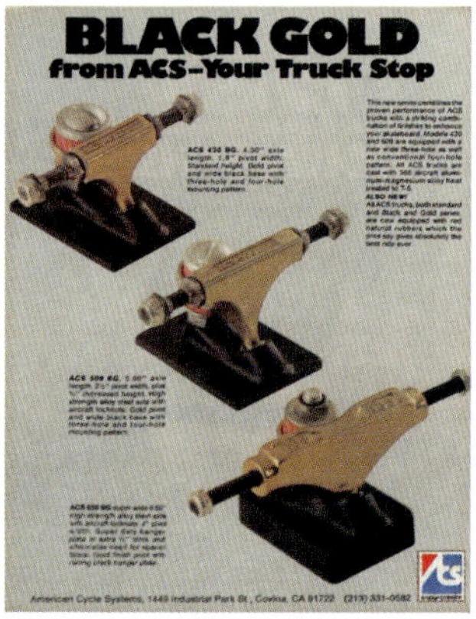
BLACK GOLD
from ACS–Your Truck Stop

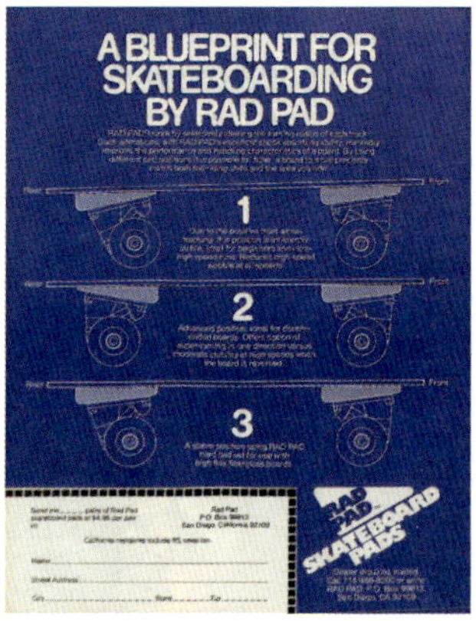
A BLUEPRINT FOR SKATEBOARDING BY RAD PAD
1
2
3
RAD PAD SKATEBOARD PADS

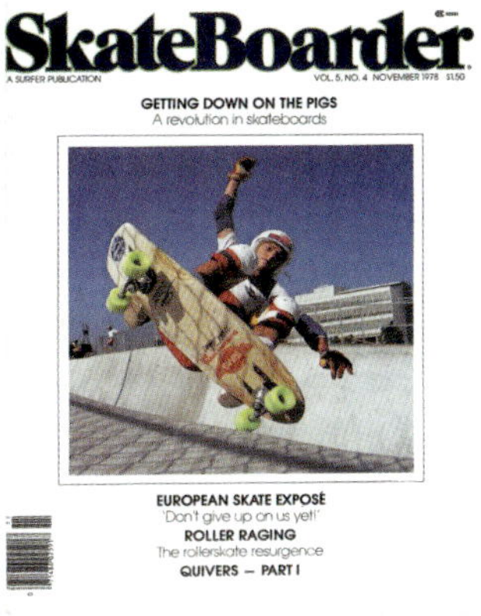
SkateBoarder
A SURFER PUBLICATION
VOL. 5, NO. 4 NOVEMBER 1978 $1.50
GETTING DOWN ON THE PIGS
A revolution in skateboards
EUROPEAN SKATE EXPOSÉ
'Don't give up on us yet!'
ROLLER RAGING
The rollerskate resurgence
QUIVERS — PART I

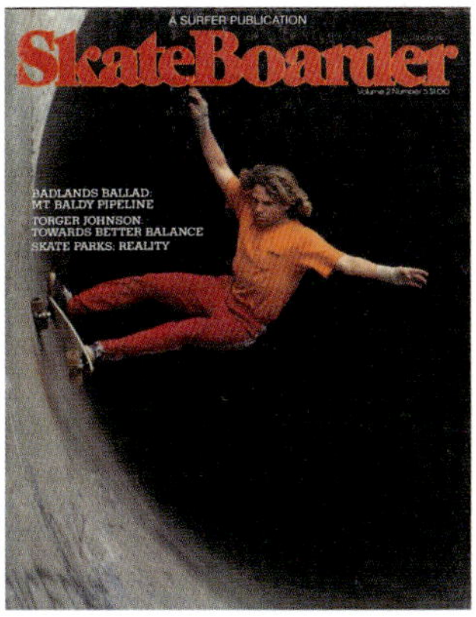
A SURFER PUBLICATION
SkateBoarder
BADLANDS BALLAD:
MT. BALDY PIPELINE
TORGER JOHNSON
TOWARDS BETTER BALANCE
SKATE PARKS: REALITY

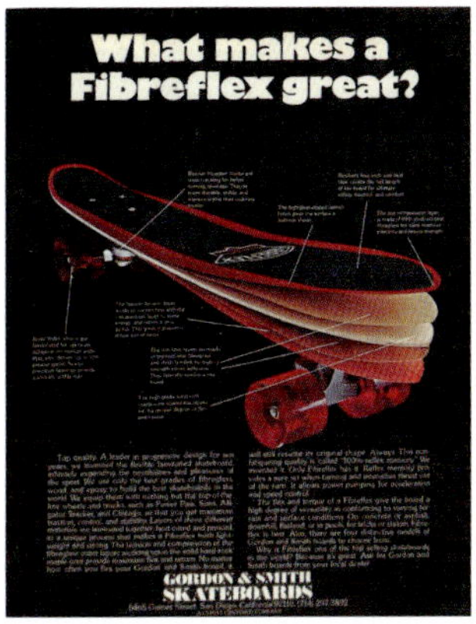
What makes a Fibreflex great?
GORDON & SMITH SKATEBOARDS

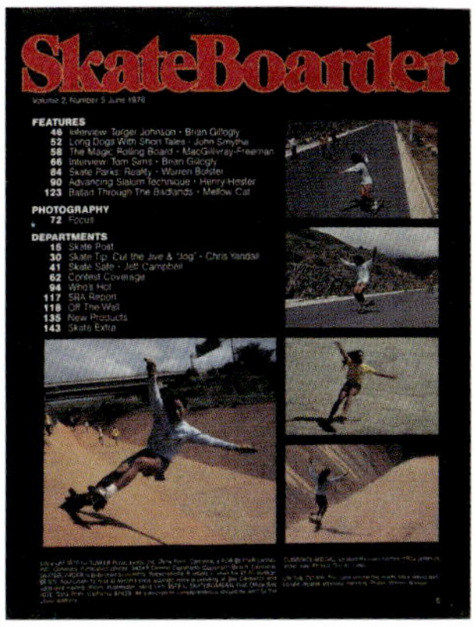
SkateBoarder
FEATURES
PHOTOGRAPHY
DEPARTMENTS

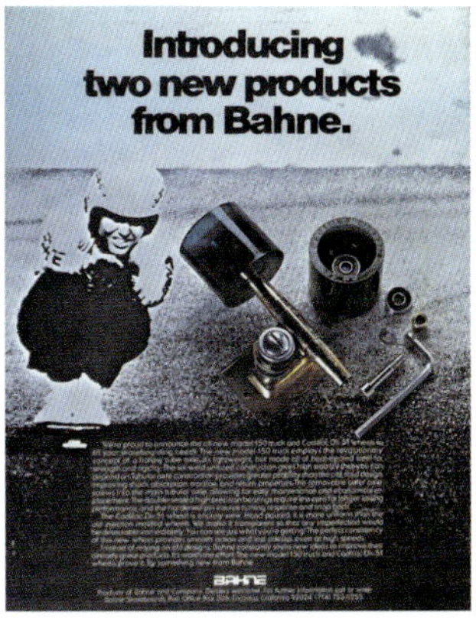
Introducing two new products from Bahne.

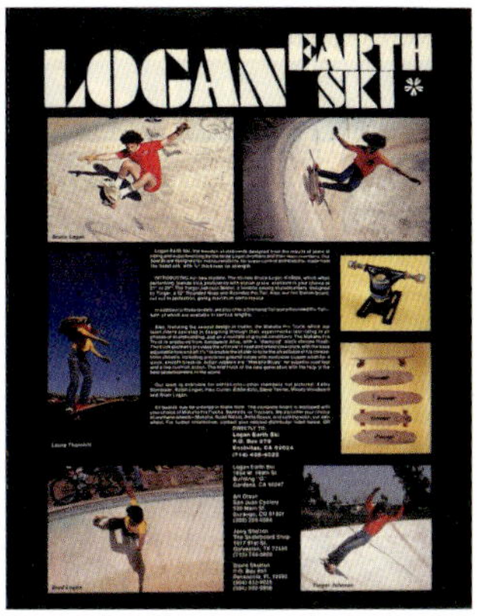
LOGAN EARTH SKI

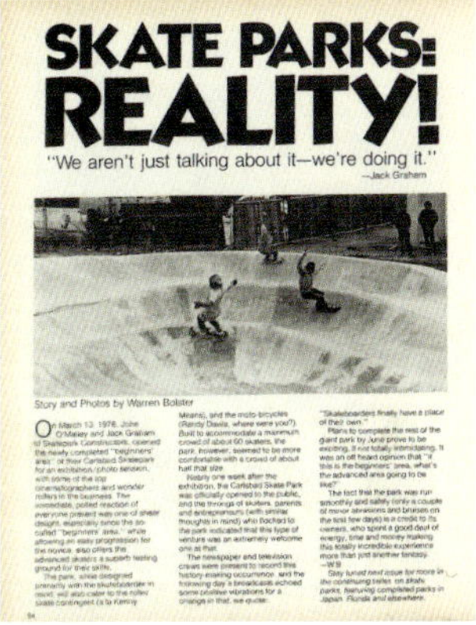
SKATE PARKS: REALITY!
"We aren't just talking about it—we're doing it."
—Jack Graham
Story and Photos by Warren Bolster

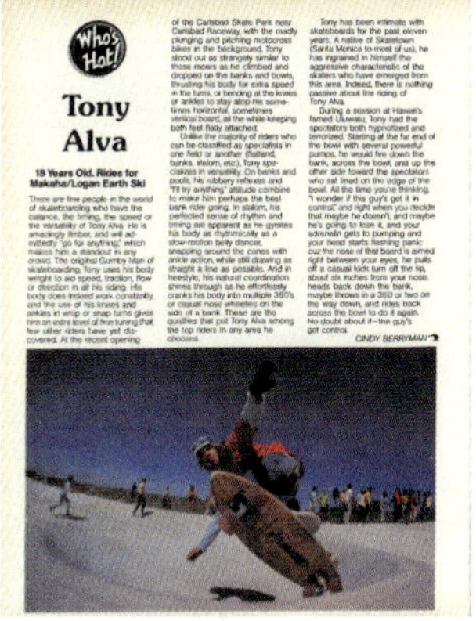
Who's Hot!
Tony Alva
18 Years Old. Rides for Makaha/Logan Earth Ski

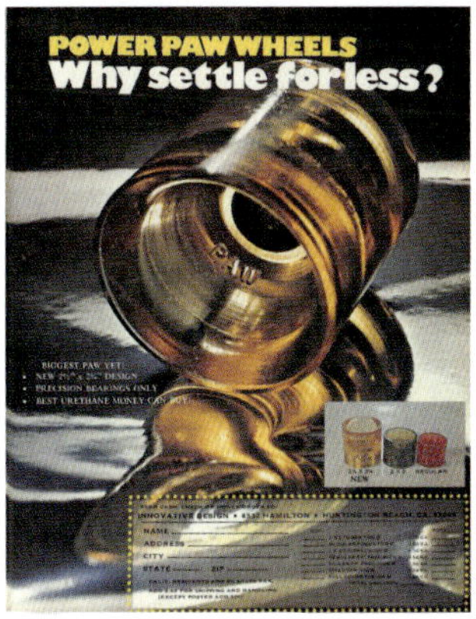
POWER PAW WHEELS
Why settle for less?

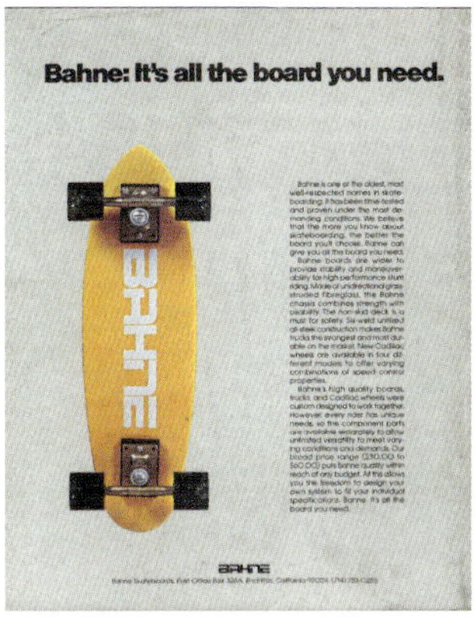
Bahne: It's all the board you need.

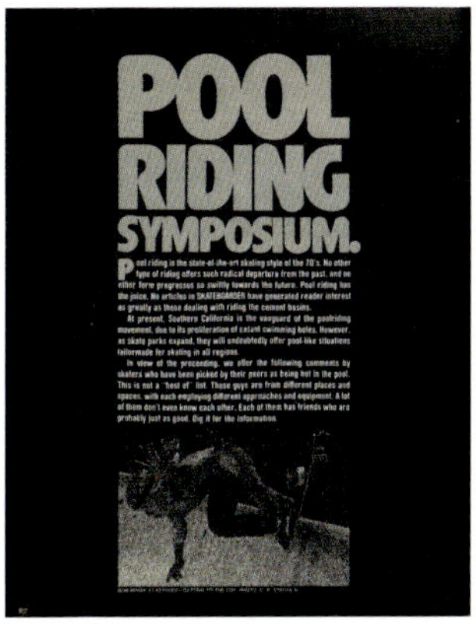
POOL RIDING SYMPOSIUM.

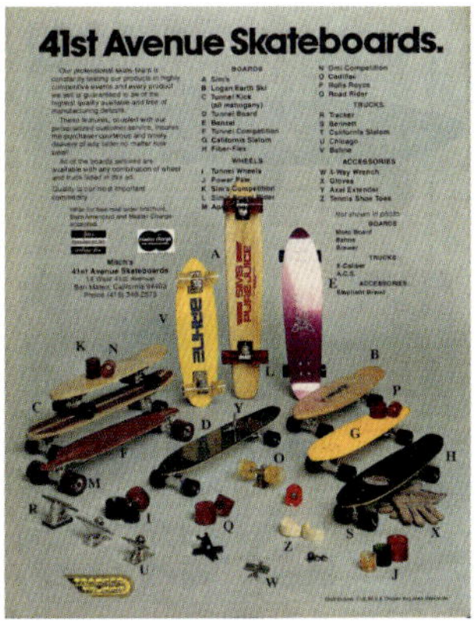
41st Avenue Skateboards.

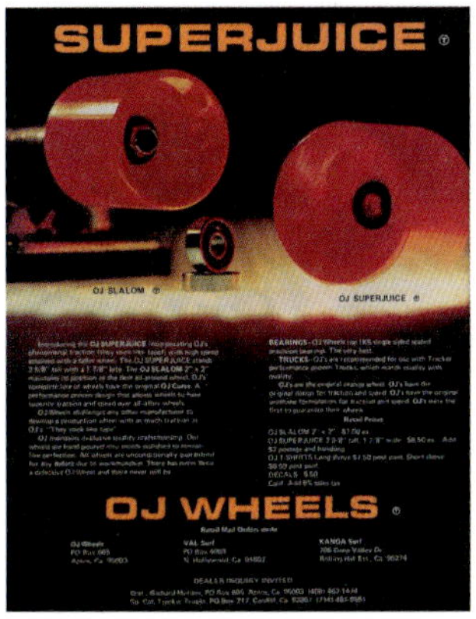
SUPERJUICE
OJ SLALOM
OJ SUPERJUICE
OJ WHEELS

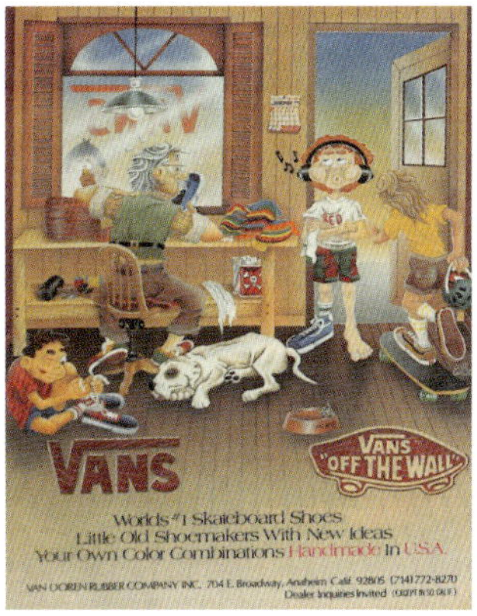
VANS
VANS "OFF THE WALL"
World's #1 Skateboard Shoes
Little Old Shoemakers With New Ideas
Your Own Color Combinations Handmade in U.S.A.

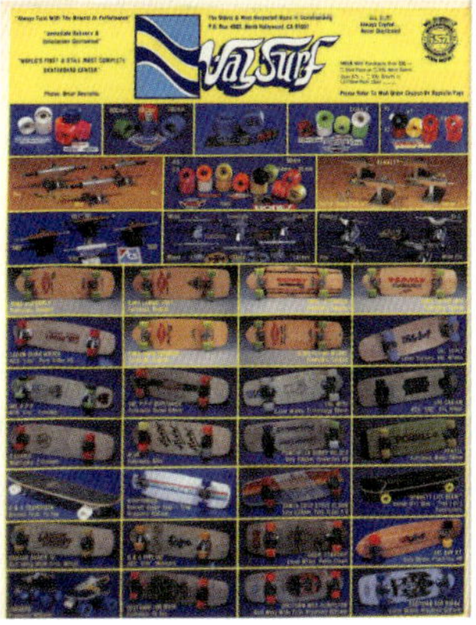
Val Surf

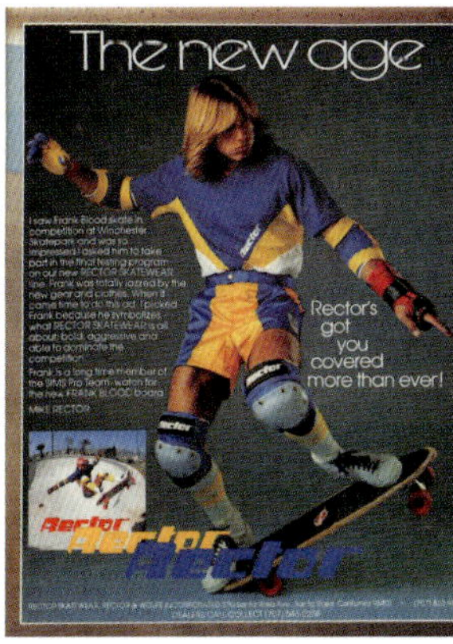
The new age
Rector's got you covered more than ever!
Rector

The Master of FibreFlex Restorations: Mark Mayers

Hidden in the coastal landscape of Cornwall, England, a Master has, for the last 20 years, been surreptitiously refurbishing some of the most sought-after FibreFlex on the market. His name is Mark Mayers, the world's leading restorer of golden-era skateboards. Blessed with an inimitable eye for detail, his holistic philosophy restoration has ensured the preservation of this foundational era in skateboarding.

Among the many people who have helped preserve the history of 1970s skateboarding, few have done so more keenly than Mark Mayers. Based in Cornwall, England, Mayers is a graphic designer by trade, but, over the past two decades, has become better known as the world's FibreFlex restorer.

In the niche world of enthusiasts driven by the design, craftsmanship, and material innovation of the original 1975–79 FibreFlex decks, Mayer's name is spoken with reverence. He is, in every sense of the word, a Master.

And like the hero of an adventure story, he was driven not by the promise of fame and fortune but by passion. Blessed with a designer's eye, he has developed, over the last 20 years, a unique skillset in the collector community, refurbishing over 150 FibreFlex boards, each one requiring its own unique combination of technical problem-solving, artistic reconstruction, and historical sensitivity.

What distinguishes Mayers's work is the integrity of his approach. His use of fibreglass, for instance, reflects original construction methods, strengthening damaged structures without altering the character of his boards. Cracks, delamination, warping, chipped tails, and fatigued layers are rebuilt with surgical precision. Then there's his acclaimed airbrush technique. Refined over years of experimentation, it allows him to match original colorways with uncanny accuracy.

This is where Mayers's boards transcend restoration. They look as though they have been stored in time capsules. Able to capture tonal variations, gradients, logos, striping, and colors, his skill with airbrushing continues to astonish collectors who know and understand every nuance of FibreFlex's products.

It all starts case by case, with Mayers evaluating each board passed to him individually. Some require simple rejuvenation; others, resurrection. Whatever the case, he approaches them with integrity, treating each deck not as an object to be "fixed" but as a piece of history. As a result, Mayers's work carries a certain prestige among collectors, who have come to regard the fruits of his labor as being the closest they will get to owning a pristine FibreFlex original.

My own introduction to Mayers came unexpectedly, via what I believed at the time to be a NOS FibreFlex Kicktail that I'd purchased from a collector in Australia. When the package arrived, however, it was in better condition than I could have possibly imagined. As I unwrapped the deck, it had an almost ethereal perfection: a clarity of finish that seemed the work of an impossibly careful hand. It was too good to be true.

After some investigation, comparing details and examining the craftsmanship, I eventually discovered the name behind it: Mark Mayers, the elusive Master. That board – my accidental introduction – thus became the beginning of a long and trusted collaboration.

Compelled by the brilliance of his work, I reached out to Mayers. Since then, he has restored multiple original decks for me. Each time, the process has involved long, inspiring conversations, discussing do's and don'ts, reviewing color tones, weighing historical accuracy, and navigating the balance between restoring and preserving. Mayers's insight is invaluable. He approaches every deck with both the seriousness of a conservator and the enthusiasm of someone who rode these boards in their heyday.

Six of the decks in this book owe their existence to Mayers. Of course, this represents a fraction of his output, but each one is nevertheless a microcosm of his skill. For people outside the FibreFlex collecting world, his fame might seem strange. But for those within it, his art is priceless – hence why his refurbs are so highly prized.

Having collected several of his skateboards already, I was driven by the desire to see the Master in action. And so, I visited Mayers in Cornwall with photographer Jörgen Brennicke, hoping to witness the magic firsthand. I wasn't disappointed. Nestled in the peaceful Cornish landscape, Mayers's workshop is an extension of his personality: unpretentious, calm, creative, and filled with stories, tools, and half-completed masterpieces. And within moments of meeting one another, we were already geeking out about a range of FibreFlex-related topics, including the '70s skate era; manufacturing quirks; restoration challenges; materials science; favorite skaters; hard-to-match colors; and the joy of bringing a board back to life.

For Mark, it became clear, FibreFlex isn't just a skate brand but a totem of skateboarding's golden era; an emblem for the period in which the sport came of age. As such, his work is a matter of devotion: the techniques he employs are part of a holistic philosophy of restoration that balances skill and authenticity. In turn, the visit showed me that, far from being a mere hobby, the process of collecting and restoring these objects is as much a practice as it is an obsession.

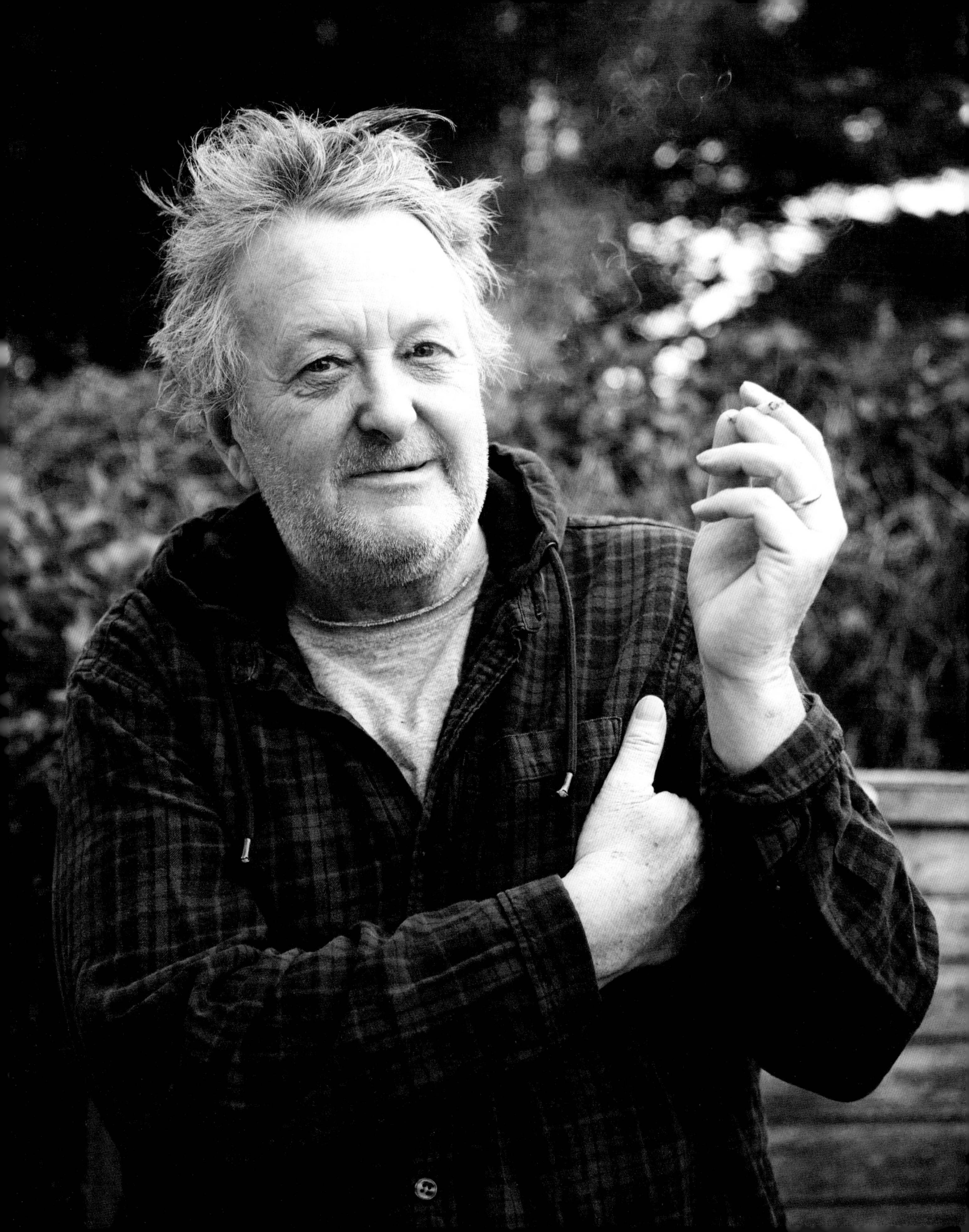

Team Riders & Signature Models

Steve Cathey: Versatility, Experimentation, and the YoYo Wheel

Steve Cathey, born in 1959 in La Jolla, California, moved effortlessly between freestyle, pools, parks, downhill, and slalom, driven by curiosity rather than specialization. His skating reflected a Southern California sensibility rooted in surfing, where style functioned as both aesthetic and philosophy, an approach drawn from Hawaiian surfers such as Gerry Lopez and Larry Bertlemann. For Cathey, skateboarding wasn't an alternative to surfing, but its continuation on concrete.

As a result, he naturally gravitated toward terrains demanding precision, creativity, and sensitivity; a tendency that would define one of his most influential contributions to the sport: YoYo wheels. Despite their superior grip and ride compared to their clay predecessors, early urethane skateboard wheels had flat outer edges that proved ill-suited to the evolving demands of skateboarding. Banked turns, coping transitions, and freestyle maneuvers required smoother rides and more forgiving shapes. Cathey's solution was crude but effective. By mounting his Road Rider wheels on an electric drill, he was able to reshape them as they spun around. The act was typical of the period: riders solving problems manufacturers had not yet recognized.

What eventually emerged from his experiment was the famous YoYo Wheels brand that revolutionized pool and ramp riding in the 1970s. Its path to glory, however, was hardly smooth. Not long after Cathey had turned pro for Gordon and Smith in 1976, the company's sales lead, Dave Macintyre, approached Road Rider regarding a Steve Cathey signature wheel incorporating this rounded-edge concept. Road Rider declined, unwilling to invest in new molds for a design that diverged from their established production. Convinced by the importance of Cathey's idea, Macintyre found an alternative manufacturer, and thus YoYo Wheels was born. Soon, adverts for the brand featuring Cathey began appearing, with "His Wheels" printed in bold at the bottom.

Cathey's involvement in the creation of YoYo Wheels captures the era's pragmatic ingenuity. In the mid '70s, skate companies often developed equipment through quickly sketched ideas. What mattered were the specs: height, width, and – most critically for Cathey's signature model – the radius shaping the wheel's edge profile. The factory producing YoYo Wheels determined its durometers: harder urethane for speed, softer for grip. Thus even the company's distinctive two-color construction carried functional reasoning beneath its visual identity.

The long-term impact of YoYo Wheels far exceeded its modest origins. The principle of its rounded-edges, initially conceived to improve

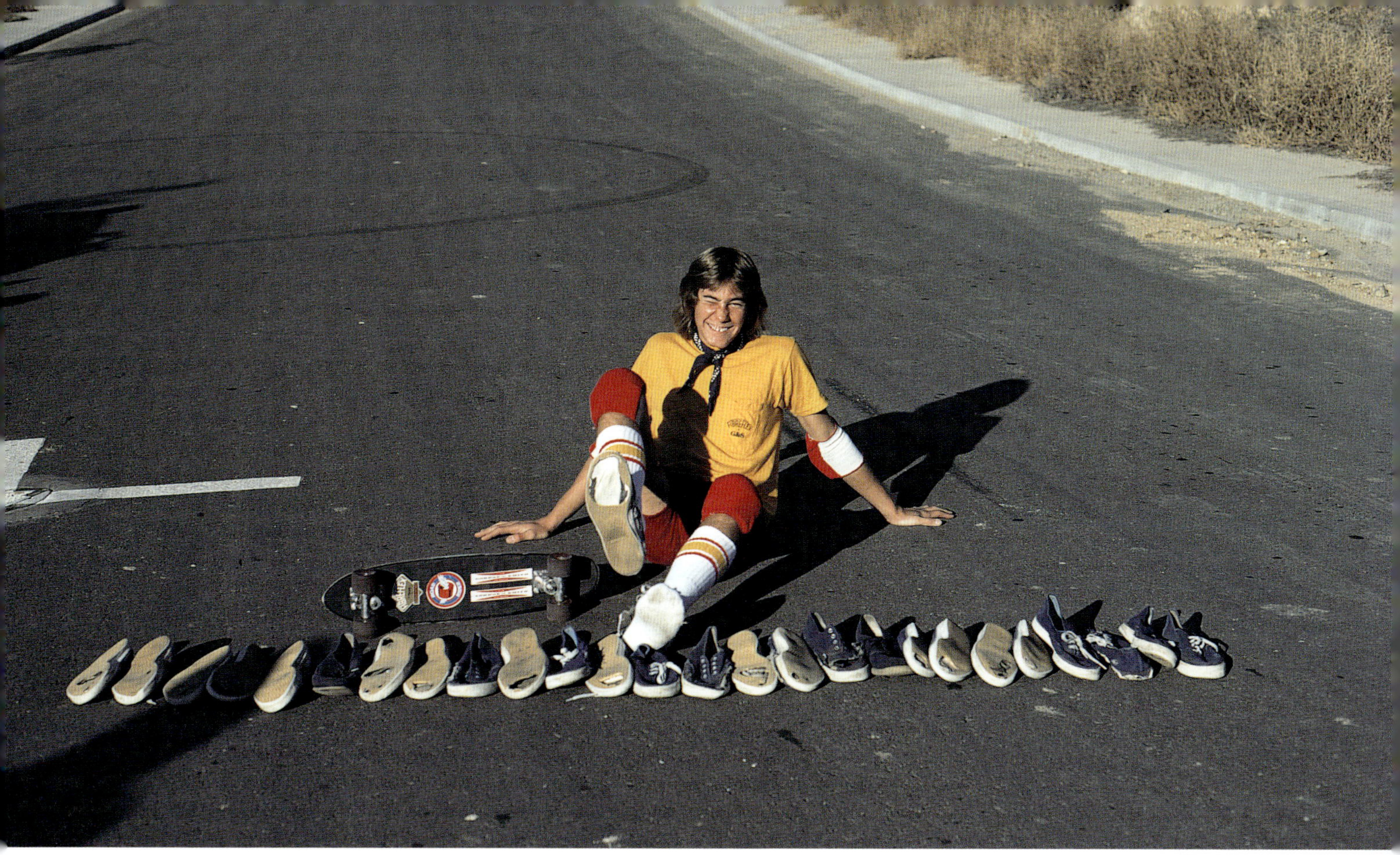

transition, release, and lateral response, became foundational across skateboard wheel design. What began as an individual rider's adaptation evolved into a new industry standard, its logic becoming ubiquitous. Cathey's design instincts extended beyond wheels, too, with his signature FibreFlex deck reflecting a continued dialogue between material behavior and skating demands. Launched in 1977, the board modified early flex-oriented constructions, optimized for cruising and slalom, through the addition of laminates and a longer tail, making it ideal for freestyle skating.

Hotly anticipated for its advanced shape, the dimensions of his subsequent Gordon and Smith (G&S) Proline SC deck were almost immediately adopted as the subject of skateboarding myth. While the initials "SC" were intended simply to denote Cathey's name, they were commonly interpreted as meaning "side cut," a misunderstanding based on the board's narrow midsection, intended to reduce weight. Cathey and G&S let the confusion persist, however, creating an accidental alignment between rider identity and (perceived) design logic. It also hinted at a general shift within skateboarding, as signature models increasingly competed with company-branded products in a market that was becoming more visually and commercially driven.

Cathey's legacy is therefore manifold. A preternaturally gifted skater, his sporting philosophy not only informed the development of the sport but its equipment too. After his innovative experiment with wheels, skate technology was transformed for good. Subject to a process of constant refinement, skateboard equipment came to be seen as a medium through which sporting progression could be achieved. It was therefore no longer fixed or sacrosanct: Following the emergence of YoYo Wheels, versatility and mechanical curiosity were inseparable from performance itself. In the trajectory of Steve Cathey's career, it's possible to discern a defining principle of skateboarding's evolution, one in which its most enduring advancements originated not in laboratories or boardrooms, but in the imaginations and skills of skaters themselves.

Henry Hester: The Instinct of Speed

Like many skateboarders in the '70s, Henry Hester's professional life began with surfing. For him, however, these pursuits were extensions of one another. The street was simply another surface to interpret, a place where balance, timing, and momentum mattered more than spectacle. Early skateboards were crude, often made from plywood and disc-shaped, yet the limitations of the equipment did little to constrain his obvious gifts.

With its speed and graceful carving style, slalom unsurprisingly became Hester's instinctive domain. While many skaters at the time were drawn toward tricks and emerging freestyle forms, Hester preferred smoothness and precision. The appeal was neither strategic nor ideological but physical. Surfing had hardwired his body for continuous pumping, for generating speed through subtle shifts rather than abrupt force. Slalom rewarded the same economy of movement; speed, in this context, was not aggression but rhythm.

Hester made his name through sessions at La Costa and the Black Hill in northern San Diego County, a spot favored by downhill and slalom riders. While many racers attended this self-styled asphalt "church," Hester was on any given way, the fastest of them all. The years he'd spent surfing on short, fish-shaped boards had demanded constant balance and control, qualities that prepared him for skating. While other riders took time to perfect their style, Hester intuitively knew how to move a board quickly and maintain momentum.

Central to this was his understanding of flex dynamics. Boards shaped with convex "cambers" did not merely bend when riders stepped on them; they responded. Energy compressed and returned through turns, creating propulsion. Slalom riders therefore did not simply pivot around cones but interacted with the board's rebound, tracing arcs rather than angles. For Hester, this responsiveness aligned perfectly with his experience as a surfer, a sport in which movement is prescribed by timing, not force.

Hester was consequently deeply engaged with the development of skateboard equipment, and was part of a new generation of riders who treated hardware as an extension of performance. Trucks were swapped, wheels were tested, and skateboard setups were endlessly refined. For Hester, this was more than novelty: He believed that subtle mechanical changes could unleash new styles and ways of skating. Despite this outlook, Hester was never a technophile per se. At its heart, he insisted, skating was simply the art of moving a board mounted on four wheels across a surface – no more, no less.

This interplay between intuition and refinement culminated in FibreFlex's Henry Hester signature

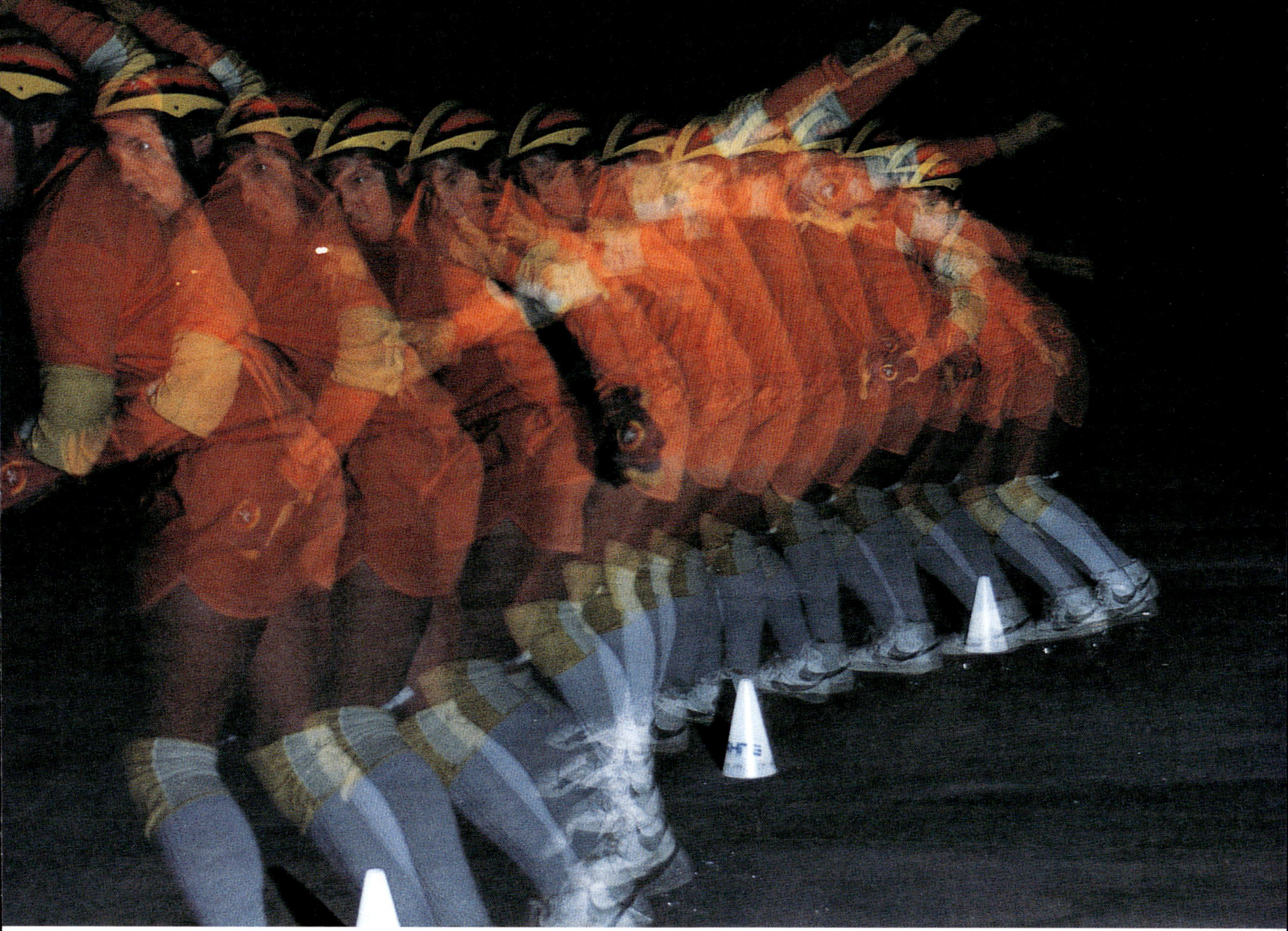

model, a design milestone the significance of which only became clear with time. In an era before the aesthetics of skateboards became dominated by graphics, the Hester was comparably sleek, minimal and functional. Its narrow dimensions reflected Hester's needs; its geometry was shaped by the logic of slalom rather than by visual statement. Put simply, his signature board was a performance tool.

In the mid to late '70s, competitions were contested by a community of riders who were largely – like Hester himself, who grew up in Long Beach and San Diego – from California. Race days were therefore as much about rivalry as they were camaraderie. Entry fees were diminutive, as were the prizes, and the bonhomie and occasional disputes between riders created an atmosphere that was paradoxically both relaxed and fierce. Teams existed, loyalties were real, but the slalom scenes Hester frequented were intimate, driven by experimentation, shared curiosity, and the collective pursuit of speed.

Indeed, if the spirit of slalom riding in the '70s could be distilled, its essence would be the balance between speed, intuition, and technology that Hester embodied. Rooted in a style of skating based on the harmony between the rider, their board, and the terrain beneath them, his legacy is a way of thinking about skateboarding itself; an ethos composed of rhythm, responsiveness, and the quiet mastery of motion.

Dennis Martinez: Transition, Trajectory, and the Flying Aces

One of the kingpins of the California scene in the late '70s, Dennis Martinez was unique in that he excelled at both freestyle and pool and ramp riding. Today, though, he's largely remembered – thanks to photoshoots in *SkateBoarder* – for his rough, ready, but always technically impressive style of vert skating. Ornament and technique never interested Martinez; on the contrary, what drove him was how a board carried momentum, whether traversing the ramps, bowls, or flying in the air.

Much of this sentiment is evident in Martinez's collaboration with fellow San Diegan skater Doug Saladino on the FibreFlex Teamrider deck. Launched in 1978, their design arose as a response to the evolving demands of pool and ramp skating. Moreover, Martinez and Saladino's involvement in the board's creation reflected a trend for skaters moonlighting as designers, translating their experience into material logic.

This trajectory of refinement culminated in Martinez's FibreFlex signature model, the Flying Aces. More than just a personal endorsement, the deck captured a broader directional shift. Thick, wide, and featuring a slightly raised kicktail, it was tailored to vert riding, a discipline demanding rigid, durable, and stable decks able to support aerial maneuvers. Vert skaters duly embraced the Flying Aces with open arms; alongside other ramp-dedicated models also featured in these pages, it not only helped these riders land tricks but boosted the growth of one of the sport's most recognizable styles today.

As the last model FibreFlex made in the '70s, the Flying Aces marked an endpoint for the brand's previous exclusive commitment to making flexible boards catering to slalom and downhill racing. Although FibreFlex continued producing its older, bouncy models after it released the Flying Aces – and still does – skateboarding had nevertheless gone through a paradigmatic shift that it couldn't ignore. The writing, as the saying goes, was on the wall.

The abruptness of this shift in the sport was embodied by Martinez's departure from FibreFlex shortly after the Flying Aces' launch. Around 1979, he released another pro board with one of FibreFlex's rivals, Variflex. As skateboarding styles began to proliferate through the use of new types of hardware, everything, it seemed, was up for grabs. Thus as vert riding accelerated, brands reflected these changes in both the products they sold and the riders they sponsored. Martinez's move to Variflex was therefore not just a personal choice but a consequence of the seismic transformations in skateboarding in general.

Today, it would be easy to label Martinez as simply a vert skater, which is how he ultimately found fame. That, however, would be a drastic simplification. As discussed, he was also a talented all-rounder, who just happened to excel at pool and ramp riding around the time they were gaining in popularity. More than that, however, he was also a gifted designer, able to turn his varied experience riding skateboards into products that caught the zeitgeist, as both his collaboration on the FibreFlex Teamrider model and his Flying Aces signature board demonstrate. As skateboarding's paths diverged in the '70s, Martinez was able to see which way the wind was blowing – and he used his enormous gifts to ensure it carried the sport with it.

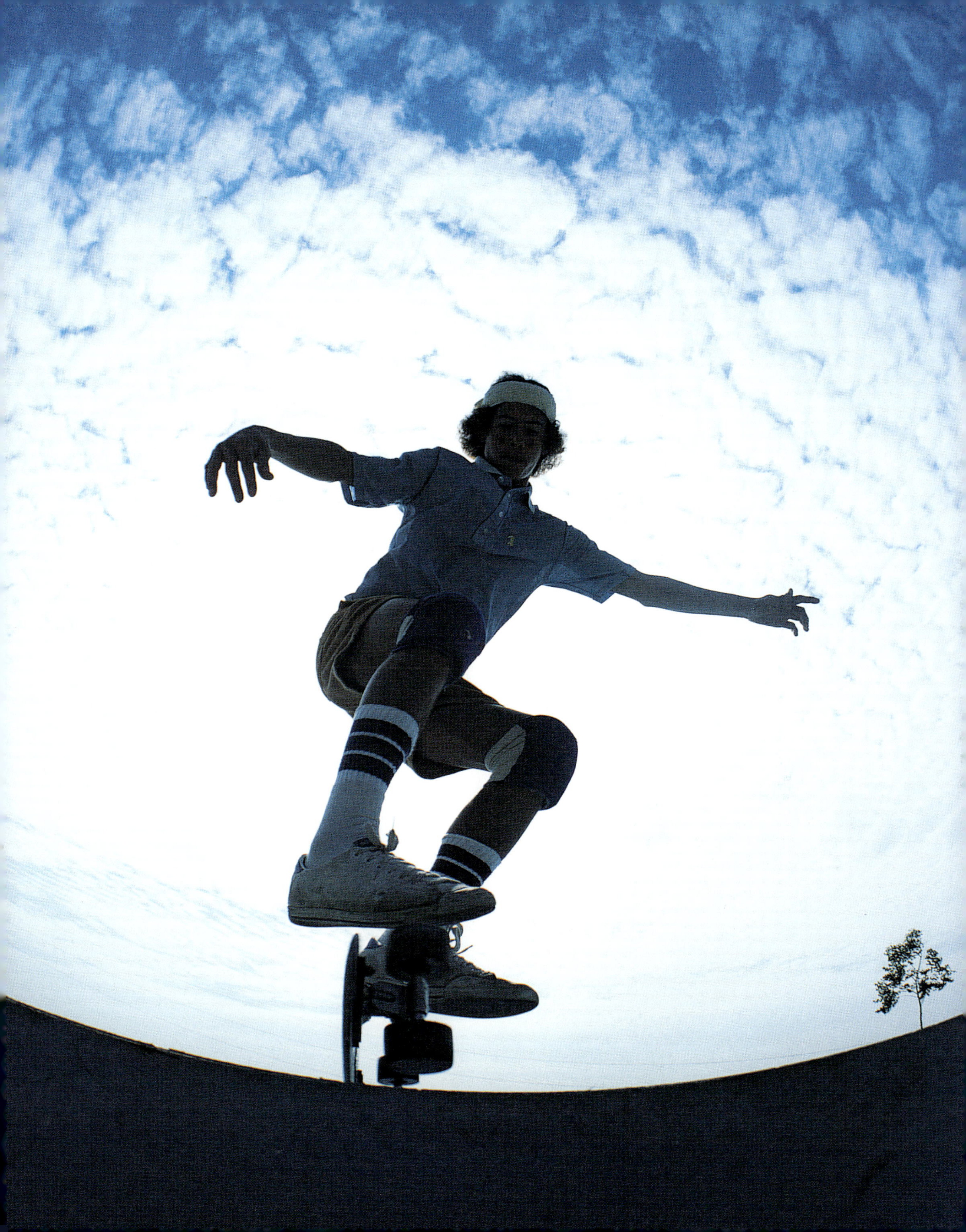

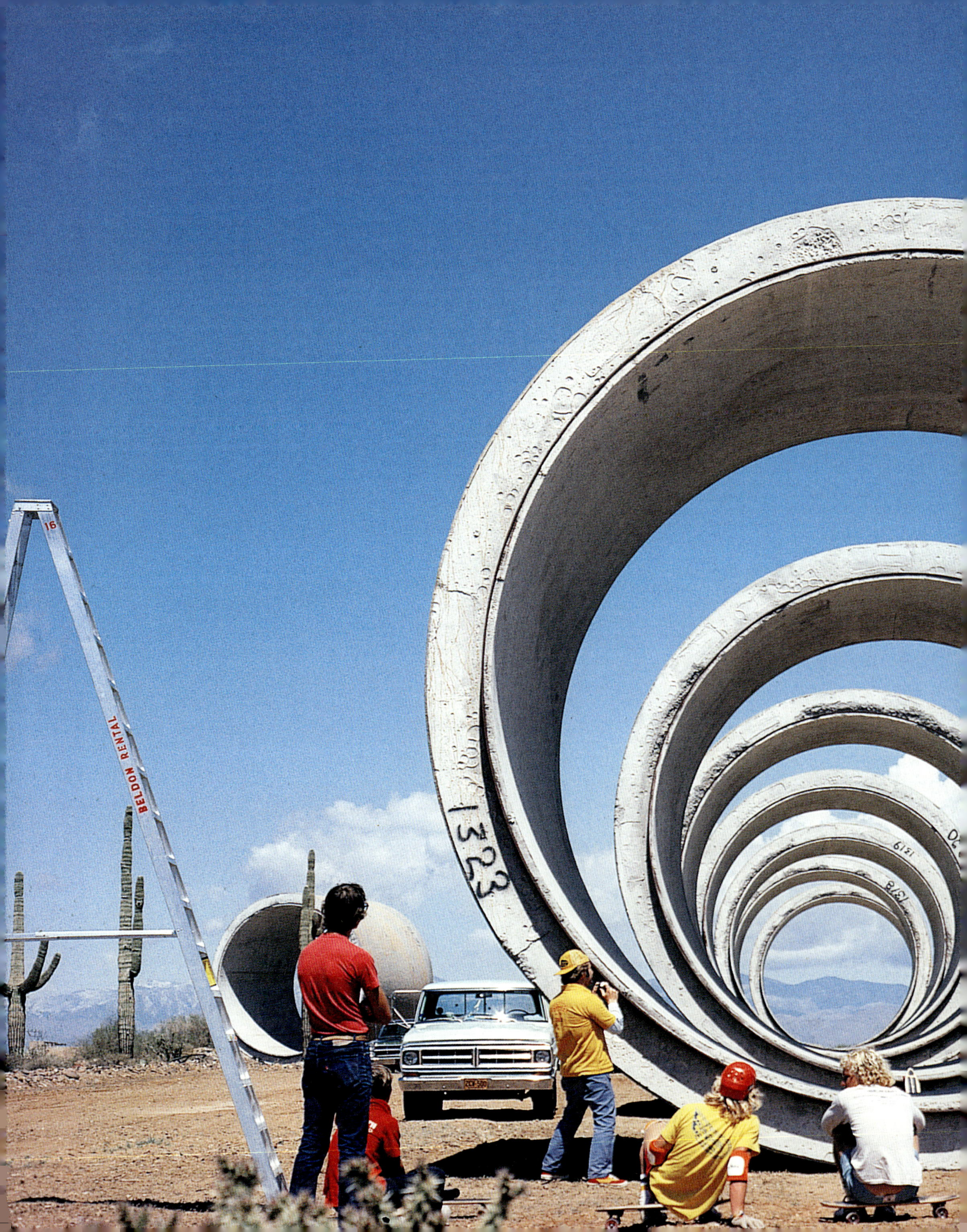
16
BELDON RENTAL
1323

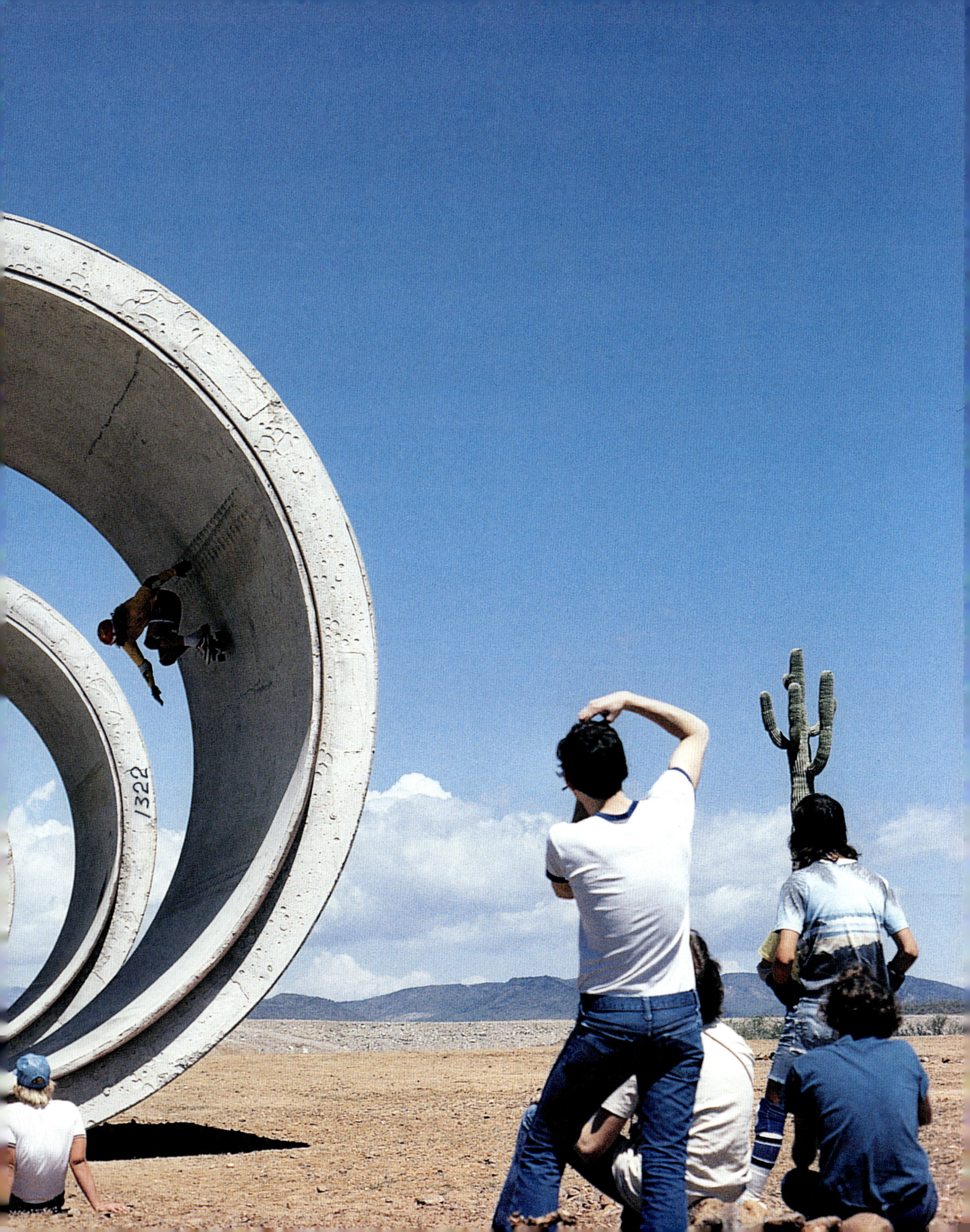
1322

The Golden Age of the California Skatepark

The emergence of skateparks in the late 1970s was another pivotal moment for the sport. Alongside the revolutions taking place in equipment design, the appearance of spaces dedicated to skateboarding was utterly transformative. With the opening of the Carlsbad Skatepark in 1976—one of the first purpose-built examples of skate architecture—riders finally had a place to call home. And while the honeymoon period for skateparks may have been short-lived, thanks, among other things, to high insurance costs, things were never the same again. Here are some parks that put skateboarding literally on the map.

Carlsbad Skatepark
1976, Carlsbad, CA

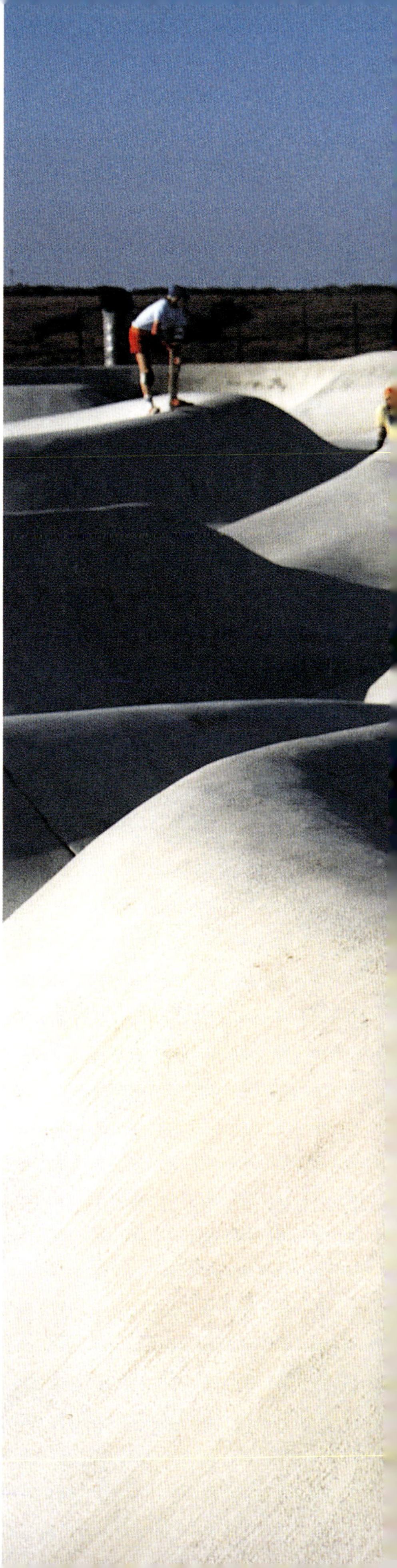

Opened in March 1976, the Carlsbad Skatepark was the first modern environment dedicated to skateboarding. Its terrain – snake runs, a rolling "Mogul Maze" inspired by skiing, and early bowls – were modelled on the natural contours of ditches and drained pools, yet elevated them to the level of architectural ingenuity. Its creators, skaters John O'Malley and Jack Graham, weren't traditional building designers. Relying on intuition, they shaped the park's concrete curves like artists. Indeed, the legend goes that the park was built with minimal planning, guided mostly by feeling. The result felt organic: fluid lines, "camel back" humps, rising berms, and transitions that mirrored skateboarding's improvisational spirit.

In time, Carlsbad became a hallowed site to which skaters from across the world made pilgrimages, each paying homage to its foundational form. The template for every park that followed marked the beginning of a new volume in the sport's history.

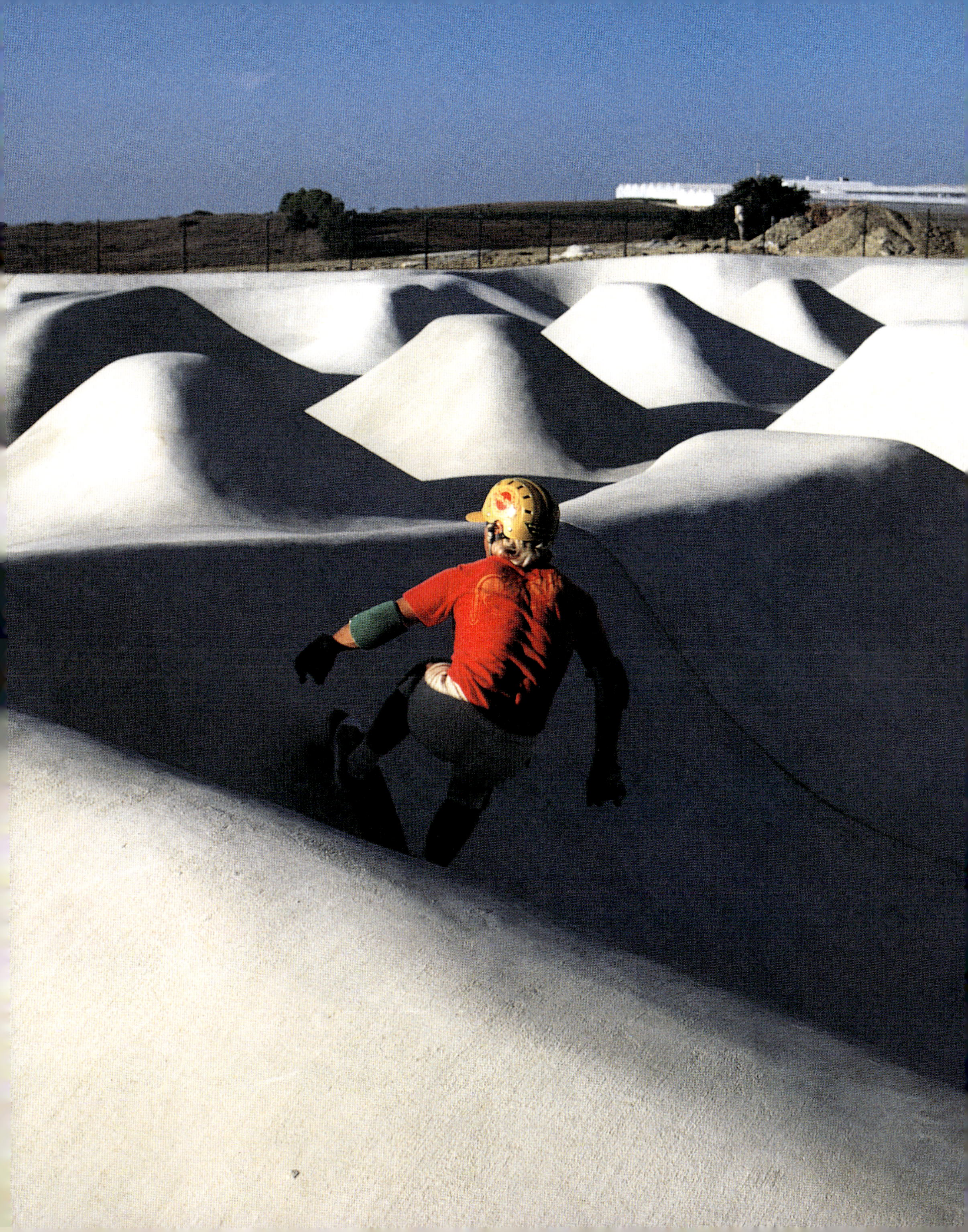

Concrete Wave
1976, Anaheim, CA

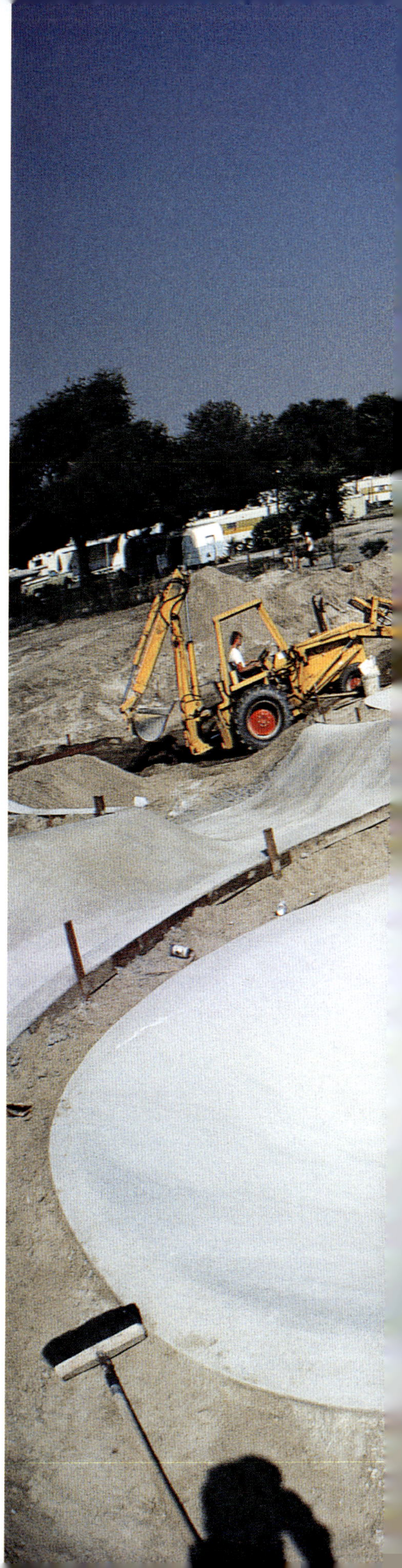

Indicative of the intuitive approach many skatepark designers took to designing in the 1970s, Concrete Wave in Anaheim – also home to Disneyland – is a veritable adventure park for skaters. Opening the same year as Carlsbad in 1976, its experimental, snakelike curves sought to capture what it might be like to ride on concrete waves.

By modern standards, the park's abrupt transitions between sections, uneven corners, and unusual shapes seem spontaneous and at times erratic. Yet even at the time, this was considered part of its charm. While other parks were smoother and/or required advanced skills to ride, visitors to Concrete Wave were rewarded with a unique terrain anyone with patience could use. As a result, it isn't as famous as other purpose-built skate locations. Despite this, its remarkable form continues to be a reference for skatepark designers, especially those seeking to add an element of unpredictability to their creations.

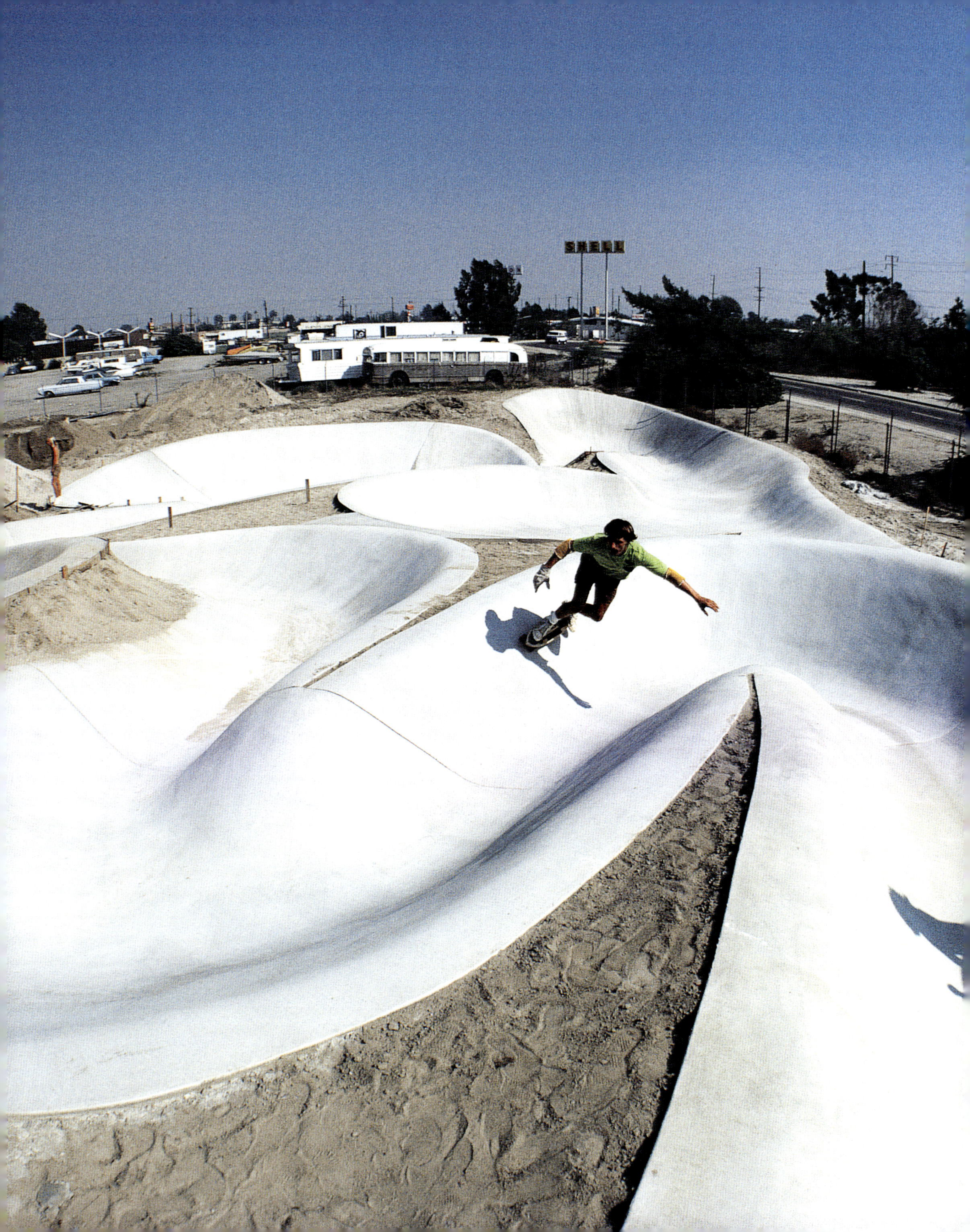
SHELL

Skatopia
1977–1982, Buena Park, CA

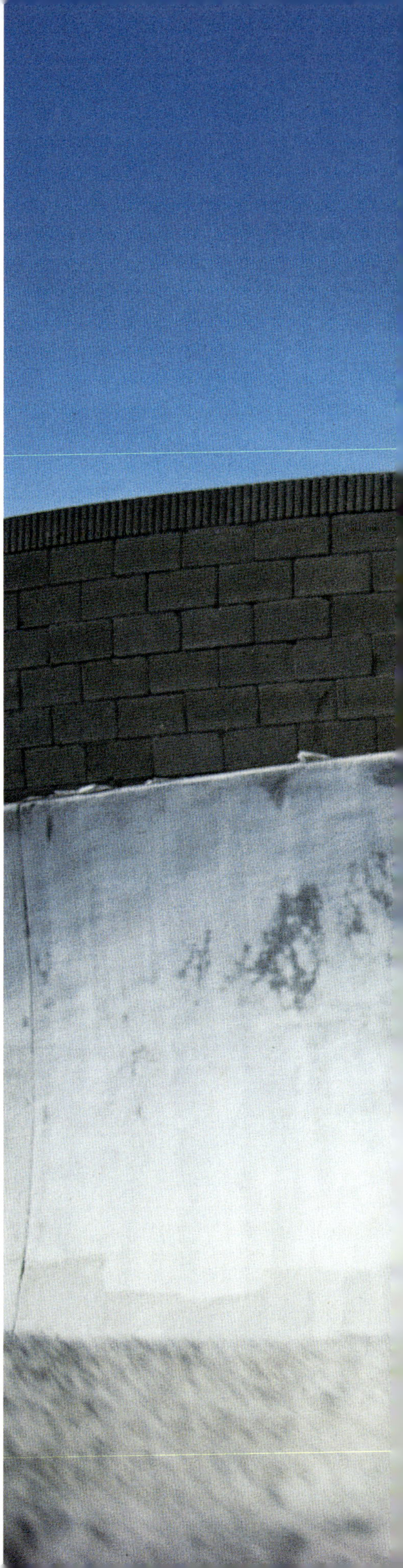

Skatopia in Buena Park operated almost like a cultural crossroads, part training ground, part hangout, part competitive arena. With seven bowls and a halfpipe, it offered a variety of terrain that attracted professionals and ambitious amateurs alike. Skate sessions were known for their intensity: fast and technical, the park was often crowded with riders who were trying to out do one another in terms of air time and trick complexity.

Skatopia's well-attended competitions draw participants and spectators from far and wide, making it a perfect place to meet other skaters. To this extent, it was perhaps the place to be seen riding. After it closed in 1982, another, unaffiliated Skatopia opened in Rutland, Ohio. Yet it could never compete with the original, which remains woven in the very fabric of California skateboarding.

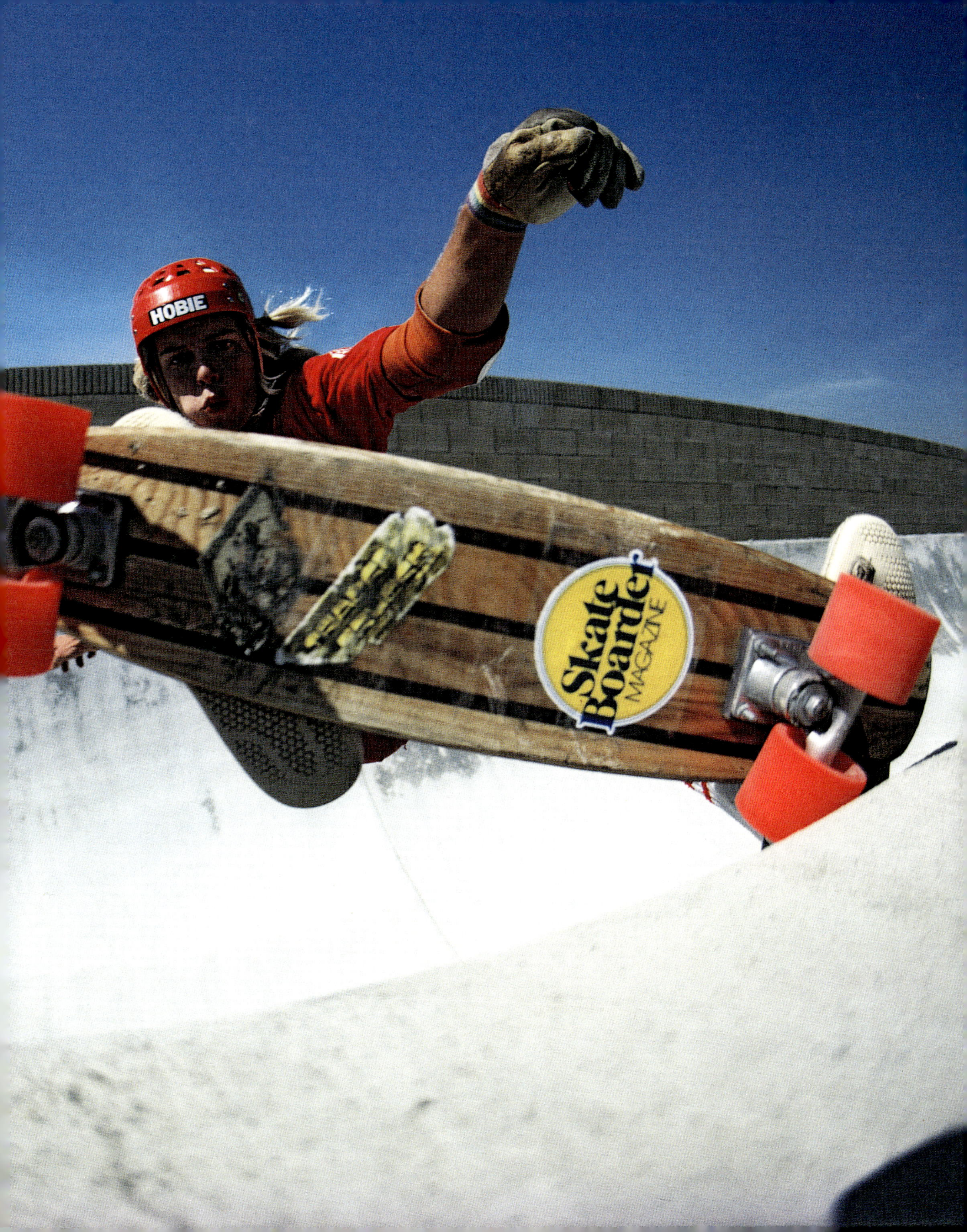
HOBIE
Skate Boarder
MAGAZINE

The Pipeline
1977–1988, Upland, CA

The Pipeline skatepark was the heart of what's called "transition" skating, where riders carve around bowls, ramps, and other curved surfaces Also known as Badlands, its concrete wasn't polished, and its dimensions were sometimes unforgiving, but for the time, it was visionary.

With its marriage of square and round sections, it demanded a level of ability from its guests, especially its full pipe and "pro bowl." The latter, for instance, featured a near-vertical 6 foot (2m) "tombstone" area where skaters could "drop-in," and became a rite of passage for any aspiring vert skater in California at the time.

The park's Hester Series competitions amplified its reputation, bringing the best riders of the day to the site, pushing the limits of the sport with every trophy. Skaters like Steve Olson and Steve Alba found celebrity in skating circles via appearances at The Pipeline, their styles becoming synonymous with it.

Even after its closure in 1988, The Pipeline's influence was so strong that recreations and homages continue to appear in modern parks today. While all of the parks listed here are important, few have shaped skateboarding so profoundly.

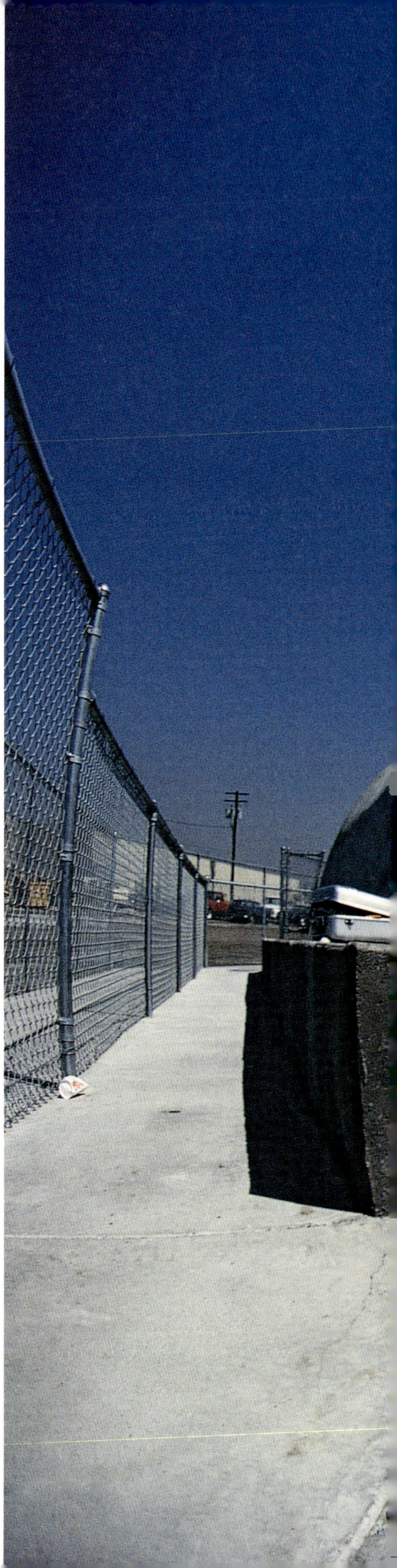

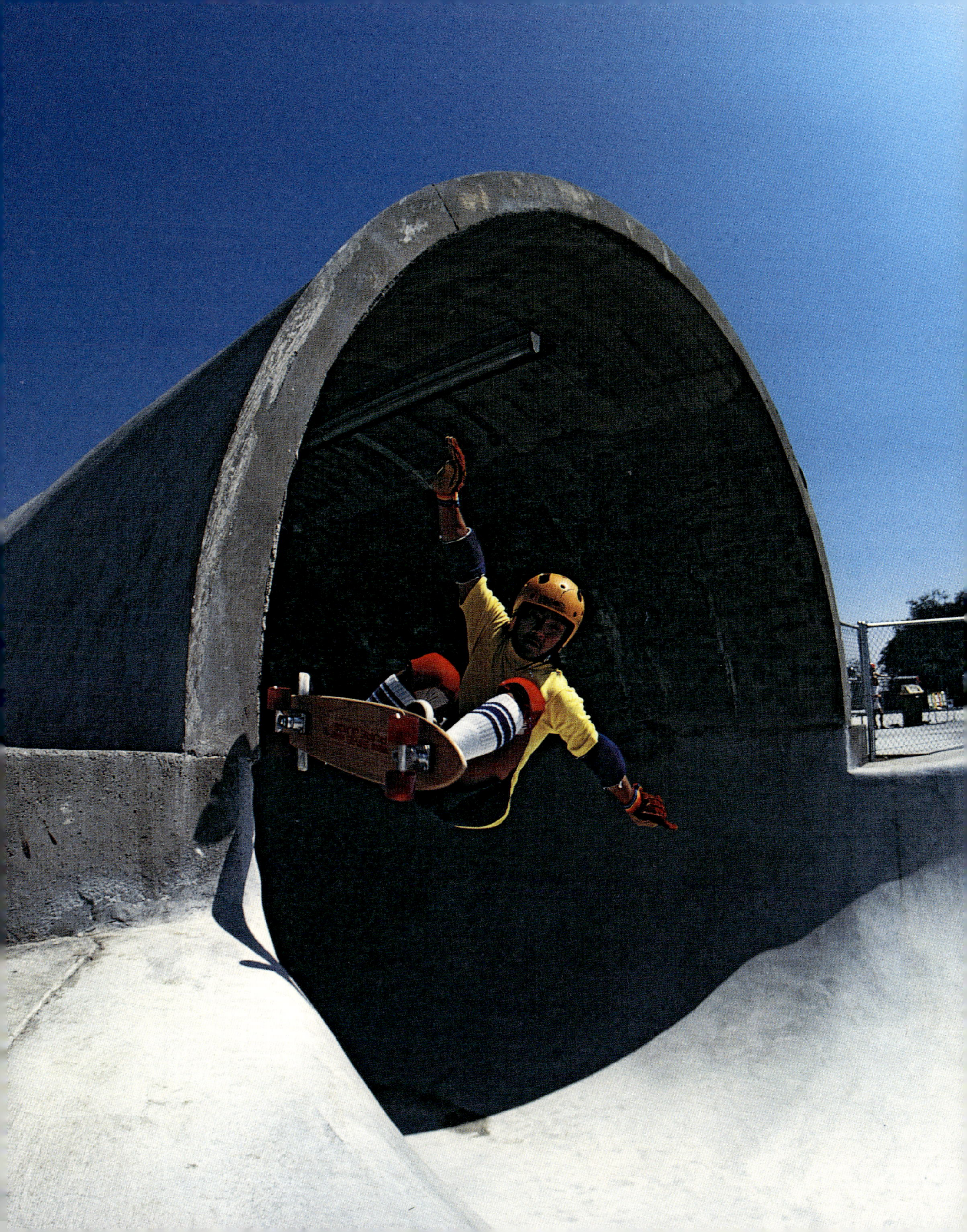

Oasis Skatepark
1978–1980s, San Diego, CA

Located in the neighborhood of Mission Valley, San Diego, Oasis Skatepark's varied terrain was a hotspot for competitions, which became a core part of its identity. Its pool and freestyles trophies were highly sought-after, leading to droves of skaters to visit the park on event days. One famous tournament was the 1980 Oasis Freestyle Contest, where a young Rodney Mullen – a pioneering skateboarder, famed for his technical ability, who invented the kickflip – claimed his first major victory.

Boasting an ice-white bowl, Oasis was a social hub for skaters from all over San Diego and California too. Like many parks of the era, it succumbed to insurance problems, but its influence lives on in its celebrated trophies as well as the friendships it helped forge.

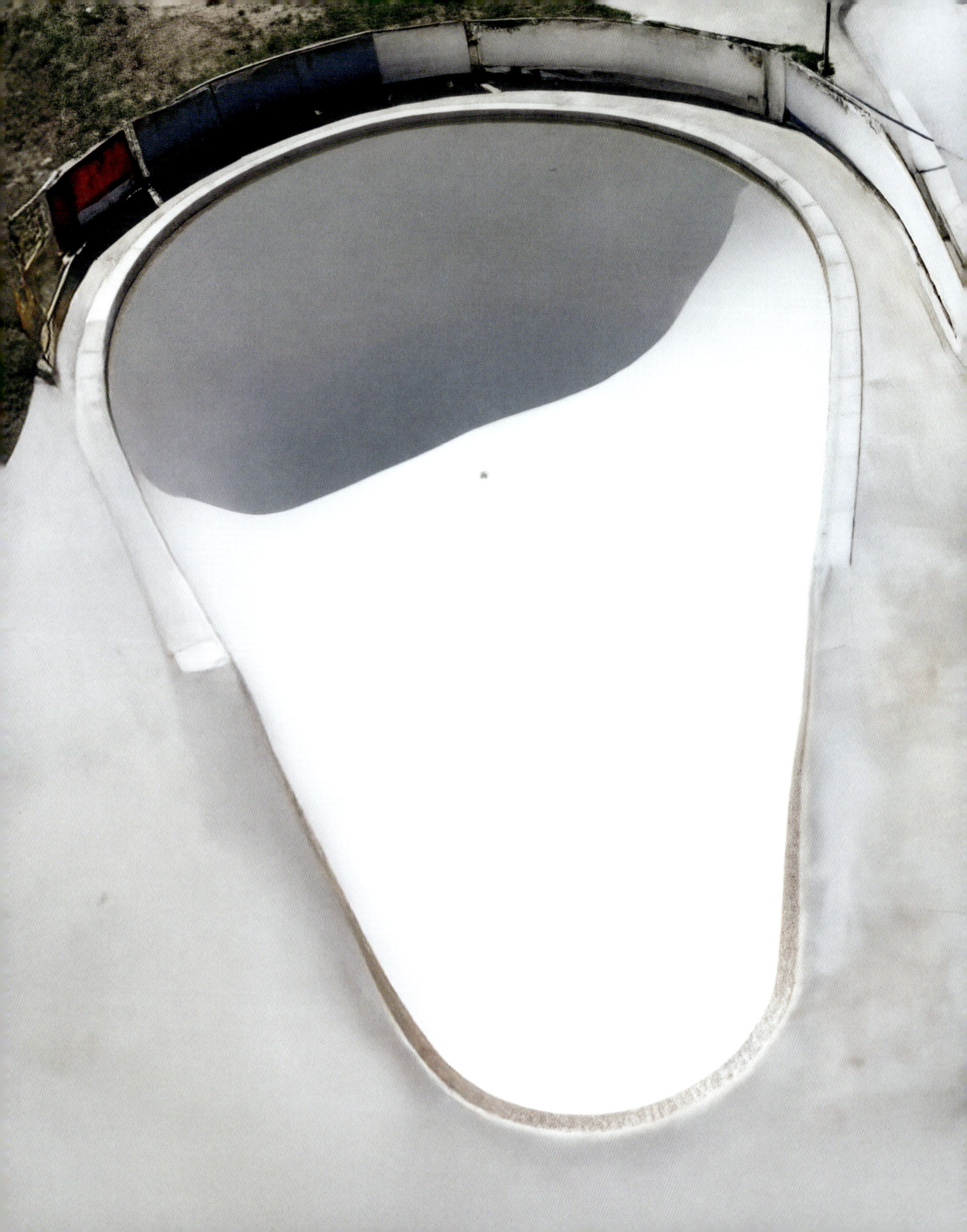

Skateboard Heaven
1978–1980, Spring Valley, CA

Skateboard Heaven was a park built for ambitious and skillful riders. When it was inaugurated in 1978, the sport was beginning its obsession with vertical surfaces, and its terrain reflects that trend. The layout emphasized bowls and curves that rewarded speed, power, and fearlessness, leaving little room for hesitation. This was not a casual park; it demanded courage from the moment your wheels touched the concrete.

What set Skateboard Heaven apart was its atmosphere. Sessions here were always competitive, with riders feeding off one another. It became a place where skaters tested themselves against both the terrain and their peers, sharpening styles that leaned increasingly toward air and amplitude. Though its lifespan was short, Skateboard Heaven made a big impact, turning the skate park into a theater for athletic excellence.

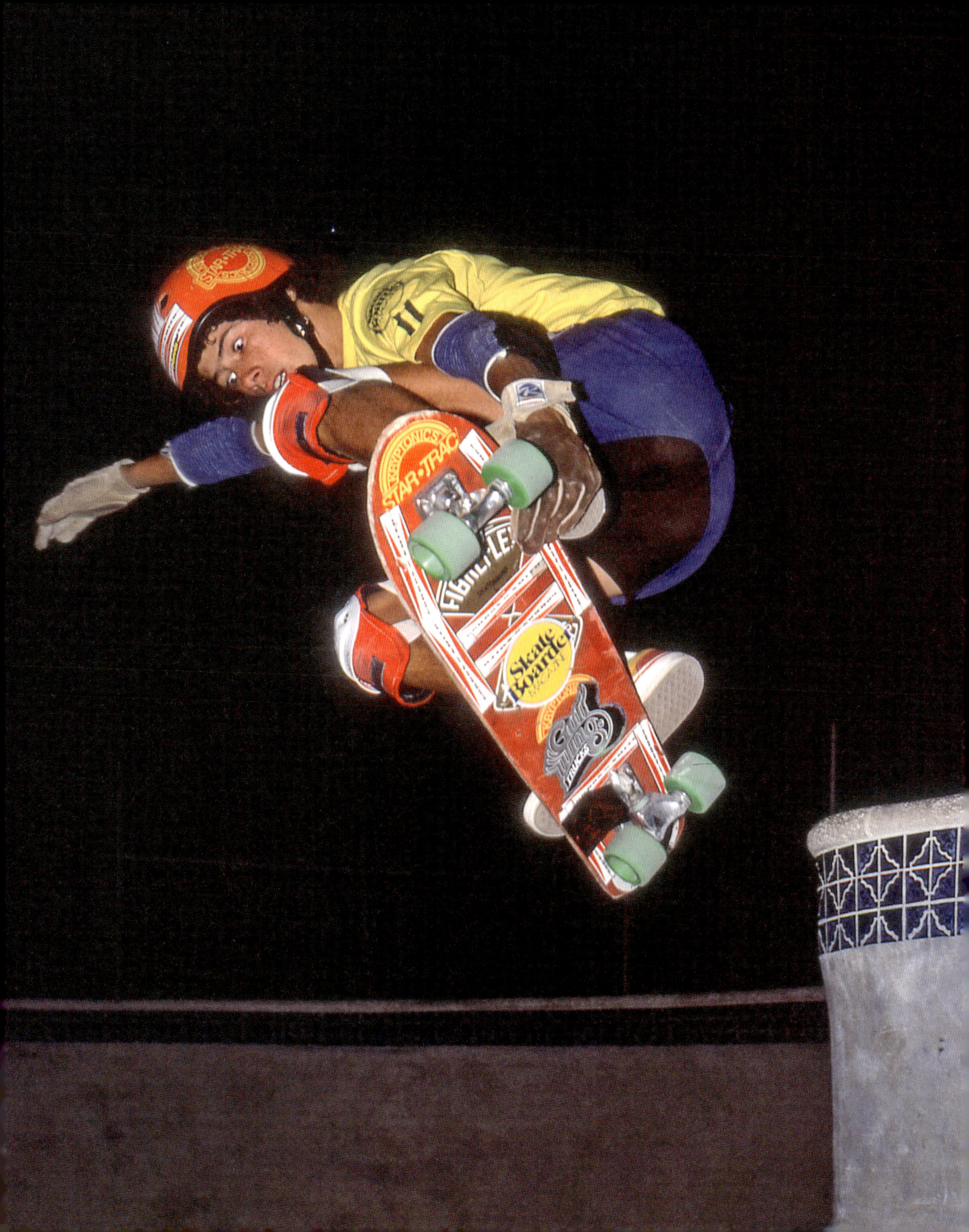
STAR-TRAC
Skate Boarder

Marina del Rey Skatepark
1978–1981, Los Angeles, CA

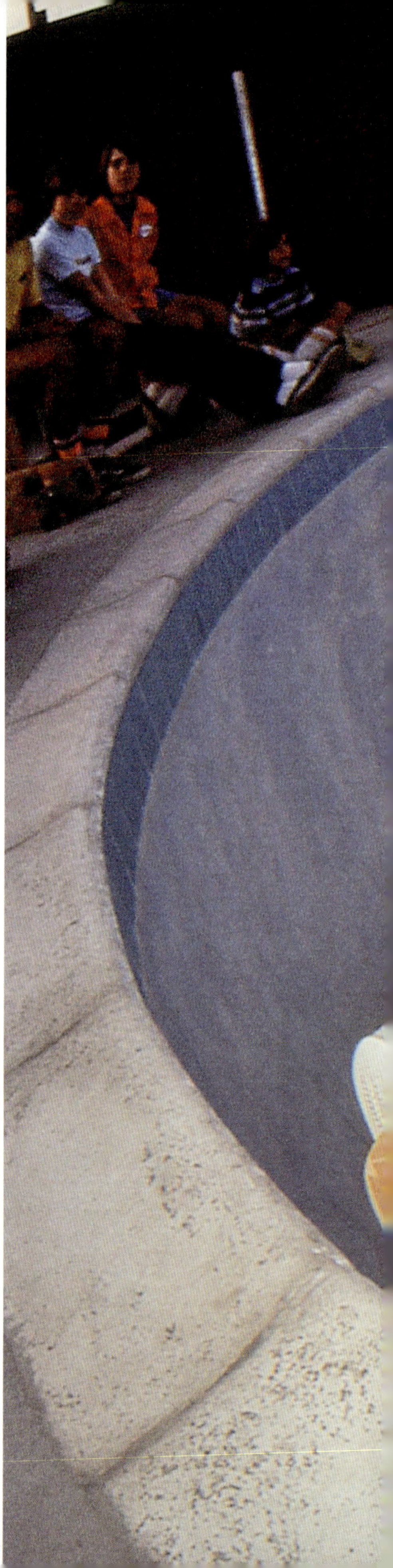

Marina del Rey holds a special place in the mythology of skateboarding for both its terrain and cultural gravity. Situated on the outskirts of the city of Santa Monica and L.A.'s Venice Beach neighborhood – an area buzzing with surf and street energy – the park was inaugurated in 1978.

Today, its renowned "Dogbowl" is still spoken about with reverence. Perfectly shaped, it was steep enough to require serious commitment, but smooth enough to reward those who had the courage to skate it. Soon, it became a canvas for some of the era's best riders.

Alas, it couldn't last. Three years after opening, it closed. But during those years, it hosted numerous contests and skaters, including the local Dogtown Crew, which featured one of the sport's founding fathers, Stacy Peralta. Now derelict, the park nonetheless remains an important site for the sport.

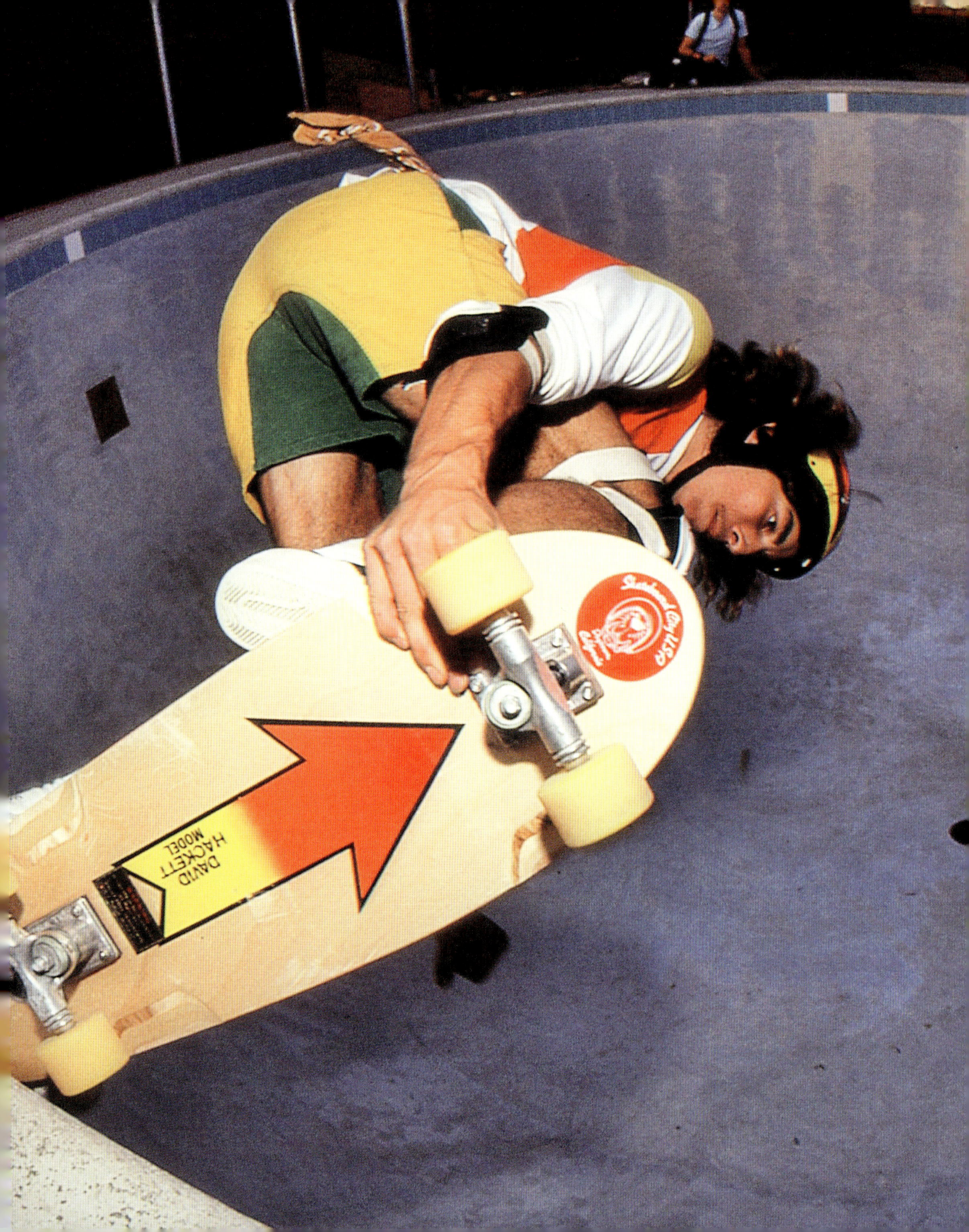
DAVID
HACKETT
MODEL

Surf de Earth
1978–early 1980s, Vista, CA

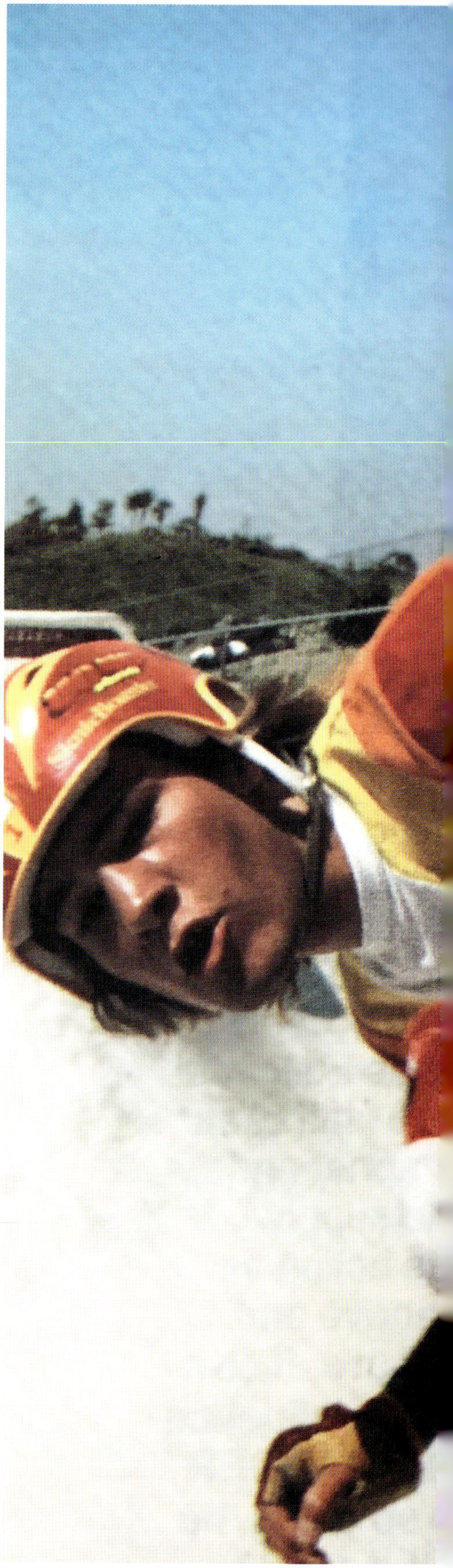

Located in the Californian city of Vista, just east of Carlsbad in San Diego County, Surf de Earth, also known simply as the Vista Skatepark, typifies the skatepark scene of Southern California in the late 1970s. Offering combined bowls, banks, and flowing lines in a layout that encouraged versatility rather than specialization, it wasn't as extreme as The Pipeline or Skateboard Heaven, but its moderate design helped skaters cultivate their skills.

A popular hangout for riders in the area and beyond, Surf de Earth was a local skate spot with big dimensions and an even greater number of visitors. Online lore has it that the park was created by a pool builder and skater next to their showroom. Whatever the truth, Vista, which was open from 1978 to the early 1980s, is remarkable for being both well-designed and community-centered – facets that define the very best modern skateparks too.

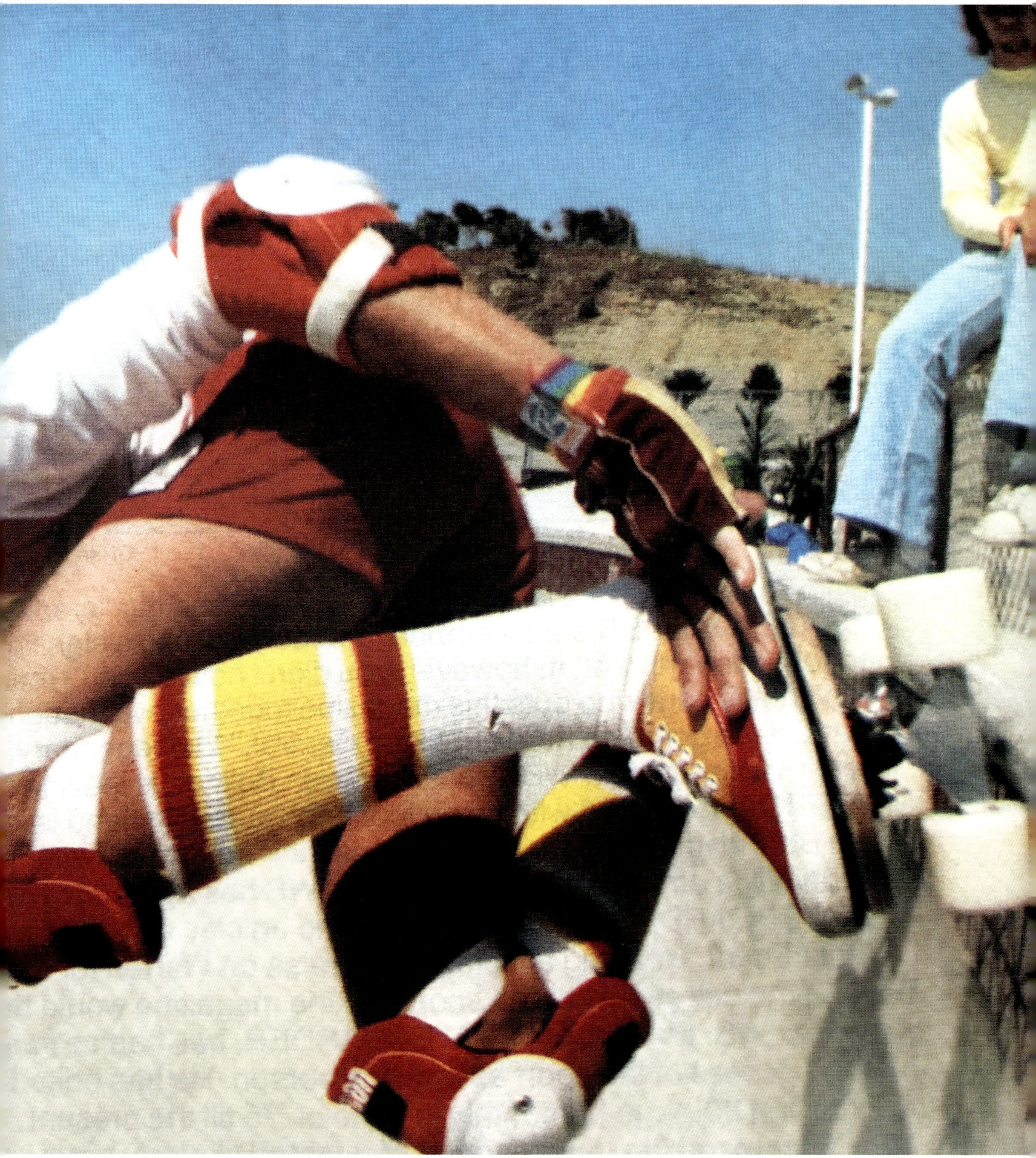

Del Mar Skate Ranch
1978–1987, Del Mar, CA

Del Mar Skate Ranch was a moment of consolidation in skateboarding's rapid evolution. Arriving after the most experimental phase of skatepark design had passed, it opened in 1978 when the art of building bowls and ramps was no longer guesswork. As a result, Del Mar was able to build on the lessons of Carlsbad, The Pipeline, and Marina del Rey, creating a considered, nuanced environment for skaters to express themselves.

For starters, its terrain was simply smoother and more sculpted than earlier parks. Its bowls were clearly modelled on those drained pools that California skaters used to frequent, but they now had consistent curves, encouraging progression rather than risk-taking. The snake run, which emphasized speed and rhythm, was conceived with a similar logic, rewarding skaters of all abilities with clean, flowing lines.

In short, Del Mar's refined design made it arguably the first modern skatepark. While its predecessors were based on ingenuity, Del Mar's polished dimensions were based on studied observation. Here, skaters were able to perfect emerging styles, particularly in its bowls with vert sections, which have become the bedrock of skateboarding today. After 11 years, it closed. But its spirit lives on in practically every park that's open today.

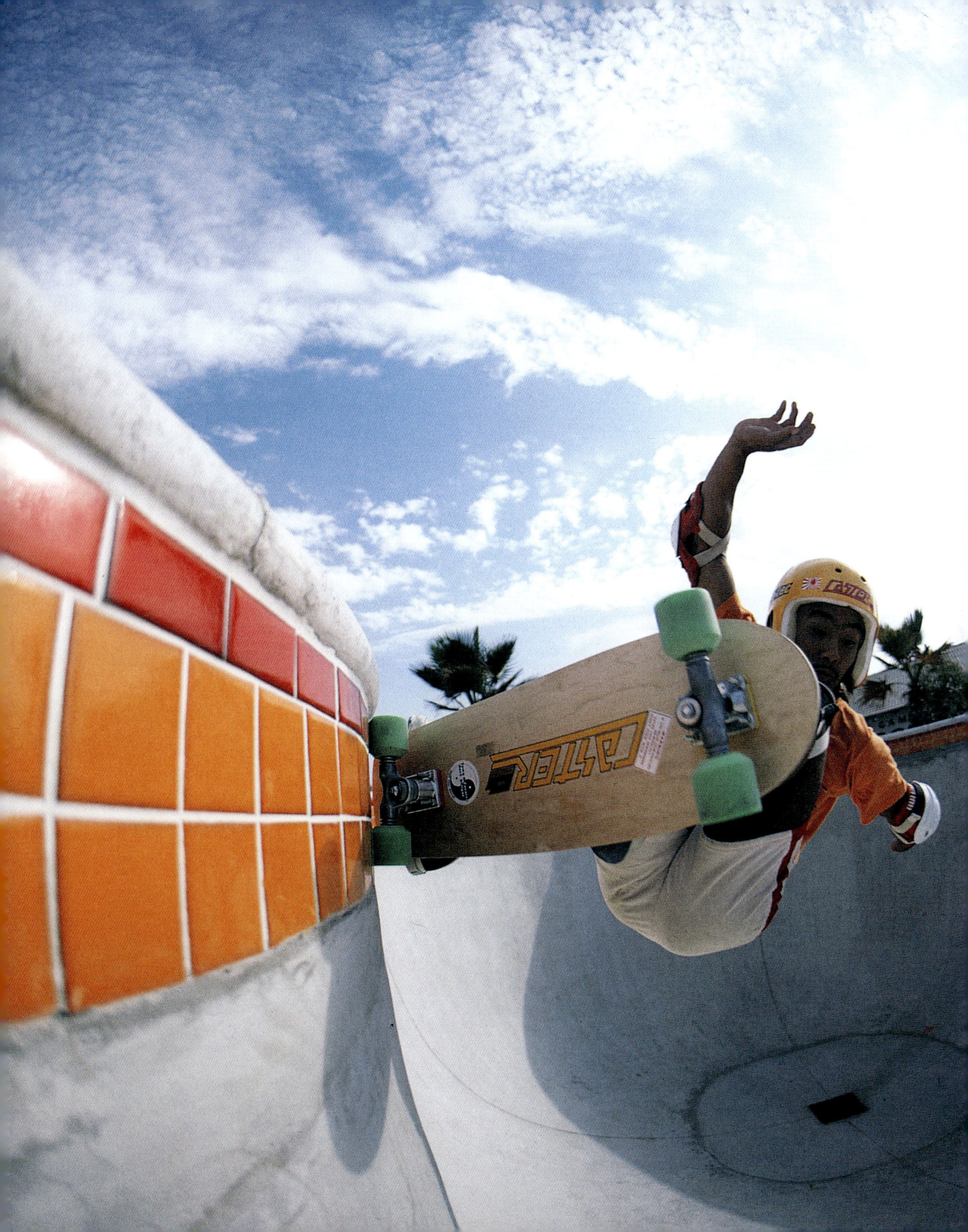
CASTER

Pools, Ramps, and Venues

When *SkateBoarder* magazine relaunched in 1975, its cover—a drained concrete pool somewhere in California—announced a new frontier in the sport. Now, it declared, skateboarding was entering a sculpted environment in which speed, fearlessness, and dexterity were everything. Like all great historical occurrences, chance was at play: in the mid 1970s, a drought in California drained all the backyard pools. Henceforth, the sport became transfixed by curves, leading to the sloping surfaces of the first skateparks. Before that, however, pools ruled supreme. These are the spots everyone dreamed of riding.

Water Drainage & Ditch Banking

The droughts in California during the mid '70s created opportunities for skaters that no one could have predicted. As reservoirs ran dry, miles of concrete storm drainage ditches sat empty and exposed. These places were utilitarian by design, but sculptural by accident: long, sloping angles, and curved troughs that stretched further than any pool. (For the perfect example, watch *The Search for Animal Chin.* Shot in 1986, it was among the first skate videos, and features the Bones Brigade riding several.)

Skaters instinctively understood the potential, with the ditches in L.A.'s Laurel Canyon becoming a hub of experimentation. In 1975, photographer Hugh Holland turned his lens on the scene, having stumbled upon it while driving in the area. Filled with images of skaters blending surf style with the then-newfound control provided by urethane wheels, his photos captured the youthful energy of these riders as they explored this unique terrain. With time, new spots, such as the Brea Spillway in Fullerton, Orange County, and the drainage ditches of Malibu, achieved equal popularity. Here, riders carving downhill learned to negotiate steep banks and shoot across the flats with finesse. These locations were where the continuous, fast-moving style of modern skating was born. Long before bowls and parks existed, ditch riding honed the techniques that would be instrumental in skating vertical ramps.

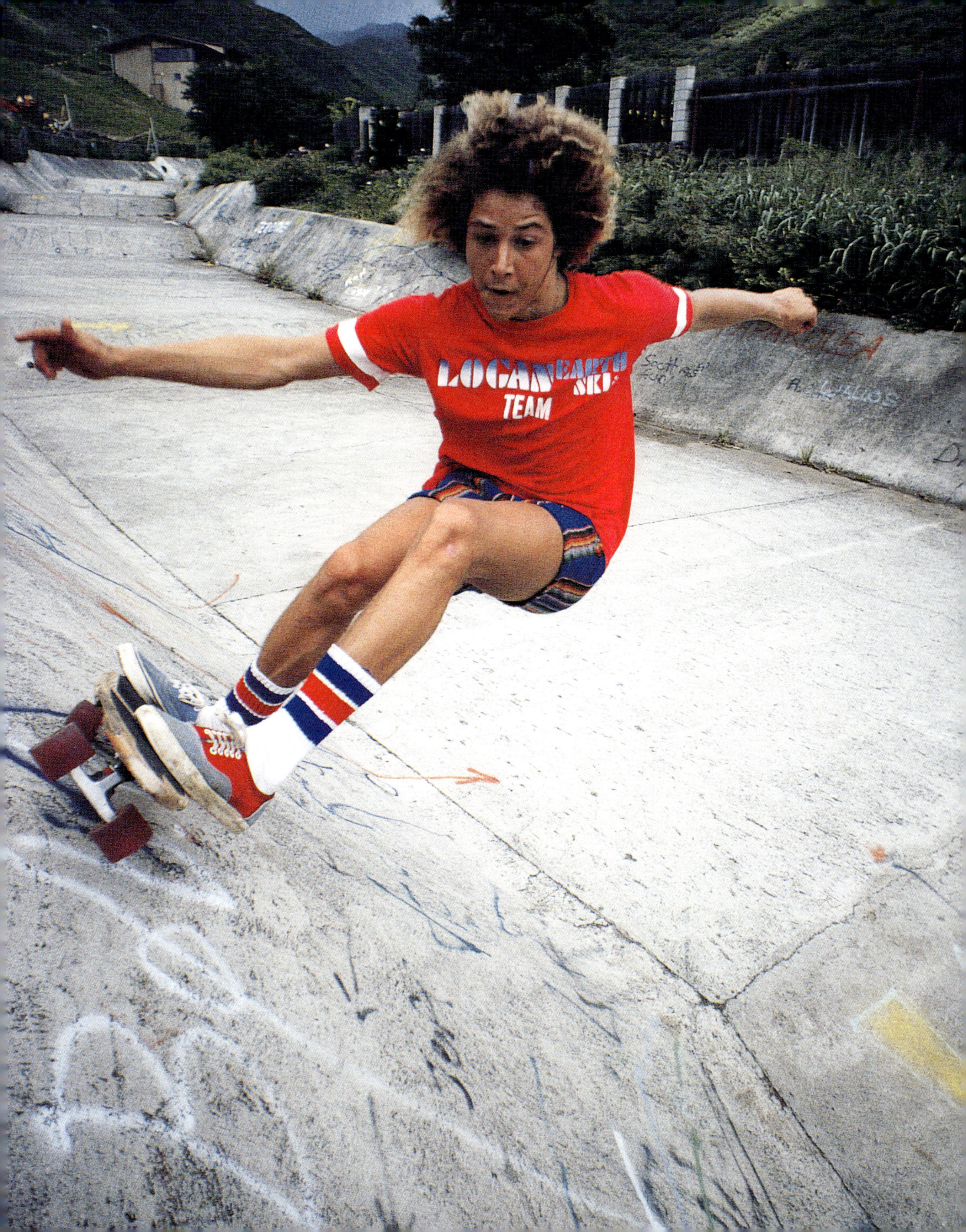
LOGAN
EARTH SKI
TEAM

The Arizona Desert Pipeline
Phoenix, AZ

Once located about 400 miles (640 km) east of California near Phoenix in the Sonoran Desert, the temporary, free-standing Arizona Desert Pipes still feels like legend. Cinematic and otherworldly, it was, for a brief moment in 1977, arguably the greatest skate spot on Earth.

The story goes like this: One day, *SkateBoarder* editor and photographer Warren Bolster received a tip-off in his office that some giant concrete sections of pipe for the new Central Arizona Pipeline – a huge waterway – were standing unguarded. He soon gathered a group of acclaimed riders, including Stacy Peralta and Gregg Weaver, and visited the pipes on three trips, documenting their exploits in the surrounding arid landscape, creating some of the most striking images in skateboarding history.

A series of massive, hollow cylinders formed from smooth concrete, the Arizona Desert Pipes gave Bolster a once in a lifetime opportunity to capture skaters conquering a unique terrain. While some sections were connected, others stood alone, providing the ability to both carve and ride up and down, as high as possible. Compared to the limits of pools and ditches, the circularity of the pipes allowed riders to push themselves harder than ever.

But the pipes were also unforgiving. Some connecting joints were flawless; others had abrupt shifts or huge gaps. Riders had to learn how to manage these obstacles quickly. Then there were the dozens of individual pipes: isolated rings with perfect radii and dramatic natural lighting. Skaters moved between them, chasing the best angles, the most dramatic backdrops. The desert itself infused the experience, with heat shimmering off the concrete.

Over the next few years, other skate crews visited different locations along the CAP's construction, mostly notably the Z-Boys of Dogtown in 1978. Few of these subsequent sessions, however, captured the magic of Bolster's images, which have a fairytale quality; photos documenting the thrill of discovering a new realm of skateboarding.

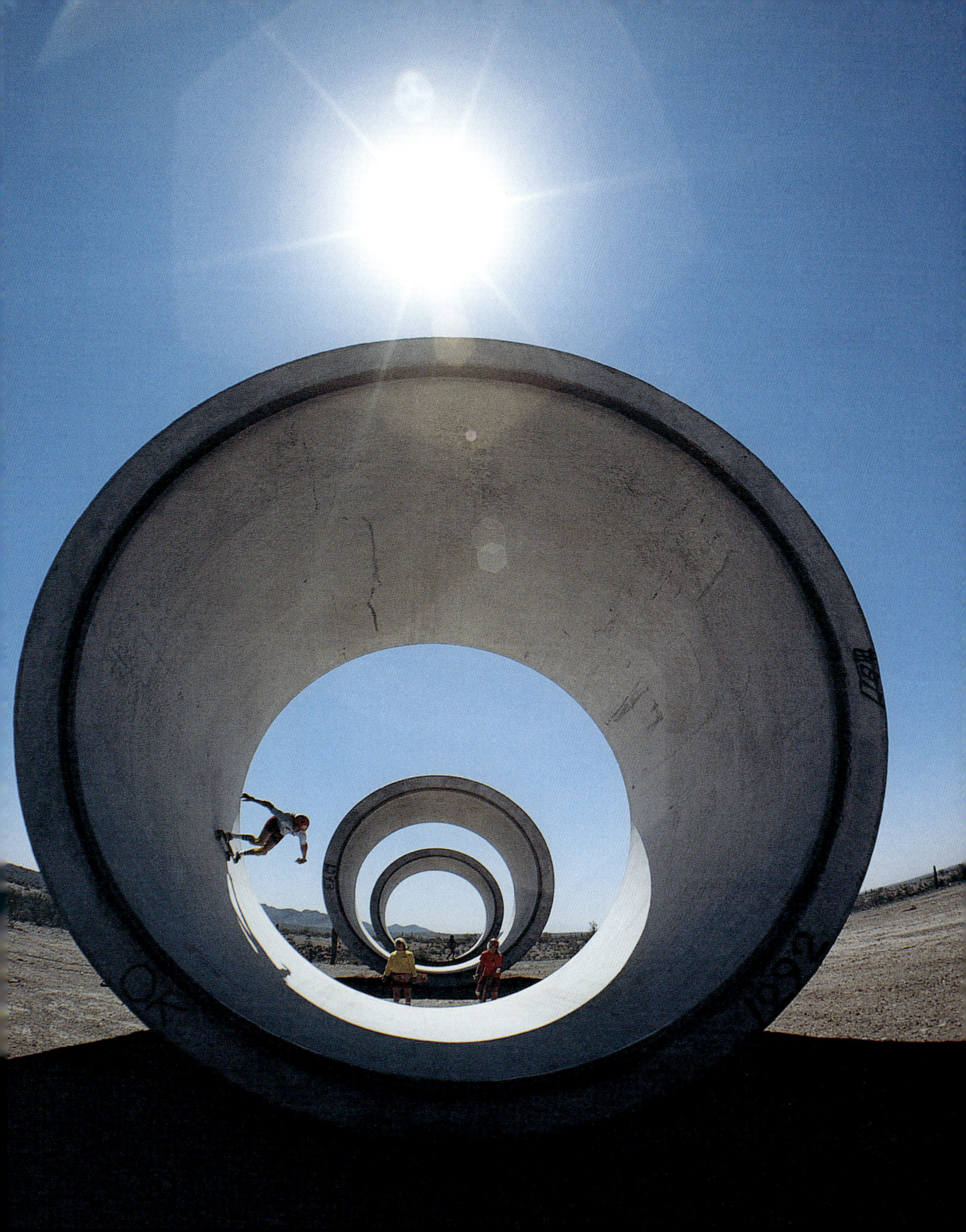

La Costa & the Black Hill
Carlsbad, CA

Situated in Carlsbad in northern San Diego County, La Costa and the Black Hill consisted of a long, untouched asphalt road, perfect for downhill slalom. Smooth, fast, and virtually free of traffic most of the time, it was, unlike the haphazard nature of ditches or backyard pools, almost tailor-made for skating. What's more, its relatively gentle incline was just steep enough to test riders' skills without pushing them too hard or overwhelming novices. It was, in short, the perfect spot for skaters of all abilities.

The Black Hill, as it was known for short, subsequently became the place for the pioneers of slalom and downhill to test and develop their skills before transferring them to harsh climes. Here, Henry Hester refined his turns; brothers Bill and Bob Bahne, of the eponymous skate brand, experimented with deck flex and wheel formulas; and Steve Cathey and Greg Taie explored various speed-demon techniques. A melting pot of ideas, the spot became a setting for brands to improve their equipment, and for skaters to perfect their styles.

The atmosphere at this self-styled "church," was above all communal. Spectators lined the edges during informal races, while freestyle skaters used the flats to invent new tricks between downhill runs. In many ways, the Black Hill was an open-air laboratory, one in which the idea of skating as a spectator sport first began to emerge.

Though the area has since been developed, the Black Hill's legacy is still discernible in the equipment of the era, particularly those responsive boards made by brands like FibreFlex, as well as in the speed-driven styles of skating that are still performed today.

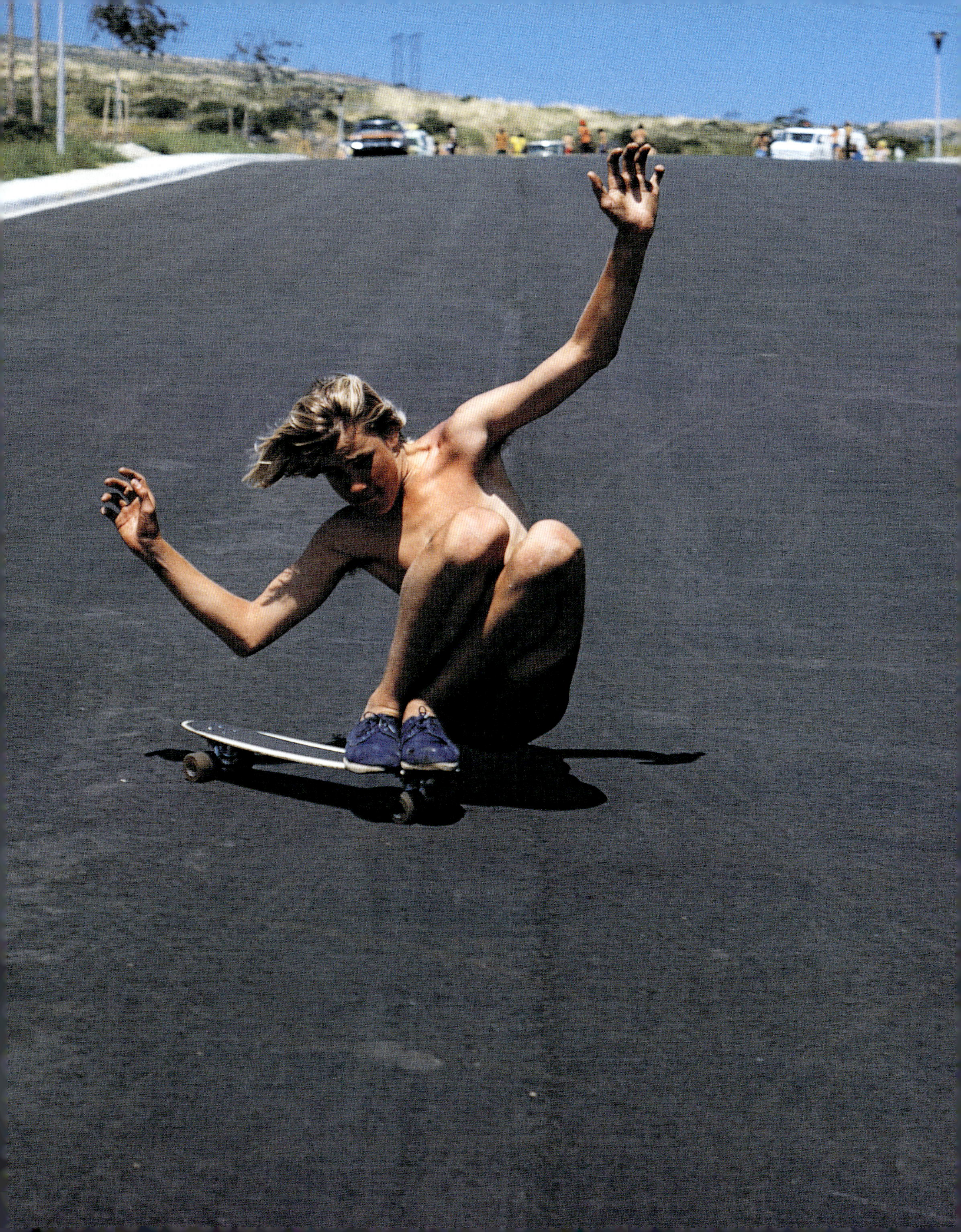

Tom Stewart's First Halfpipe
Encinitas, CA

After Warren Bolster's legendary sessions at the Arizona Desert Pipes, things were never the same again in skateboarding. Hungry for similar experiences, skaters began dreaming of how they could emulate the perfect curves of those waterway sections. Enter Tom Stewart, a skater from Encinitas, a city south of Carlsbad. Using his carpentry skills, he mapped the exact arc of those pipes near Phoenix, translating them, using wood, into the world's first half-pipe.

Built in his backyard the same year as Bolster's sessions in the desert in 1977, Stewart's pipe was a masterpiece. While ramps during that period were often rough, inconsistent, and improvised, his creation was made with the skill of a craftsman. In doing so, he provided skaters with a semi-permanent place to enjoy a virtually identical experience to the riders who made it to the Arizona Desert Pipes. Word spread quickly. Skaters not only flocked to his backyard but were soon asking him to make another.

Stewart and his brother responded by selling professional blueprints detailing measurements, materials, and structural supports. Riders around the world ordered them, and tens of thousands of copies were printed and shipped.

The effect was revolutionary. Backyard vert skating exploded. Teens who had never seen a drainage ditch – let alone the pipelines of Arizona – could now practice vertical riding daily, refining airs, lip tricks, coping grinds, and all the foundational elements of vert skating. In turn, this cultivated the beginnings of a generation of professional skaters who grew up skating ramps built from Stewart's plans. To put it mildly, without Stewart's precise ingenuity, the sport today would look very different.

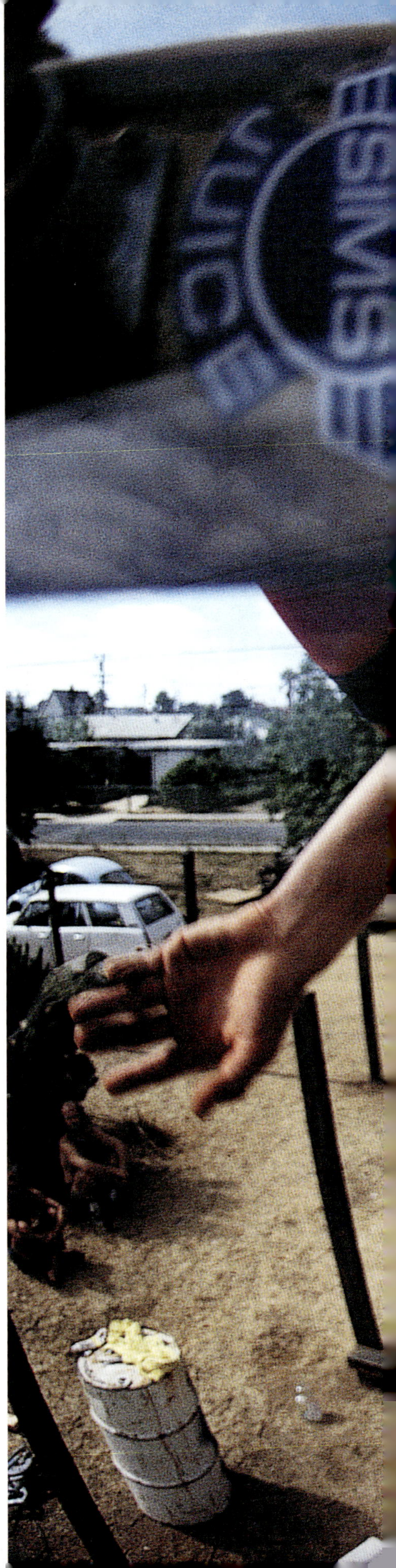

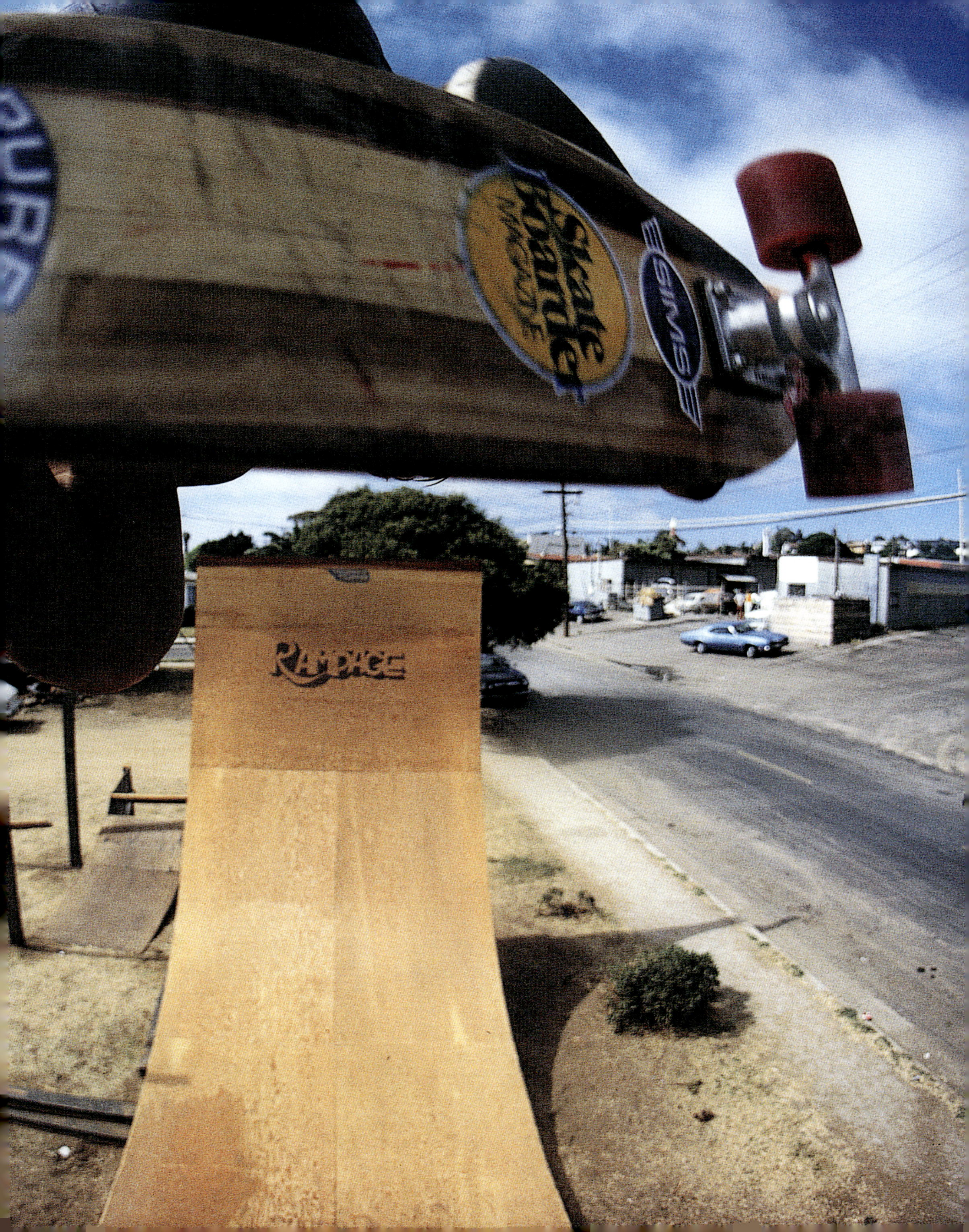
SIMS
RAMPAGE

The Dog Bowl
Santa Monica, CA

In the late ’70s, the Dog Bowl wasn’t just a pool but a crucible of style and attitude. Part of a private residence at 1525 San Vicente Boulevard in Santa Monica, its kidney-shaped form became one of the most important proving grounds for riders at the time – presumably much to the displeasure of the home’s owners.

With the drought drying out backyard pools in the region, local skaters – most notably Tony Alva of the Z-Boys, who was photographed performing one of the first frontside air tricks there – briefly adopted the Dog Bowl in 1977 as a training ground, one where camaraderie and rivalry blended into a powerful creative force. Of course, many empty pools in California became temporary, illicit spots for skate sessions during the drought; a phenomenon driven by that famous cover of *SkateBoarder* in 1975. The unique thing about the Dog Bowl, however, was that, for a short period at least, it was effectively a studio for some of skateboarding’s greatest talents.

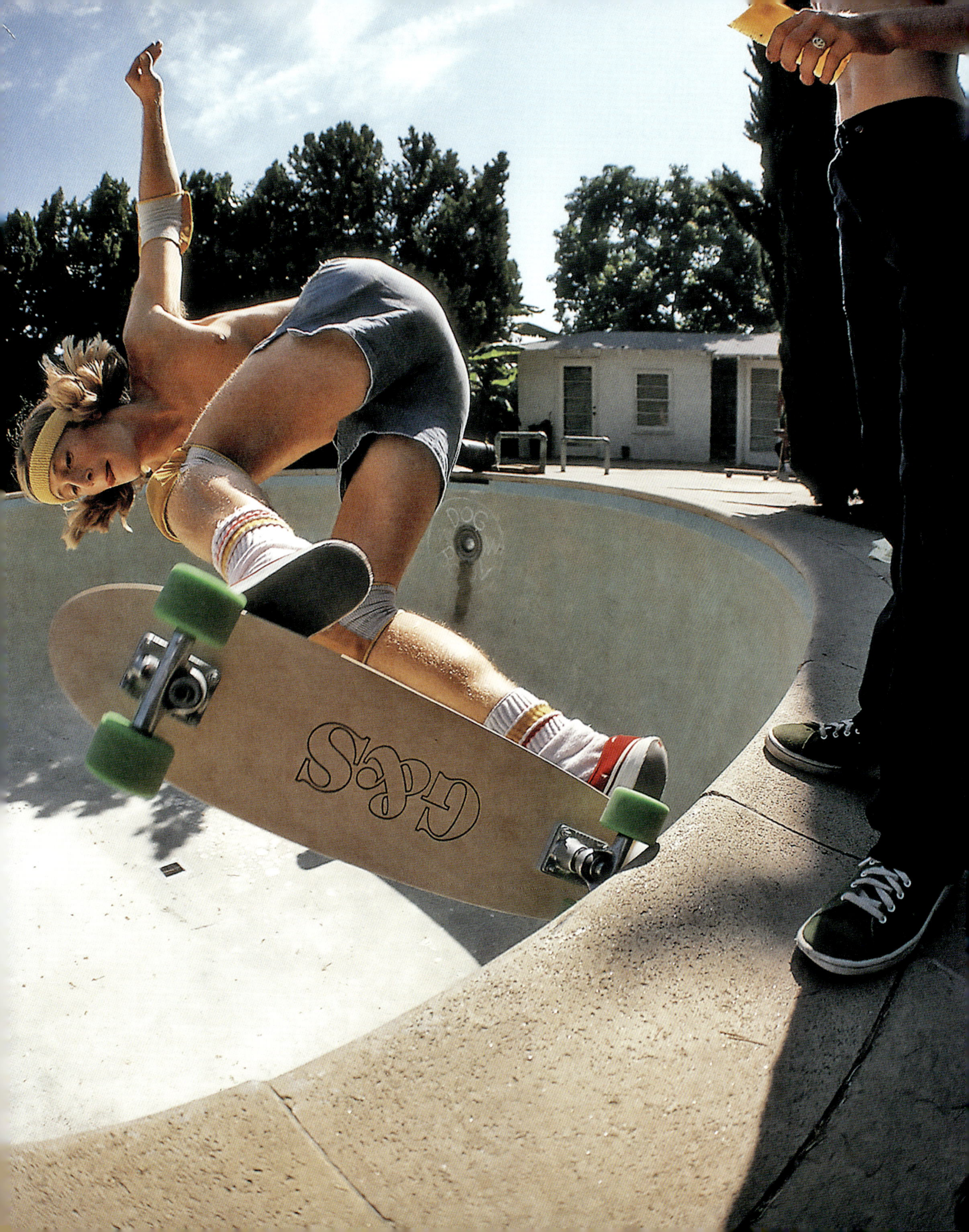
G&S

The Turning Point Ramp
Fort Lauderdale, FL

While California's backyard ramp scene was exploding with wooden ramps inspired by the Arizona Desert Pipes, a completely different experiment was underway in Florida. In 1979, Scotty Senatore, a skater from Fort Lauderdale, engineered the Turning Point Ramp, a futuristic, capsule-shaped structure built from transparent polycarbonate and aluminum: a piece of skateboard architecture that was unlike anything that had come before it – or since.

Launched that spring at the Solid Surf Skateboard Park in Senatore's hometown, the Turning Point Ramp, which was mounted on a hydraulic stand, could be raised, tilted, and even transported. Part mobile full-pipe, part sculpture, its smooth inner surface was hard and fast, allowing riders to explore deeper angles and perform more complex maneuvers. The ramp traveled around the country for exhibitions, and even appeared in the documentary film *Skateboard Madness* (1980) directed by Julian Pena, who later worked on *Tron* (1982) and *Superman IV* (1987). Every time Senatore's creation arrived in a new town, crowds saw something different, courtesy of the riders from across the US who flocked to it. Among them were upcoming stars Tony Hawk and Steve Caballero, as well as '70s heroes such as Brad Bowman, Steve Lippman, and Jim "Graystoke" Gray. But it was Scotty Senatore's brother, Kent, who made history in the Turning Point by performing a full loop of the pipe; a feat then rarely performed anywhere.

Senatore only built one version of the Turning Point Ramp, and its influence today is hardly discernible anywhere, which is part of its reputation. Shaped like a zeppelin, it was an inimitable creation that has as much in common with skateparks as it does the white cube: a singular example of ramp design that aspired to the quality of art.

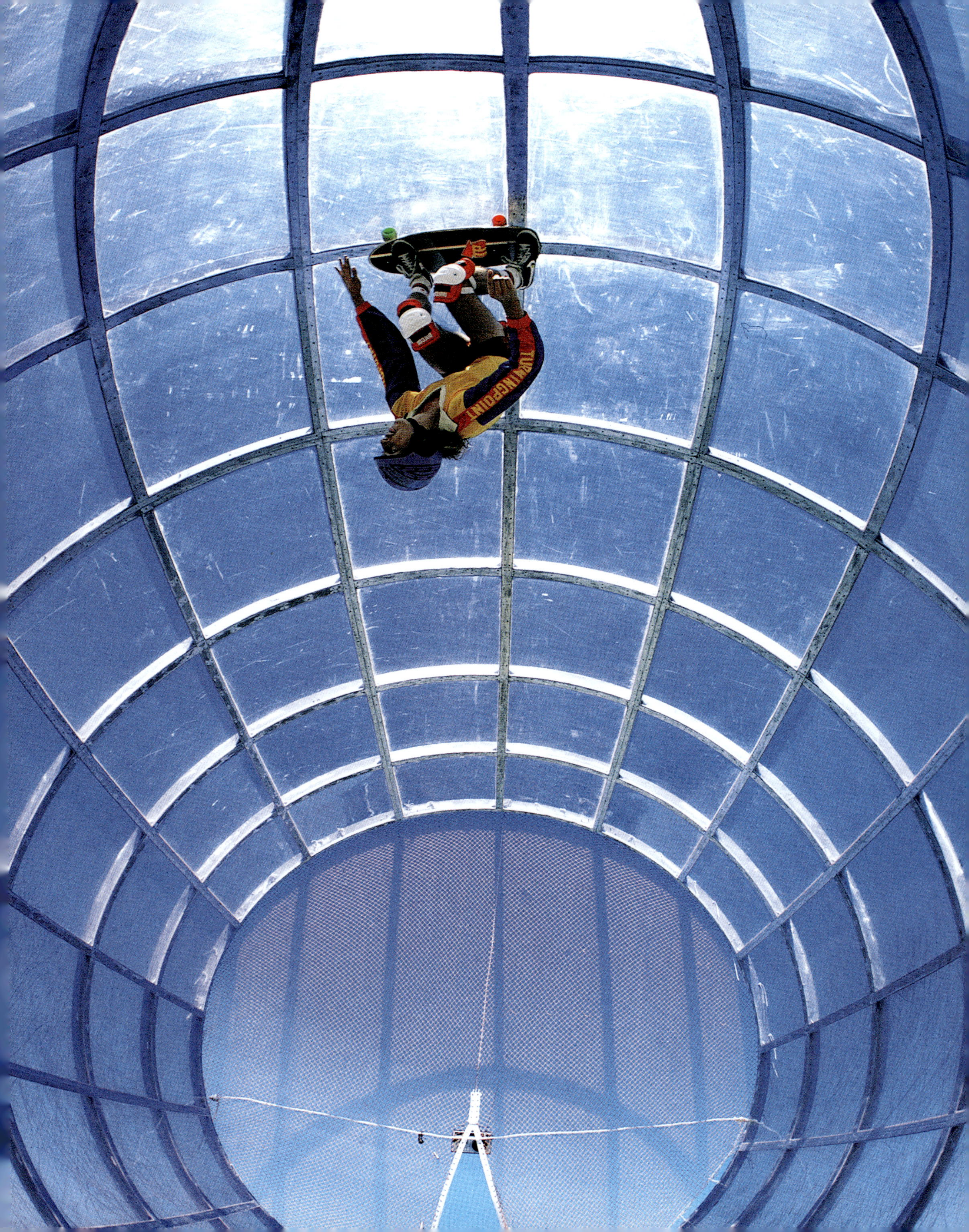
TURNINGPOINT

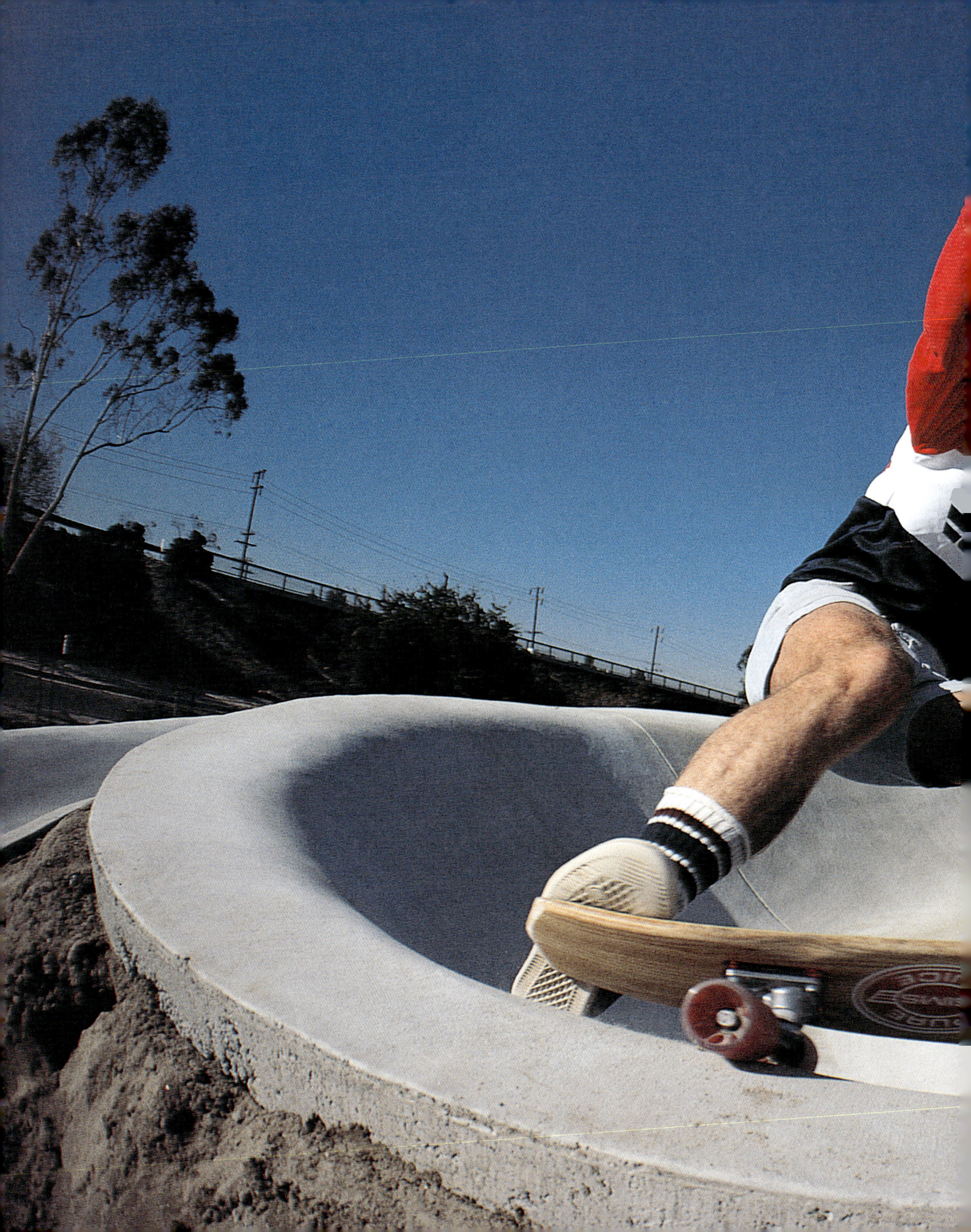

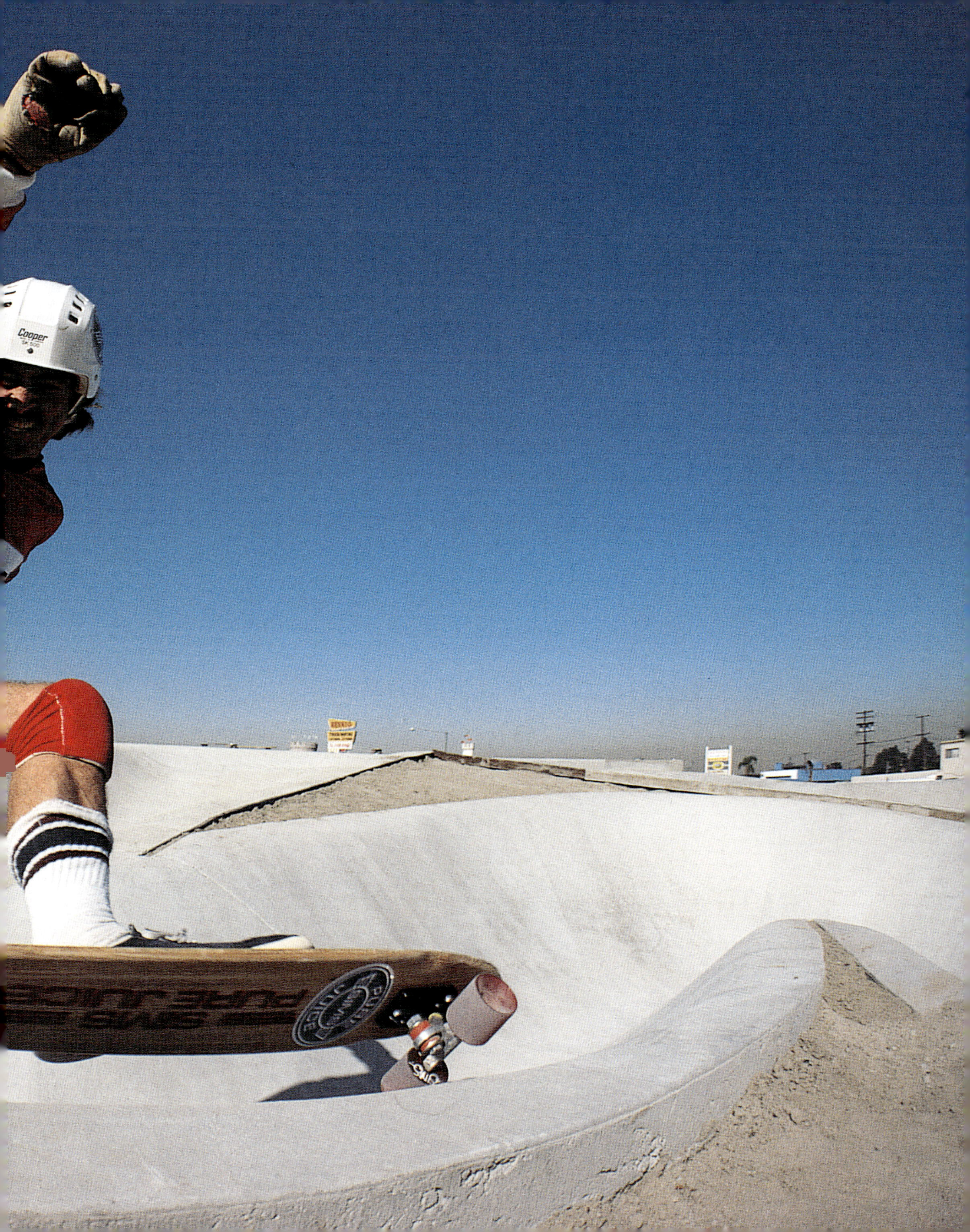
Cooper

The Competitive Meta-morphosis (1975–1979)

The rapid evolution in skateboarding during the late 1970s is no place more evident than in the proliferation of competitions during this period. From early freestyle events to downhill and slalom competitions, and, eventually, vert ramps contests, each new trophy for each new style represented a new milestone for skateboarding. In turn, they were also emblems of the sport's shift away from being a mere pastime toward becoming the professional sport it is today. The following is a brief survey of some of the most important competitions.

The Bahne / Cadillac National Skateboard Championships
1975, Del Mar, CA

The 1975 Bahne / Cadillac National Championships at Del Mar, a city north of San Diego, are often described as the birth of modern skateboarding – and for good reason. At the time Cadillac Wheels' novel urethane was providing riders with unparalleled grip and control, allowing them to explore new styles and perform new tricks; a development that was evident in the displays of technical virtuosity in Del Mar that year.

The Z-Boys team, for instance, arrived like they'd come from a different universe. While many competitors still carried the upright grace of traditional freestyle, the Z-Boys were bent low, carving deep lines with an elastic aggression that confused the judges and hypnotized the crowd. Crew members Tony Alva and Jay Adams looked as if they were surfing on concrete, and Peggy Oki skated with a radical confidence that made her one of the stars of the event.

Today, it's impossible to overstate the importance of this event for the future of skating. On the one hand, there were the old school skaters competing, whose lineage was still connected to the sport's roots in the 1960s, when skating was still mostly about having fun and cruising around. On the other, there were skaters like the Z-Boys, who were pushing skateboarding toward increased specialization and new heights of technical flair. Far from just a contest, Del Mar was an epochal clash.

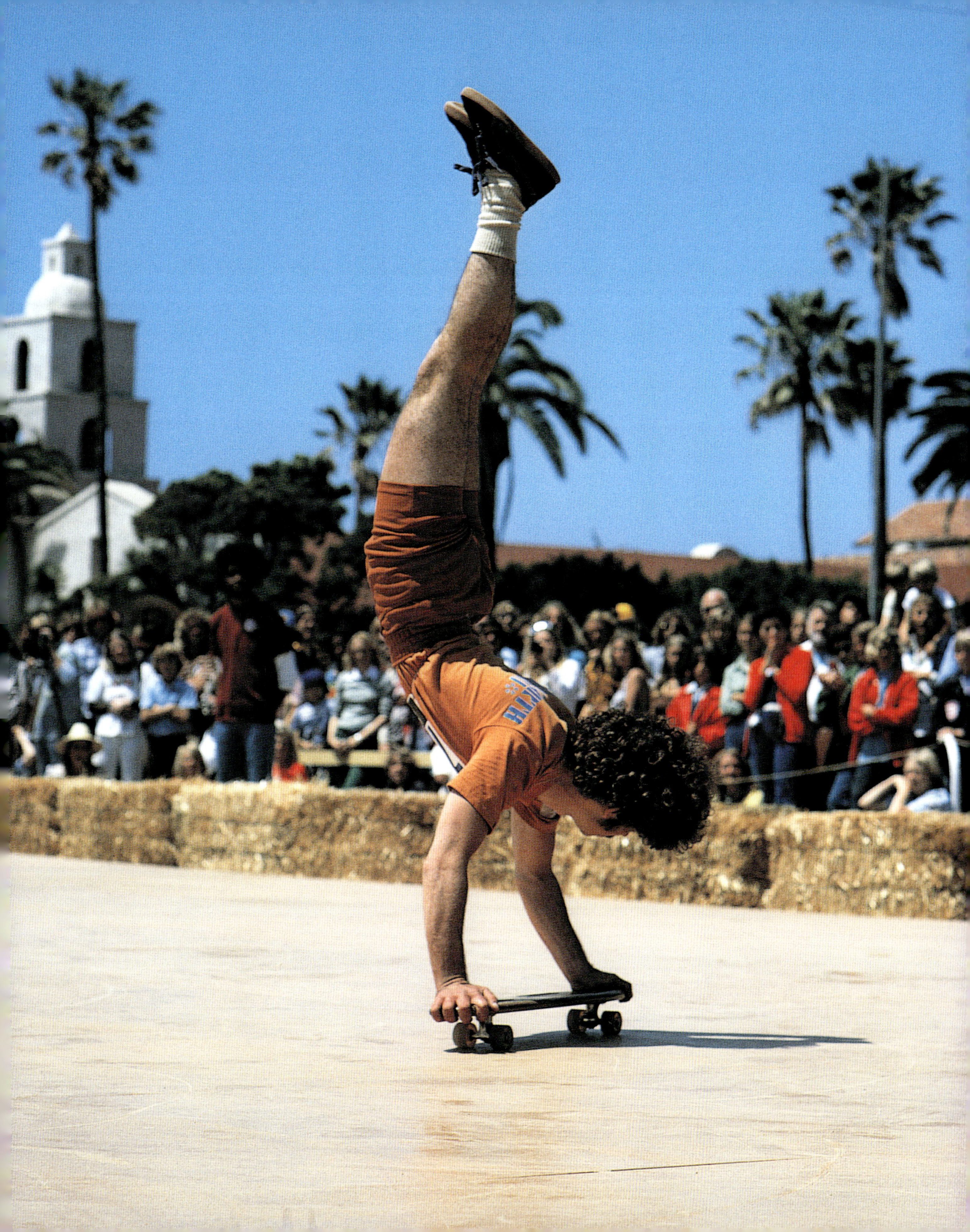

The Free Former World Professional Skateboard Championships
1976, Long Beach, CA

By the time the Free Former World Professional Championships (FFWPC) took over the Long Beach Arena in 1976, skateboarding was trying out a new identity, one that looked a little more polished and mature. In an indoor arena with lights and even bigger crowds than Del Mar, the FFWPC featured official formats and a total prize fund of $20,000 – the equivalent of $170,000 today.

Driven by both sporting excellence and the then-rare opportunity to make some money, riders – including Henry Hester, Ellen Berryman, Mike Weed – brought an unparalleled energy to the event. And like Del Mar, traditional techniques were set in stark contrast to the new styles that were emerging. The juxtaposition was fascinating, and as the latter triumphed over the former, it was clear that in Long Beach, a new dawn had arrived for skateboarding.

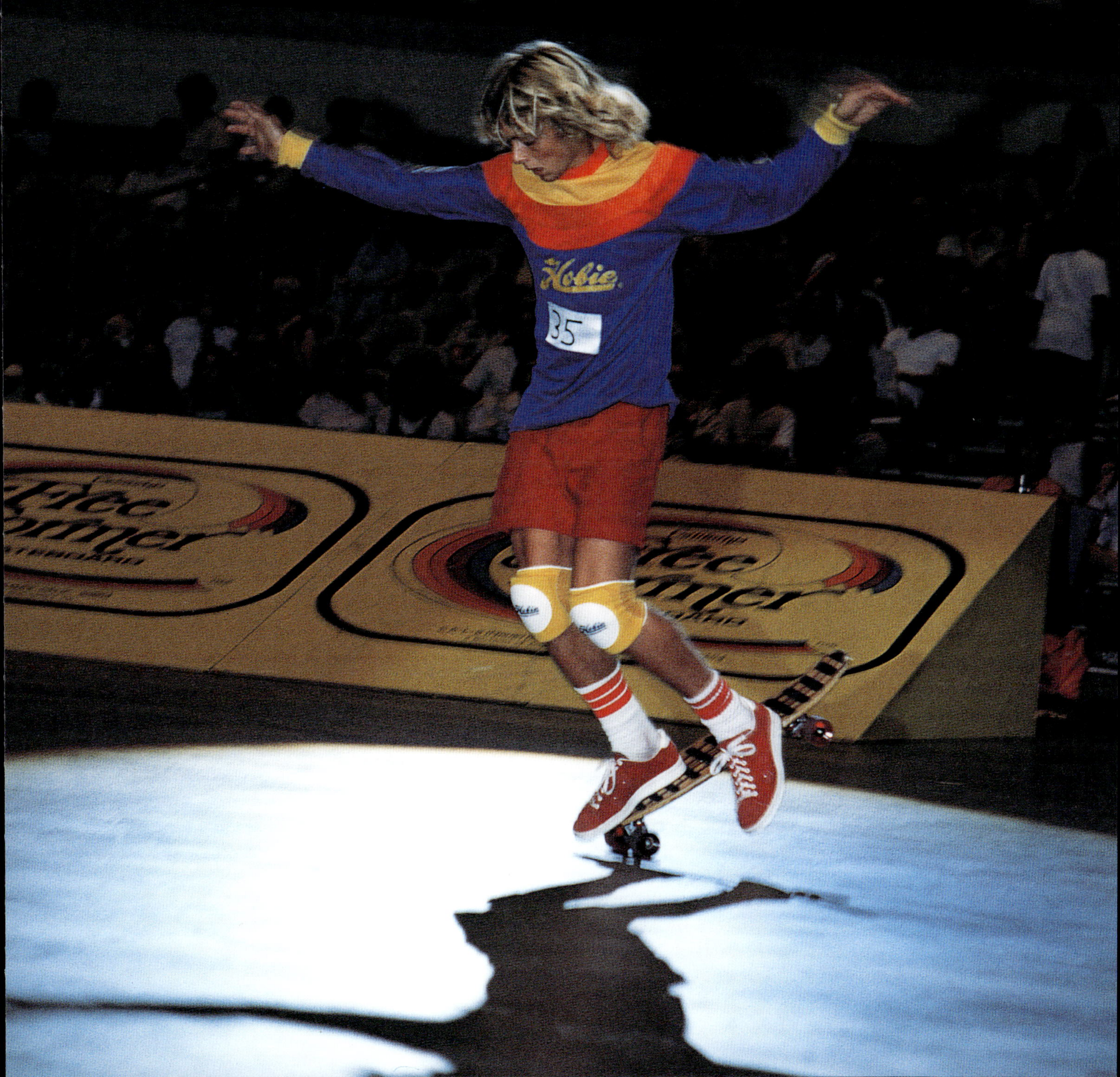
Hobie
35

The Hang Ten World Pro-AM Championships
1976, Carlsbad, CA

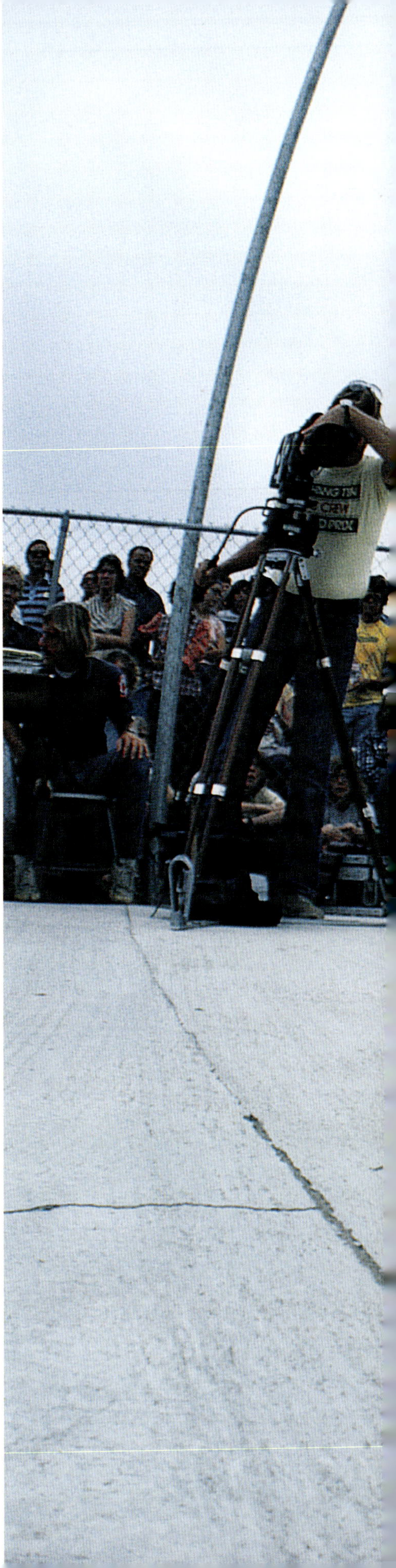

The unique thing about the 1976 Hang Ten World Pro-Am Championships was the TV cameras. Being filmed by ABC's *Wide World of Sports*, whose lenses and presenters created a sense of spectacle, resulted in a self-awareness among the event's competitors. At one of the first skateboard events to be broadcast, suddenly riders had to contend with the fact that they were being watched by people far beyond California. Santa Monica native Tony Alva rose to the occasion. Attacking bowls with an unrivalled energy, he was beaten to first place only by old school freestyle skater Bruce Logan – a sign of the affection skateboarding's establishment still had for traditional styles. On the other hand, the radical technique of women's gold medalist Laura Thornhill proved to young women and men alike that a change was taking place in the sport, one that no one could stop. A force that made victory seem almost inevitable.

Despite stepping into the national spotlight, the skaters at Carlsbad, young and old, remained true to their respective heritages. Nothing felt rehearsed or performative, with most contestants remaining virtually oblivious to the cameras. In doing so, they set a precedent for televised events that is still respected by every modest, unpretentious competition skater today.

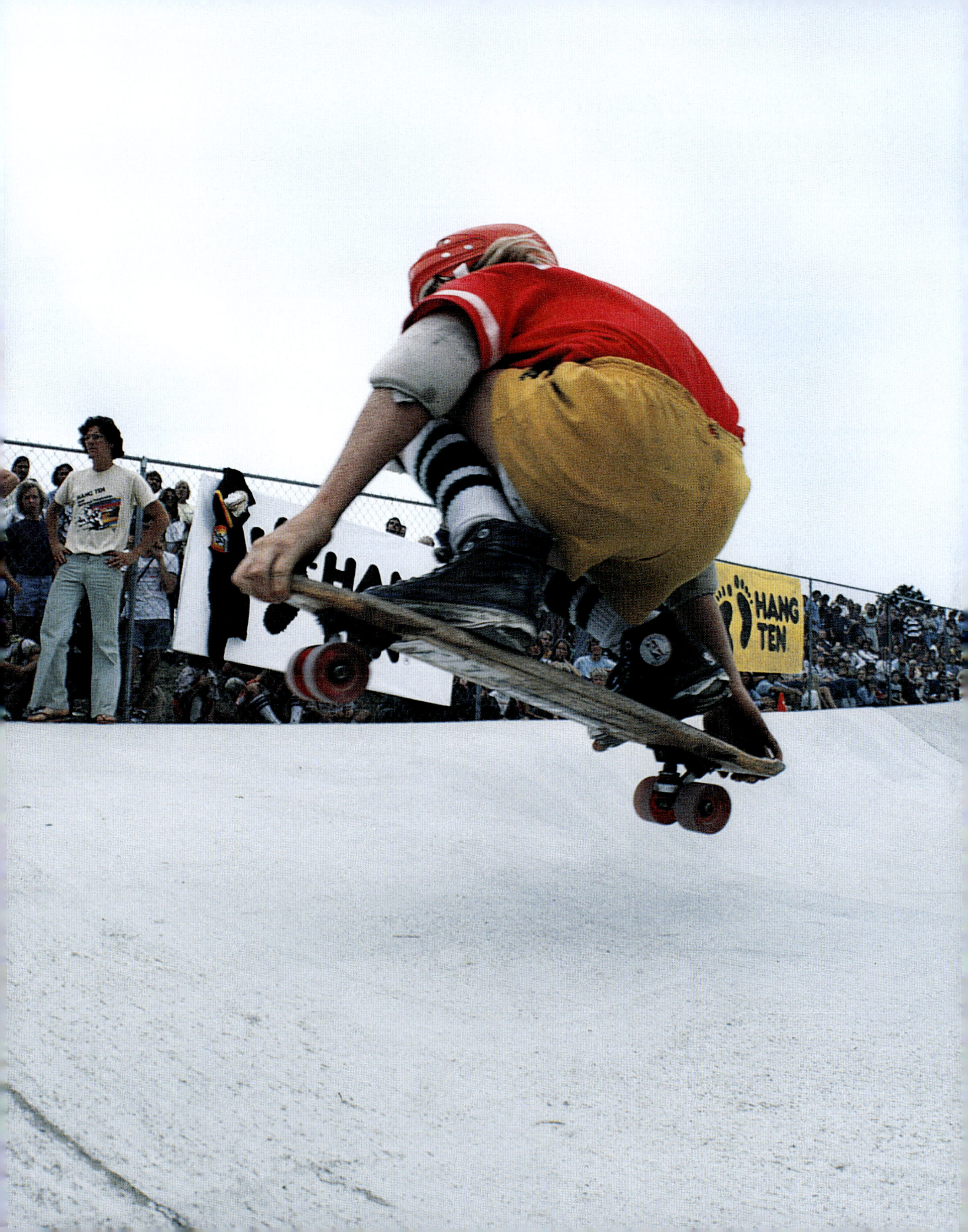
HANG TEN

The Catalina Classic
1977, Santa Catalina Island, CA

While trick-based and vert ramp riding were growing in popularity in the late '70s, racing was still thriving. And nowhere was this clearer than in the September 1977 Catalina Classic competition.

Santa Catalina, a mountainous island 29 miles (47 km) south-soutwest of Long Beach, California, was a setting whose steep, winding roads and rocky terrain made it both an ideal location for racing as well as one loaded with obvious risk.

Also broadcast on ABC's *Wide World of Sports*, the competition was fiercely contested, with the men's downhill race going down to the wire between Jamie Hart and John Hutson, both sponsored riders for Santa Cruz. In the end, Hutson prevailed, rocketing down open roads with a steadiness and confidence that, in footage from ABC still in circulation, appears almost supernatural.

Today, racing has become a specialized segment of the sport with a steady and international community of slalom skaters, while interest in downhill is growing. At its best, however, no other style could match a downhill race for intensity and thrills. Traveling at the speed of automobiles, the racers of this era were among the bravest and most skillful riders ever to set foot on a board.

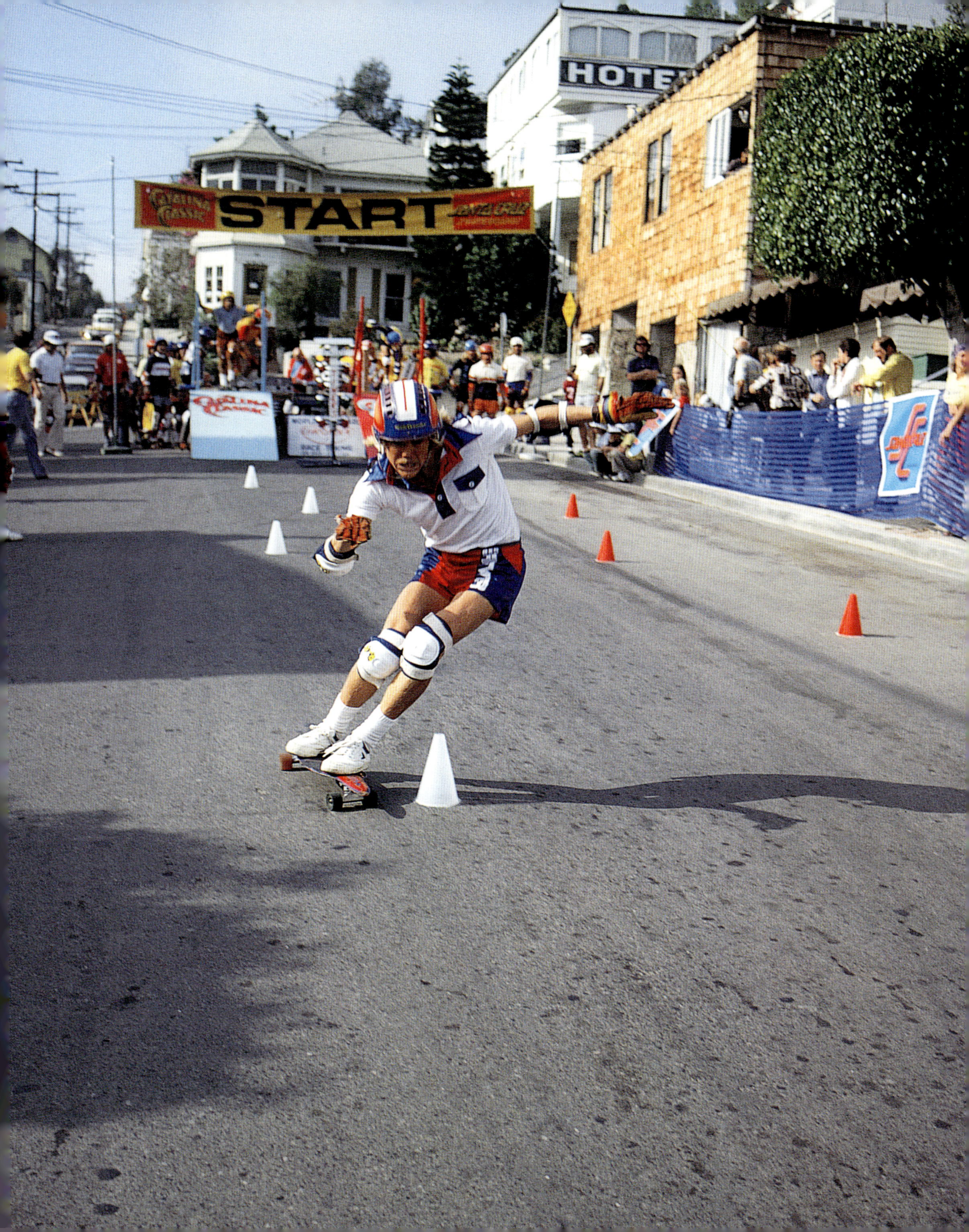
HOTE
START

The Signal Hill Speed Run
1978, Long Beach, CA

If the Catalina Classic was a thrill ride, the final iteration of the Signal Hill Speed Run in 1978 was equally ecstatic, yet troubled. Eking out only a three-year run, the annual Long Beach competition became emblematic of downhill skating and slalom's loss of status in the sport. Officially, the event closed because of Tina Trefethen's near-fatal crash, but the reality was that such styles of skating were declining in popularity as well. Nonetheless, the show went out in style, with every participant riding beyond the limits of what seemed feasible.

John Hutson set a Guinness World Record, traveling at speeds of over 53 miles per hour (85 km/h) on four wheels – a feat that remains astonishing. But what truly defined the event were its experimental "skate-cars." Hurtling around Long Beach at nearly 60 miles per hour (96 km/h), these strange aerodynamic, cocoon-like "vehicles" were a sight to behold. Of course, after Trefethen's accident, concerned onlookers began to question the risks of such exploits. But for many of its participants, the competition represented the pinnacle of the discipline.

Afterward, Long Beach banned downhill events, a decision that sped the decline of skateboard racing in general. Yet for John Hutson et al., the 1978 Speed Run was arguably the apogee of their achievements.

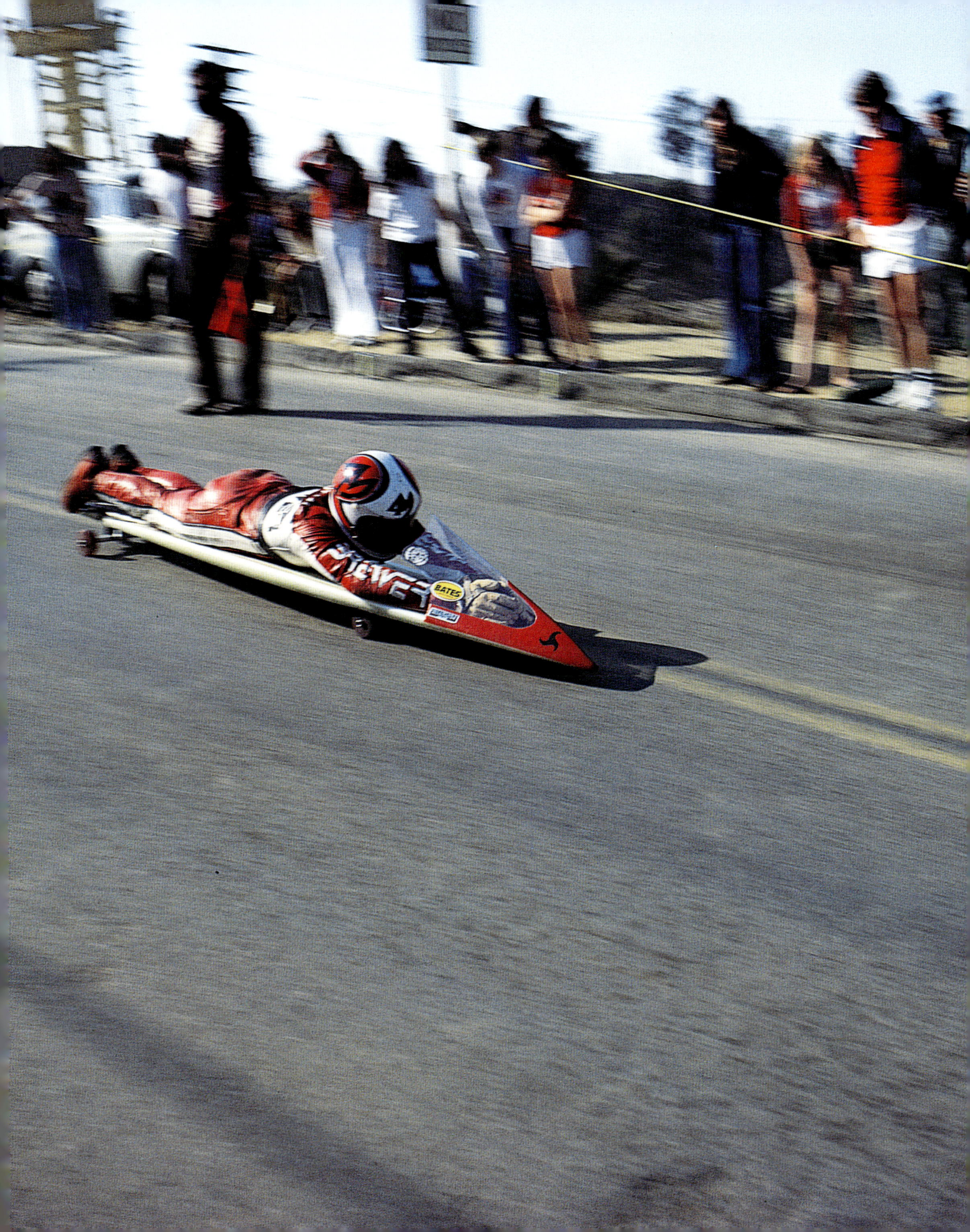
BATES

The ISA Hester Series
1978, Orange, CA

While downhill racing became less popular in the late ’70s, ramp and pool riding’s stock was rising – fast. Indeed, the ISA Hester Series, created by the FibreFlex rider Henry Hester, marked the moment vertical skating truly arrived. The series featured stops at Orange city, Spring Valley, the Pipeline at Upland, and the Del Mar Skate Ranch, among other locations, with each event being louder, more chaotic, and more fiercely contested than the last. Steve Olson, and brothers Michael and Steve Alba, dominated the series with their irrefutably new-era mix of technical prowess and fearlessness.

In similar pool and ramp competitions, judges tended to reward participants for their ability simply to complete their runs. But the judges at the Hester Series were more focussed on ambition, giving medals to riders who skated faster and displayed a commitment to style, whether or not they always remained on four wheels. As a result, a new competitive language began to emerge after the Hester Series, one that prioritized intent as much as precision. It was another paradigmatic moment for the sport, in which the art of the “slam” – those attempts to land death-defying tricks that end in glorious failure – began to take hold.

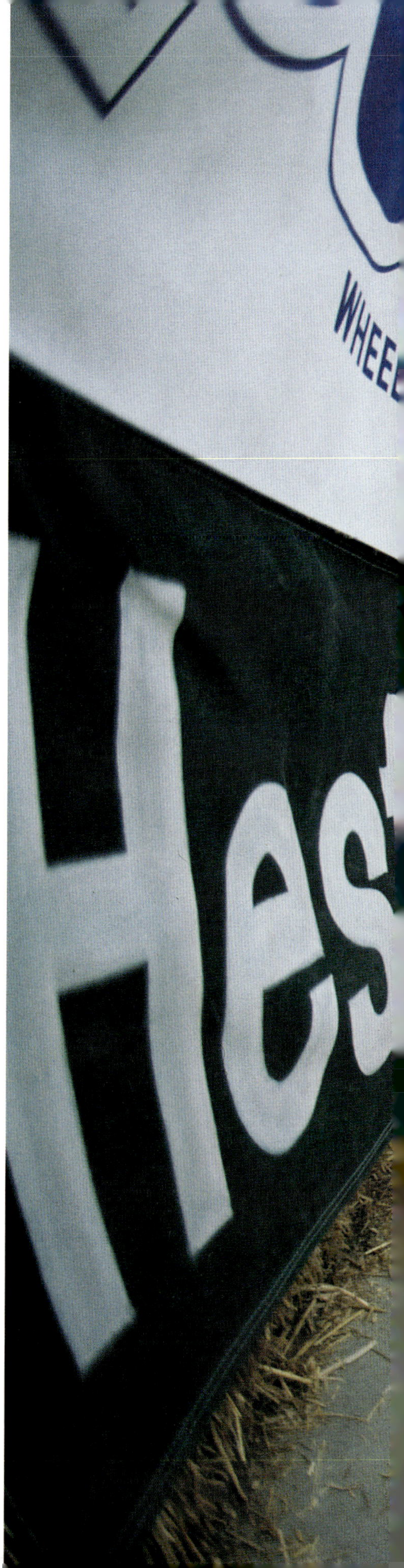

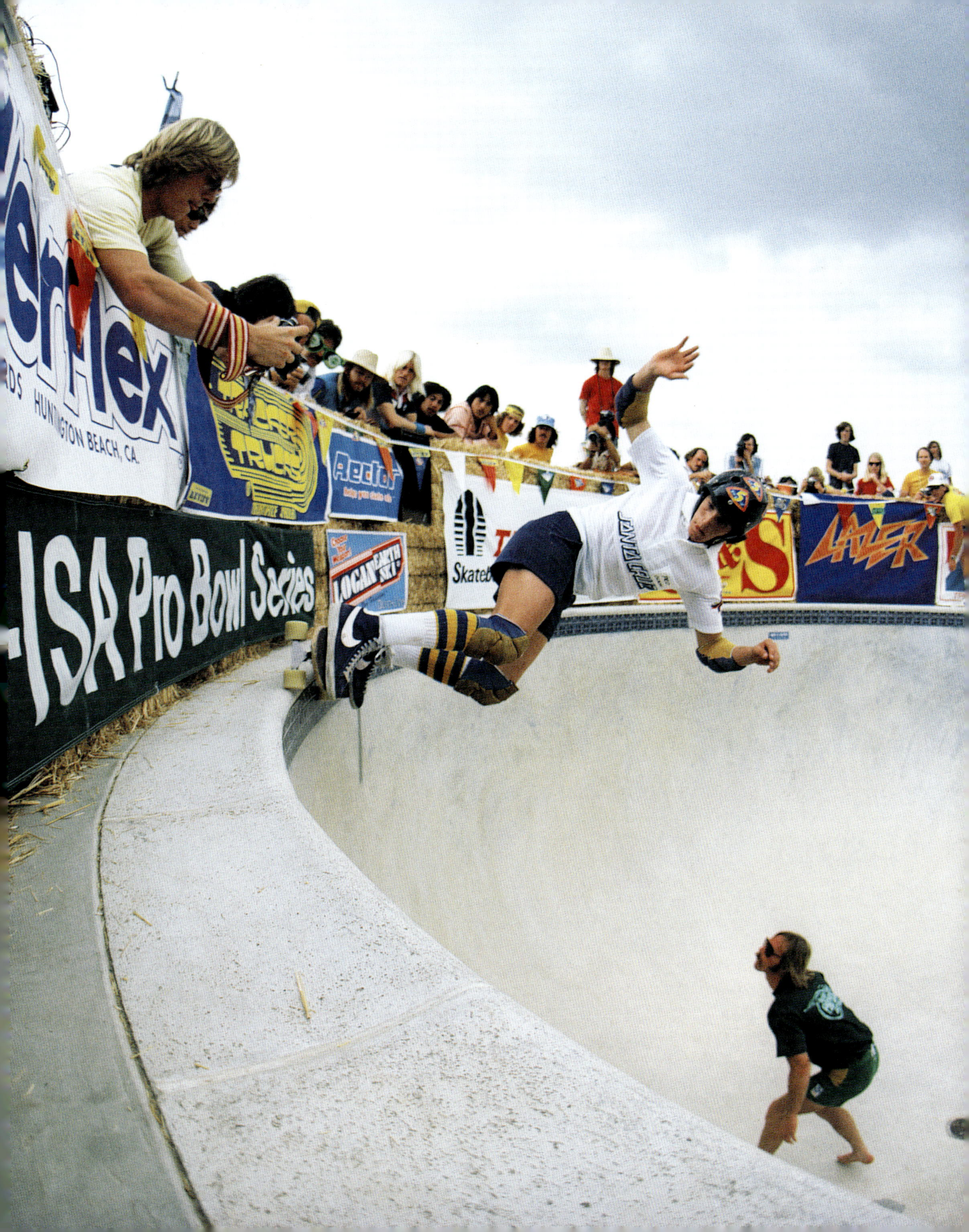

HUNTINGTON BEACH, CA.
Aector
LOGAN EARTH SKI
-ISA Pro Bowl Series
Skateb
LAZER

The Cali Contests of 1979
1979, CA Parks and Contests

1979 marked a true moment of transition. Riding broke through the surface and moved decisively into the air. An increasing number of maneuvers were executed above the coping rather than across it.

The February "Worlds" contest at Lakewood set the tone. Steve Alba led the way, winning the men's pro division with authority. Meanwhile, a new generation of riders began pushing beyond what had recently seemed possible. The level shifted visibly and irreversibly.

As the season unfolded across California's growing network of parks and contests, a quiet revolution emerged. Alan "Ollie" Gelfand, an unassuming Floridian, introduced the no-hands aerial. At first, it seemed almost incidental – a subtle release rather than a dramatic statement. Yet it carried latent potential that would soon reshape everything. The Ollie would become the foundation of modern street skating and a cornerstone of vert progression – arguably the most influential maneuver in skateboarding history.

Fittingly, this understated breakthrough marked the end of the decade. Over the previous five years, skateboarding had reinvented itself at a rapid pace. By 1979, skateboarding had found its footing and left the ground, ready for its next evolution.

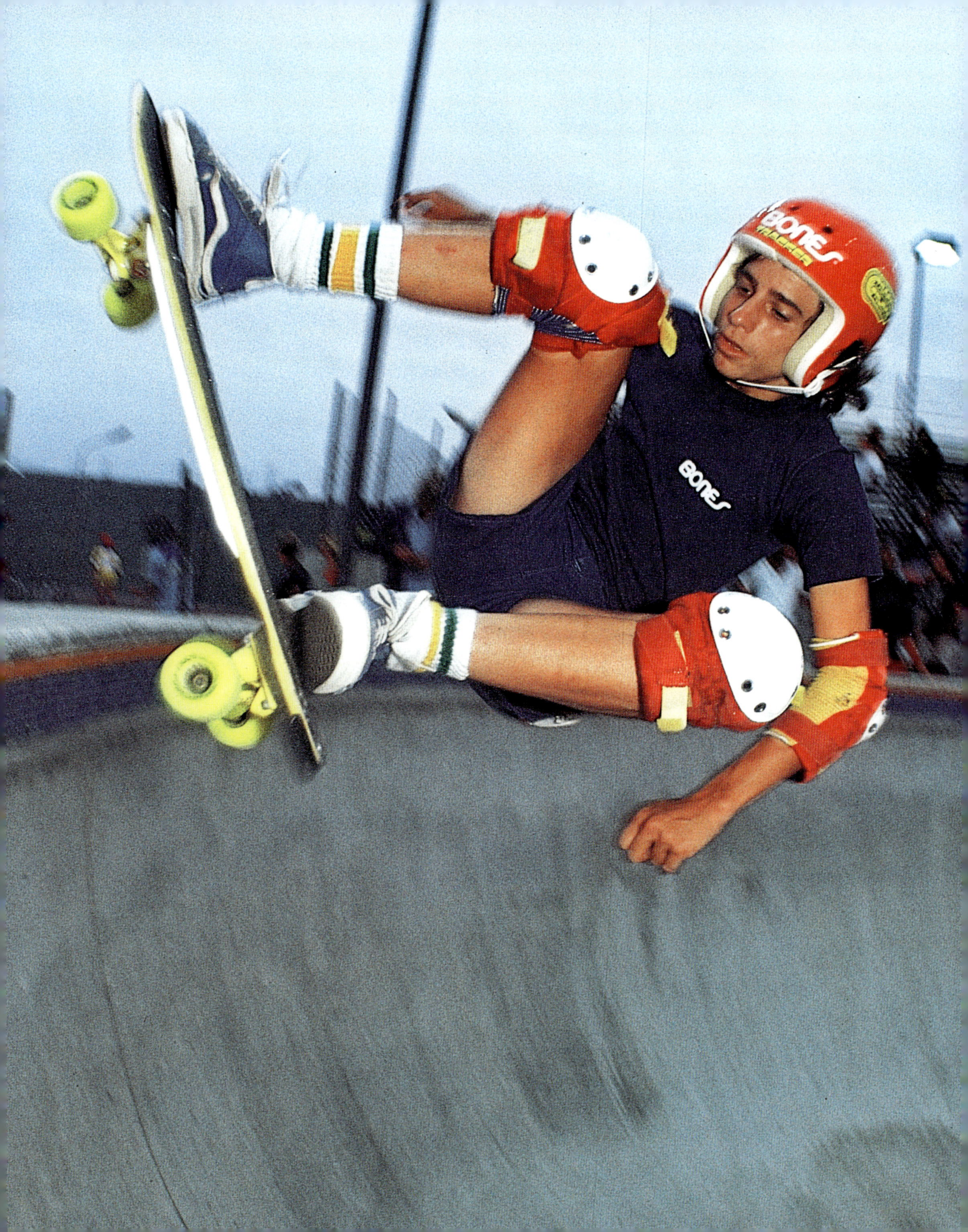
BONES
BONES

The Competitive Landscape of the Late ’70s

FibreFlex wasn't the only brand trading during skateboarding's defining years, but in 1975 and 1976, it was leading the pack. Its fiberglass composite construction and engineered flex gave riders something no other brand could match, and for a brief window, FibreFlex set the standard. By 1977, however, the sport was changing fast. As skating grew more vertical and riders began demanding stiffer, more rigid platforms, a new generation of brands emerged to meet that shift, each with its own materials, philosophies, and innovations. The competition became fierce, and the flex technology that had put FibreFlex on top gradually lost its edge. These are some of the brands that shaped the landscape alongside FibreFlex as the sport evolved between 1975 and 1979.

Bahne

An OG 1976 Bahne with OG Bahne trucks and OG Cadillac wheels

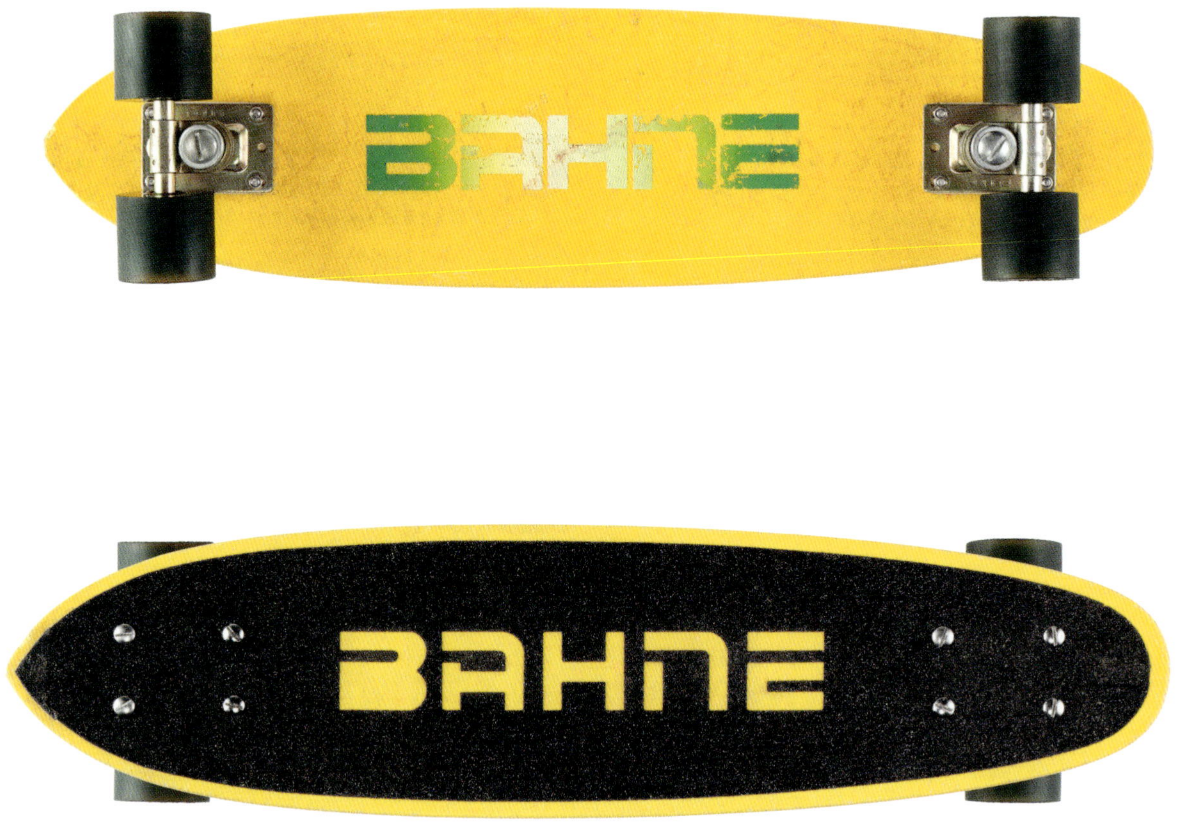

Bahne was one of the giants of the late 1970s skateboarding boom; it thrived at a scale few competitors could master. Even outside the US, where Bahne's products were unavailable, its reputation was huge. Founded by brothers Bill and Bob Bahne in Encinitas in the early '70s, the company's skateboards emerged directly from the surf industry's technical mindset. With Bill's background in surfboard design, Bahne was ideally positioned to begin producing large volumes of its prized fiberglass skate decks. During this period, the company tried to keep up with the ferocious demand for its products, which led it to become one of the biggest brands of its time. Bahne's board shapes were practical, smooth, and functional, perfectly suited for slalom, carving, and the early exploration of banks and ditches. Its foundational decks and trucks were consistently high-quality and reliable – important qualities for skaters testing their abilities. What's more, it also had a brand partnership with Cadillac Wheels, the wheel company that brought the sport into its urethane era. Through all these achievements, Bahne became synonymous with the sport's rebirth in the '70s.

Powell Quicksilver

A NOS Powell/Sims Quicksilver with OG ACS 560s and OG Road Rider 4s

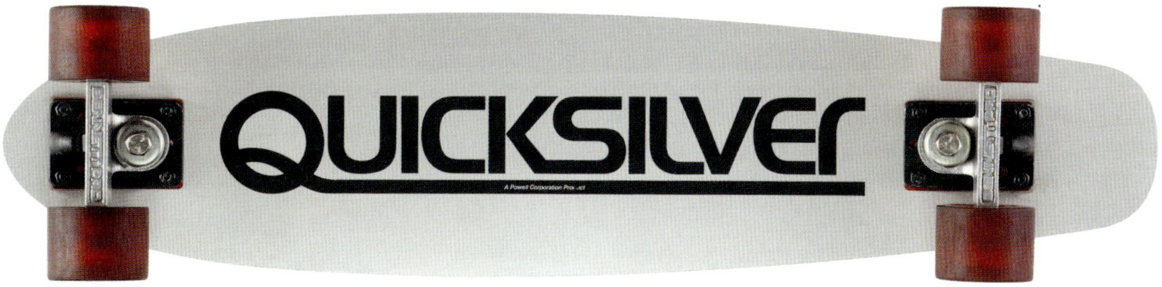

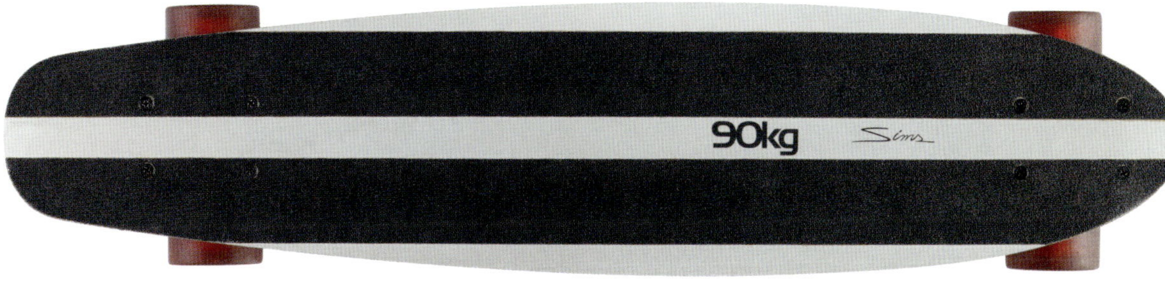

When it first appeared in ads, the Powell Quicksilver seemed to have arrived from the future. Silver and black, its spacecraft-esque shape, front-lit and placed against a jet-black background in *SkateBoarder*, like a Caravaggio, looked as if it might fly off the page. The Quicksilver, however, was no flight of sci-fi fancy. Designed by George Powell in 1976, it was an ambitious experiment: a maple core sandwiched between aerospace aluminum skins. Stiff and fast, the board was co-branded with Sims, whose name appeared on the deck, though the engineering behind it was Powell's. It quickly became a symbol of high-tech slalom performance. In an era when most companies were still experimenting with fiberglass, Powell was already pushing the conversation toward metal composites. The fruits of this innovation were short-lived. With the rising popularity of pool and vert ramp skating, demand for such a rigid board was modest. Regardless, the Quicksilver was an inimitable example of the engineering mindset that would define George Powell's career. In that sense, it can also be seen as an early precursor to Powell Peralta, where that same technical ambition, later applied to wooden laminates, helped build one of the most influential skate companies in the sport's history.

Santa Cruz Skateboards

A NOS Santa Cruz slalom model from 1977 with reissue Indy 109s and OG OJ Super Juice wheels

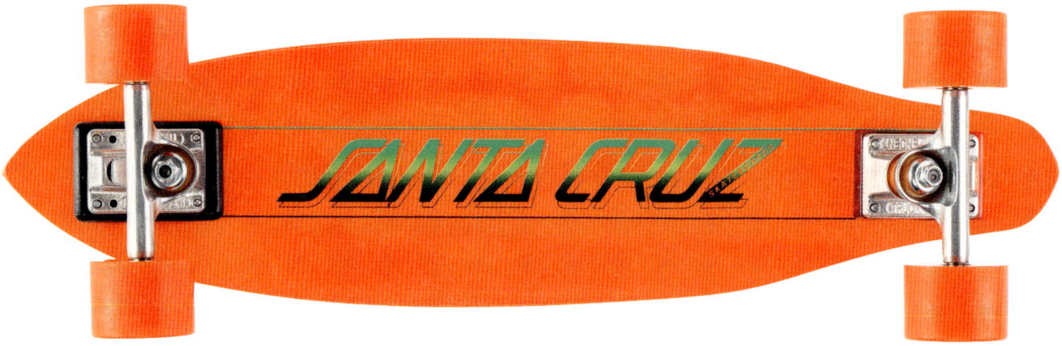

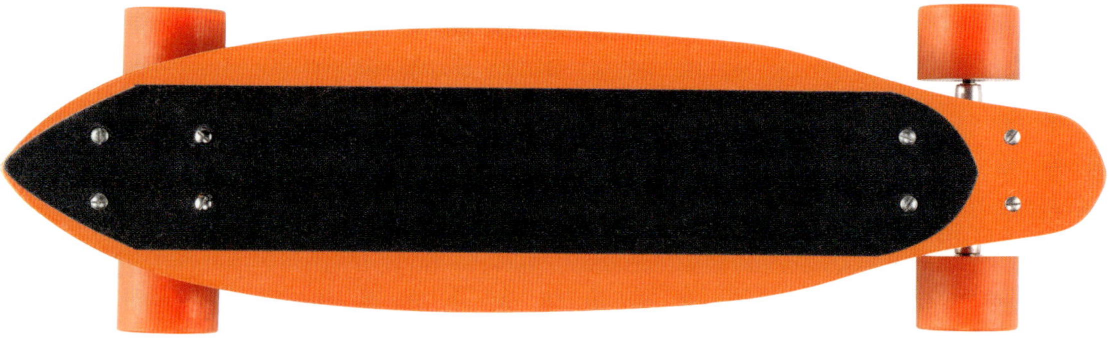

The oldest continuously operating skate company in the world, Santa Cruz Skateboards, began almost by accident in 1973. Back then, its founders, Richard Novak, Doug Haut, and Jay Shuirman, were running a struggling surf brand when a friend challenged them to make 500 skateboard decks as a possible cure for their ailing business. The boards sold out quickly, and Novak, Haut, and Shuirman never looked back. After initially making solid fiberglass decks, the company followed the trend of wooden ply-core and fiberglass, dominating slalom and downhill board constructions, with team rider John Hutson ending up dominating the discipline and soon transitioned to expertly making wooden boards. Santa Cruz's slalom models were somewhat fragile performance tools, while its pool and vert decks were built to withstand the abuse. Like Dogtown Skateboards, the company also became known for its graphics, particularly those by artist Jim Phillips, who designed its iconic logo. In moving decisively from fiberglass to wood while maintaining its commitment to quality, Santa Cruz anticipated the wider shift the industry would soon undergo.

Hobie

A 1977 NOS Hobie Flex "Bob Skoldberg" slalom deck with OG Gull Wing Split Axle trucks and NOS Road Rider 4s

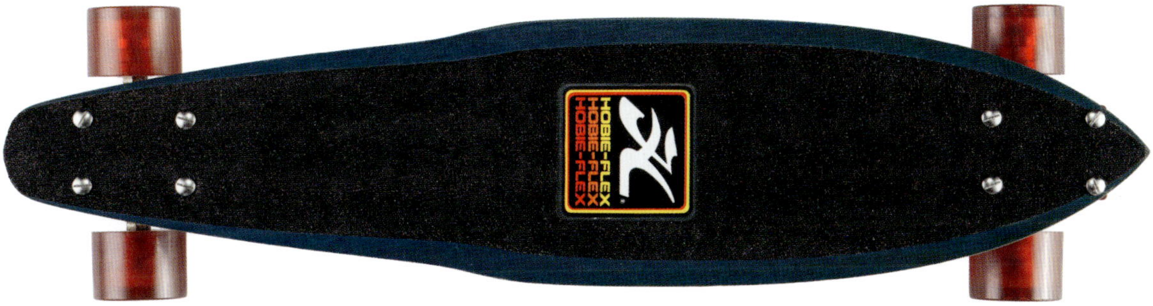

Hobie established a leading role within the 70s skateboard scene, constantly being in the forefront, developing decks, wheels and accessories utilizing the latest in terms of materials and innovation. Originally founded by surfer Hobie Alter in 1964, the brand had been making boards since skateboarding's earliest days. By the mid-1970s, its flex boards, built around a tri-ply wood core, offered a ride very close to that of FibreFlex models. Before that Hobie also produced pressure-molded fiberglass decks, a different technology altogether, closer in concept to what Bahne was doing. Refined and highly functional, its boards emphasized responsiveness, carving accuracy, and control – qualities directly inherited from the principles of surf design. Their position as one of the leaders throughout the 70s, they constantly went along, serving riders with the most accurate gear and innovation.

Turner

An OG 1970s Turner with reissue mid trucks and NOS Road Rider 4s

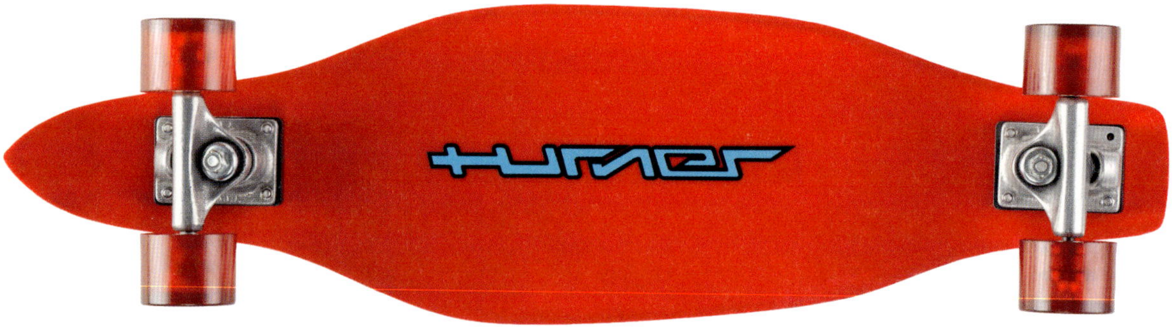

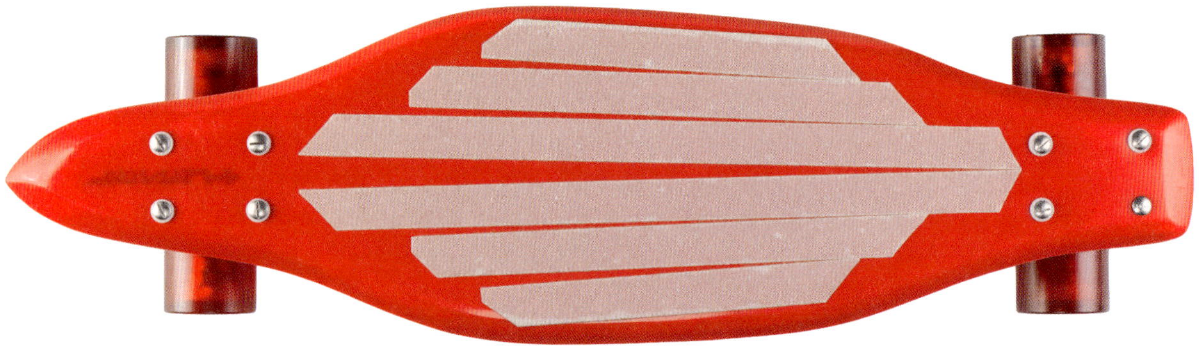

Within the slalom world of the mid-1970s, Turner Skateboards held a distinct place. At the time, riders were split between two camps: those riding flex decks like FibreFlex, built with fiberglass and wood cores, and those favoring foam-core boards constructed with polyester and fiberglass, more like surfboards in their construction. Founded by seasoned slalom rider Bobby Turner, Turner belonged firmly to the latter camp, and its boards became a reference point for riders committed to that approach. Turner's handmade SummerSki slalom decks were wide in the middle and pointed at the nose. Available in bright primary colors with striped black grip tape. Nevertheless, every model was stable and built for technical precision. Indeed, their dimensions were optimized for the low, tight, ski-like stance of high-speed slalom racing. Like other similar brands, Turner was eventually eclipsed by the thirst for vertical surfaces. But for the duration of the company's existence, its singular vision of board design defined an important chapter in the sport's evolution.

Logan Earth Ski

A 1977 NOS Bruce Logan with NOS Lazer trucks and OG 70mm 2nd-gen Kryptonics

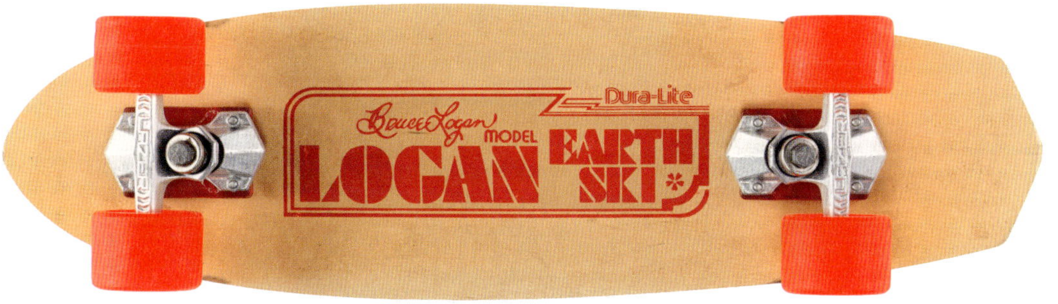

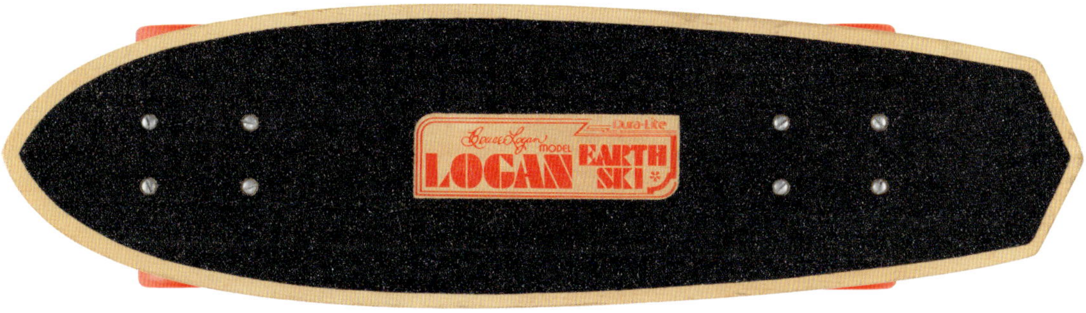

Logan Earth Ski was built on decades of experience. Officially registered as a company by Brian and Bruce Logan in 1975, the brothers had in fact been making boards in their family home in Hermosa Beach, California, since they first began skating in the 1950s. With the help of their younger brothers, Brad and Robin, who had been swept up in the new wave of skating in the mid-1970s, the Logan family launched its own company, initially making solid log decks and eventually focusing on finely crafted laminate boards. Known for balanced outlines, attention to detail, and master craftsmanship, Logan Earth Ski made its name as skateboarding was transforming from an amateur pastime into a professional sport. Overnight, the brand was everywhere. Slalom racers loved it, and so did freestyle riders and kids who wanted a skateboard that felt authentically Californian. I was one of them: my first ply board was a Robin Logan model. Sold with Tracker Haf trucks and white YO-YO wheels, it remains an emblem of skateboarding's spirit in the 1970s.

Z-Flex

A 1978 NOS Z-Wood Shogo Kubo signature model with OG Gullwing 7s and NOS Powerflex 5s

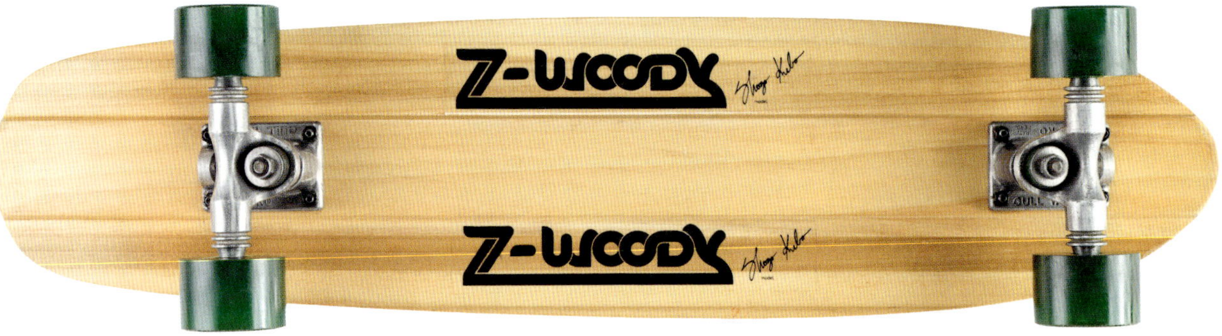

Z-Flex was founded in 1976 by Kent Sherwood after the Zephyr brand, famously promoted by its Z-Boys team, dissolved. Drawing on the Dogtown surf-skate philosophy, Sherwood created high-performance fiberglass decks built for durability and aggressive riding. With that pedigree, the brand was an instant hit with pool skaters, thanks to its stiff yet bouncy boards, tailor-made for negotiating deep curves. What's more, the Zephyr-esque minimal profile of its boards, alongside their bright colors and typically funky '70s brand font, helped Z-Flex maintain its original customer base, a loyalty reinforced by the continued sponsorship of some of the Z-Boys. As pool and vert skating placed greater demands on equipment, however, Z-Flex followed the wider industry shift from fiberglass to wood, producing laminate decks better suited to the abuse riders were putting their boards through. The Z-Wood line, including its signature models, reflected this transition: wooden construction paired with the same aggressive identity the brand had established from the start. Among the Z-Boys who rode for Z-Flex was Shogo Kubo. A pioneering skater who cut his teeth in Venice Beach and was known for his "laybacks." Kubo's signature Z-Flex board was highly sought after then and now, and the original is one of the jewels in my collection.

Dogtown

An OG 1978 Dogtown Paul Constantinou model with reissue Tracker X and reissue Gyros

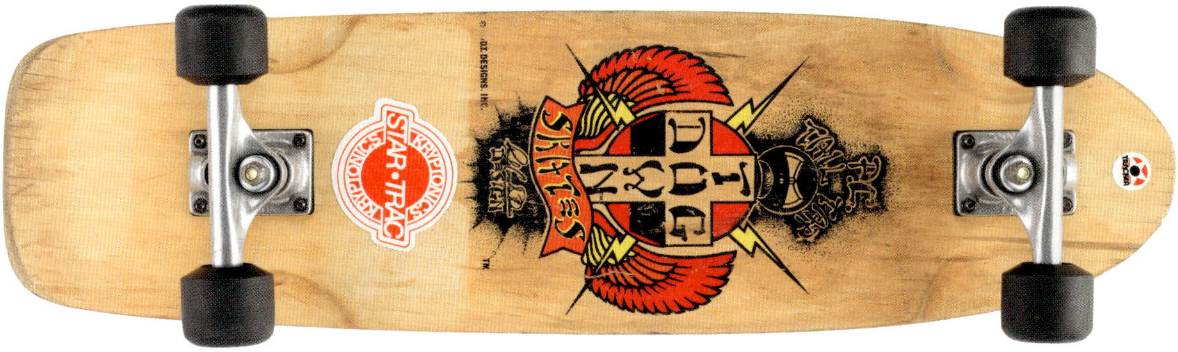

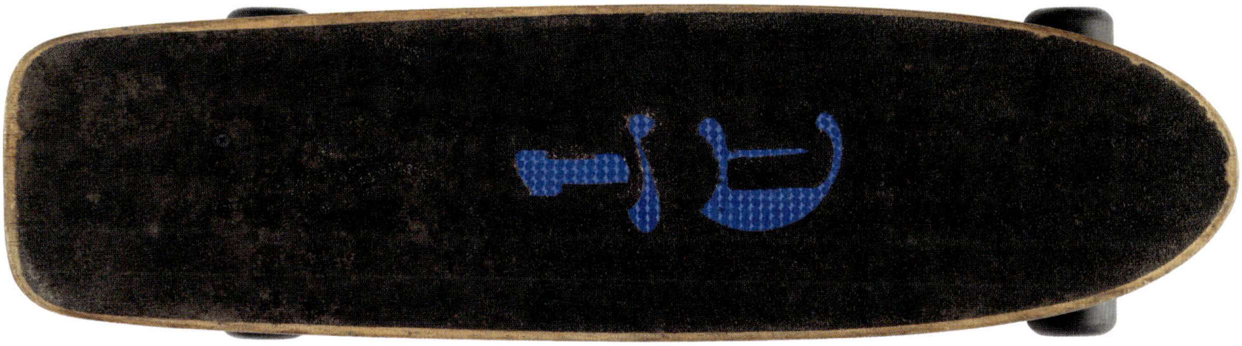

Another iconic brand to emerge from Zephyr's ashes in 1976 was Dogtown Skateboards. Owned by Jim Muir and Wes Humpston, its boards, rugged and built to survive the unforgiving world of pool skating, were best known for their distinctive visual identity. The product of Humpston's artistic gifts, his bold, gothic, and emblematic images, often resembling tattoo designs, were among the first fully developed skateboard graphics. In turn, this sparked a trend for lavishly decorated decks that remains popular today. Much like Z-Flex, Dogtown Skateboards continued to support the style of wild and technically proficient skating that the Z-Boys had championed. Its decks were less like sports equipment and more like battle tools designed for aerial "combat" in pools.

Kryptonics (Foam-Core Decks)

An OG 1978 Kryptonics foam deck with OG Mid Tracks and NOS 2nd-gen 60mm Kryptonics

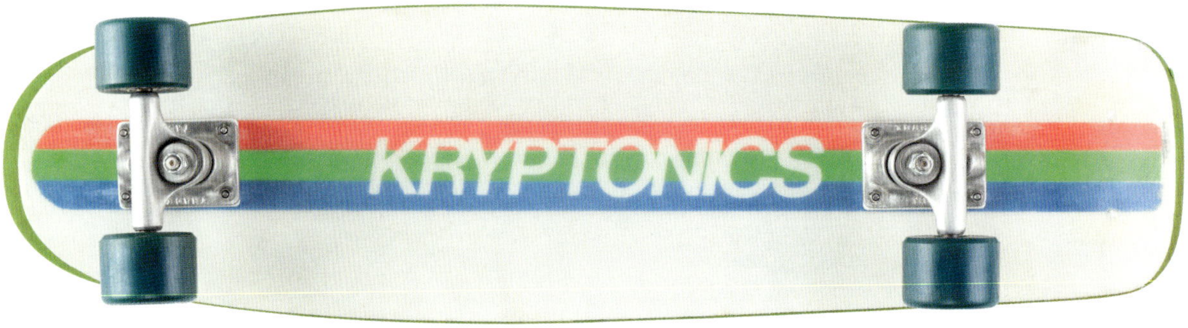

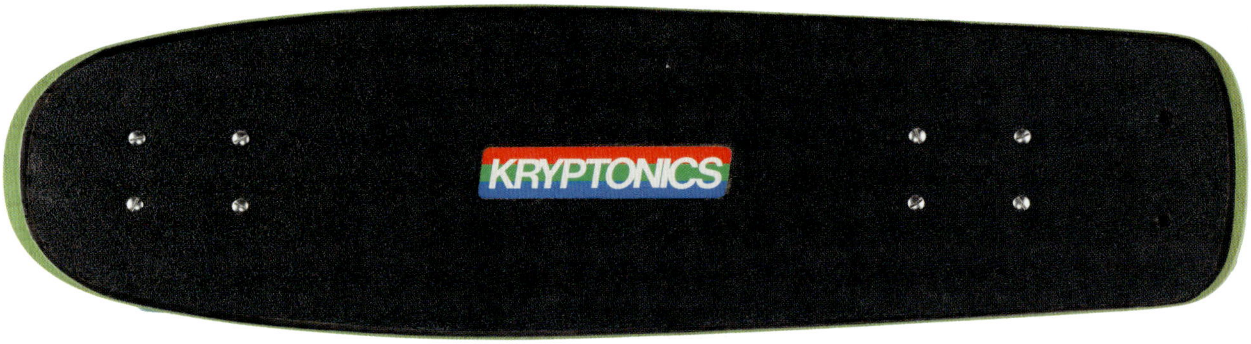

Founded in 1965, Kryptonics is known primarily for its game-changing wheels, but it was also famed for its boards. At the time, Space Age design was experiencing a revival, with sleek angles and novel materials – something Kryptonics embraced in its skateboards. Constructed from lightweight composite foam cores sandwiched between layers of fiberglass and surrounded by protective urethane rails, the decks in Kryptonics' range offered a ride that was cushioned yet responsive, marrying elements of skiing and skateboarding. Based in Boulder, Colorado, the firm brought engineering principles from winter sports into skate deck construction. Bold, experimental, and indicative of a time when skate companies still questioned how skateboards should be made, Kryptonics' decks still seem revolutionary.

Alva

An Alva reissue of the 1979 model with reissue Independent trucks and reissue Gyros

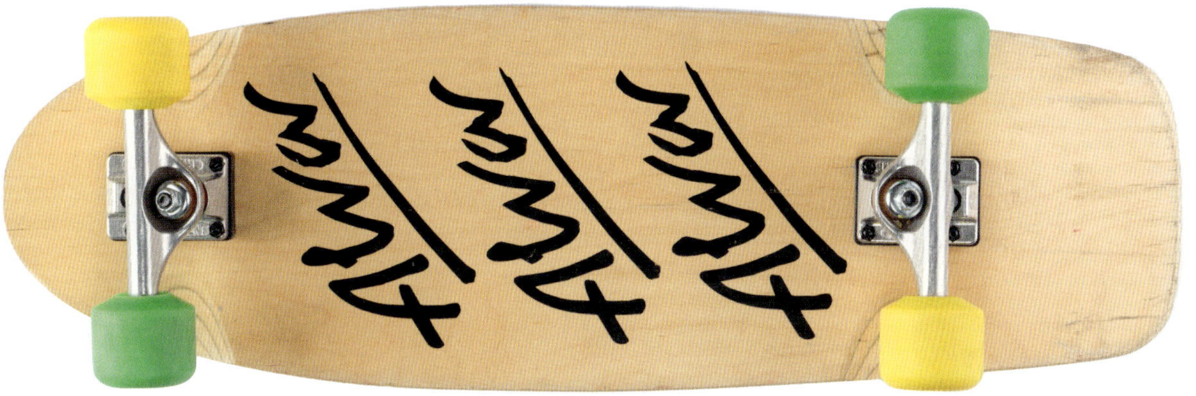

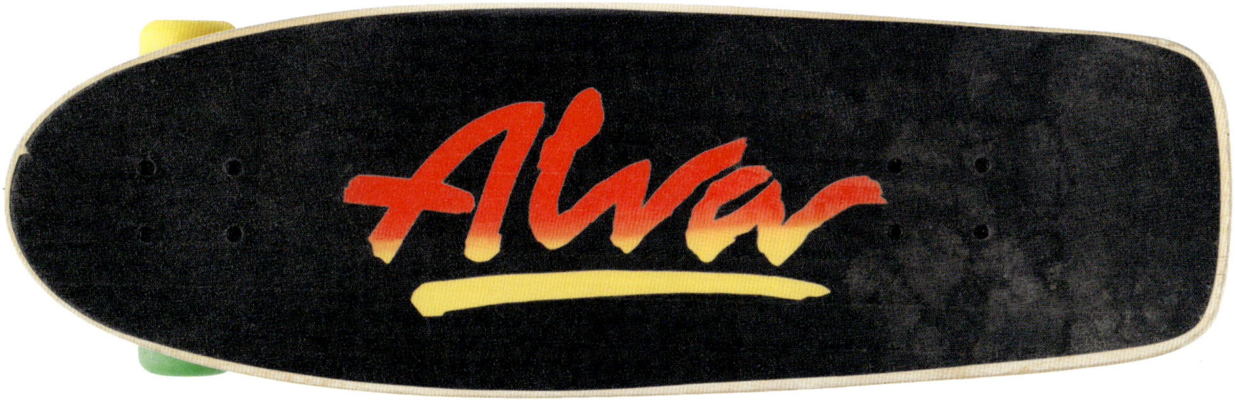

Born in 1957 in Santa Monica, Tony Alva transformed the sport. A founding member of the Z-Boys, he became known for skating vert ramps and is credited as being the first skater to land a frontside air, holding the board while launching above the lip of a pool or ramp. To put it succinctly, his audacious, rapid style changed skateboarding for good. In 1977, he launched his own line of skateboards, Alva Skates. As one of the first rider-owned brands, it signaled where skateboarding was heading: no longer a preppy sporting pursuit, but something independent, rebellious, and increasingly aligned with the punk ethos that would shape the sport into the 1980s. Early Alva boards were wide, strong, and graphically distinctive. With gradient fades and die-cut grip patterns, the Flame logo deck was among the most popular boards of the era. Physical embodiments of his aggressive style, Alva's decks were homages to the pools and ramps where he'd cut his teeth.

Sims

A 1978 NOS Sims Lonnie Toft with reissue Full Tracks and reissue Sims Pure Juice wheels

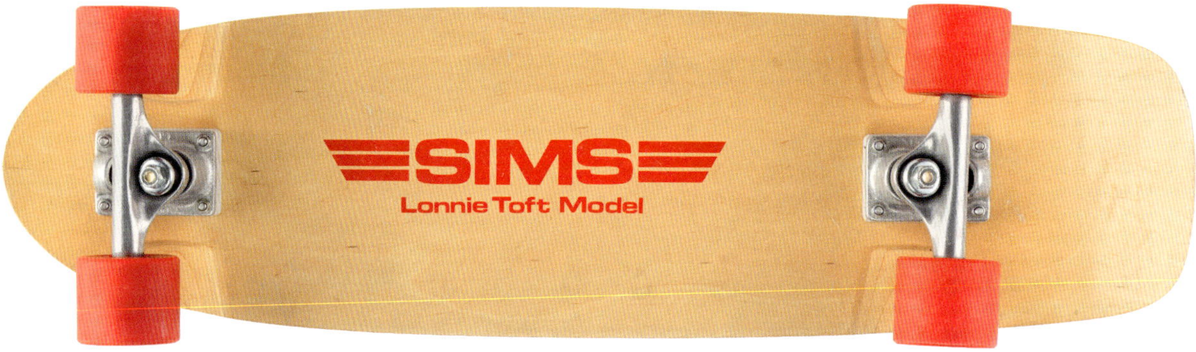

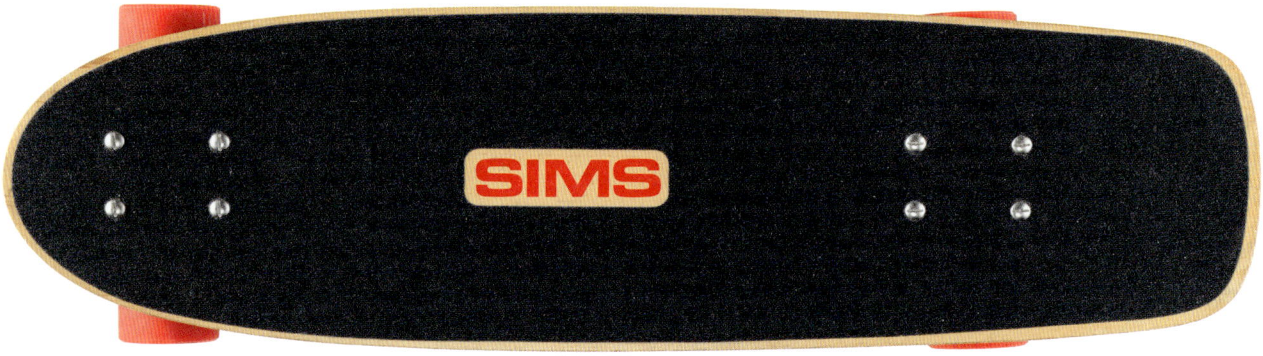

More than any other brand, Sims was responsible for catapulting skateboarding into the next phase of its evolution. Founded in California in the '60s, its early decks catered to slalom and freestyle. But by 1976–77, it began serving the growing number of vert ramp riders as well. Sims had been around since the 1960s, but what set the company apart was its ability to read where skating was heading and respond with a complete offering. More than any other brand, Sims was the first to conceptualize the vert era as a unified product vision. Its 9- and 10-inch signature decks, including the Lonnie Toft, Brad Bowman, and Taperkick models, were purpose-built for the new demands of pool and ramp riding: wider platforms, greater leverage, and greater stability. Paired with its conical Comp and Snake wheels, designed specifically for the speed and not getting stuck on the coping, required for vert skating, the lineup made an immediate impact. Within months, the rest of the industry had pivoted toward wider decks and conical wheels. Where Sims led, others followed. To call his products mere "skateboards" would be a disservice to Sims. These were purpose-built vertical machines.

Gordon & Smith

A 1978 NOS KT-30 with NOS ACS 651s and original YoYos

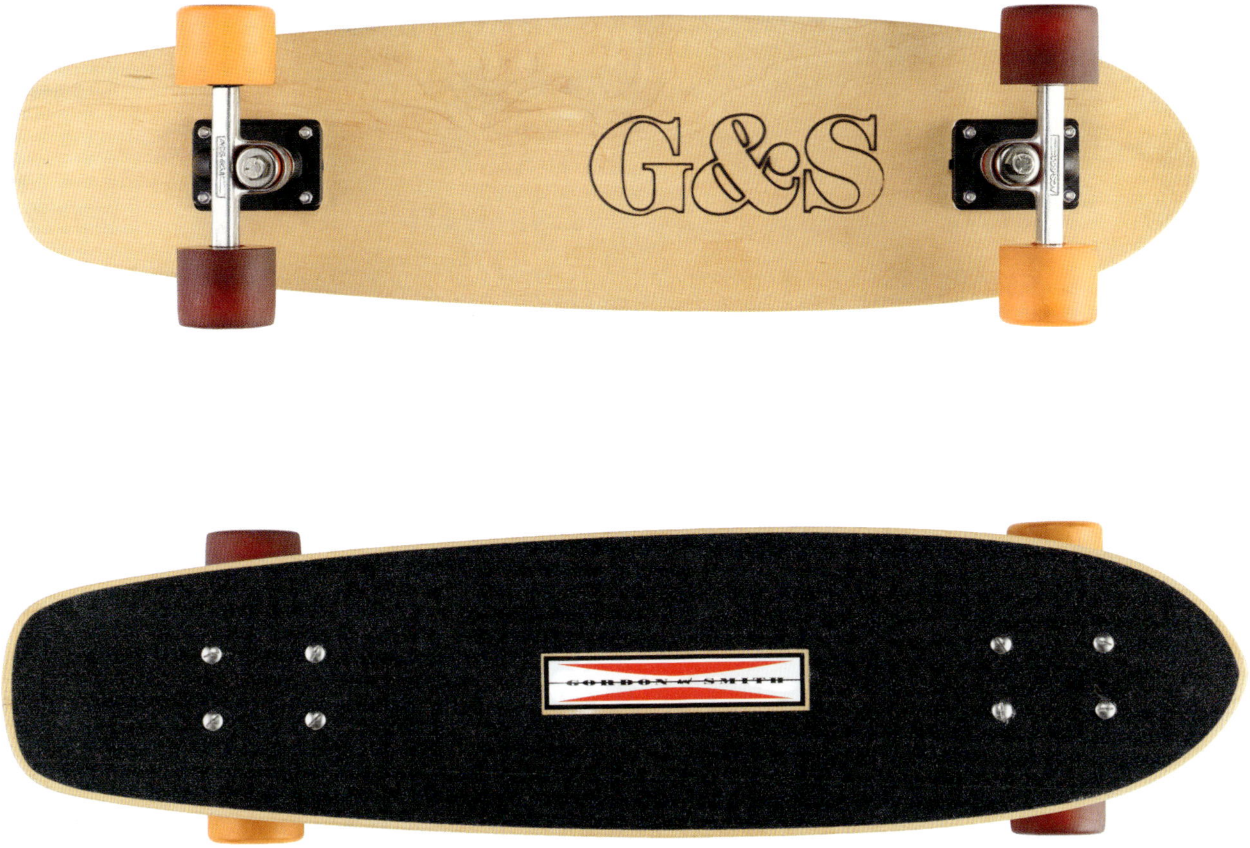

Although FibreFlex was owned by Gordon & Smith (G&S), its parent company deserves an evident place in skateboarding's hall of fame, too. Conscious of its history as a surf brand, G&S's decks, like the Warptail, a Stacy Peralta pro model, and its KT series, were beautifully shaped, extremely successful, meticulously crafted, and trusted by riders across multiple disciplines. Where FibreFlex faded, G&S kept moving forward. Committed to its wood legacy and its YoYo wheels, the company continued to develop and refine its range well into the 1980s and beyond. Decks like the Doug Saladino Pine Design, the Pro Line range, and later developments associated with Bill Ruff helped carry G&S into the future, and many of these models are still sought after by collectors or available today as reissues. In that sense, G&S proved that innovation did not have to depend on new materials. It could also come from a relentless commitment to refining the wooden skateboard.

Together, these competitor boards—Bahne, Hobie, Powell, Logan, Z-Flex, Dogtown, Santa Cruz, Turner, Kryptonics, Alva, Sims, and G&S, among others—comprised the world in which FibreFlex existed. Each represents a different facet of the creativity, ambition, and restless experimentation that defined skateboarding between 1975 and 1979. Collecting them has shown me not only how dynamic the era was, but how interconnected the innovations were. Consciously or unconsciously, each of these brands pushed the others toward greater performance, stronger identities, and more daring ideas.

As such, they weren't mere competitors. Alongside FibreFlex, they made skateboarding's golden era what it was: a time when skaters and brands pushed the sport in new directions that no one had ever thought possible. Without them, FibreFlex's story itself would be untellable.

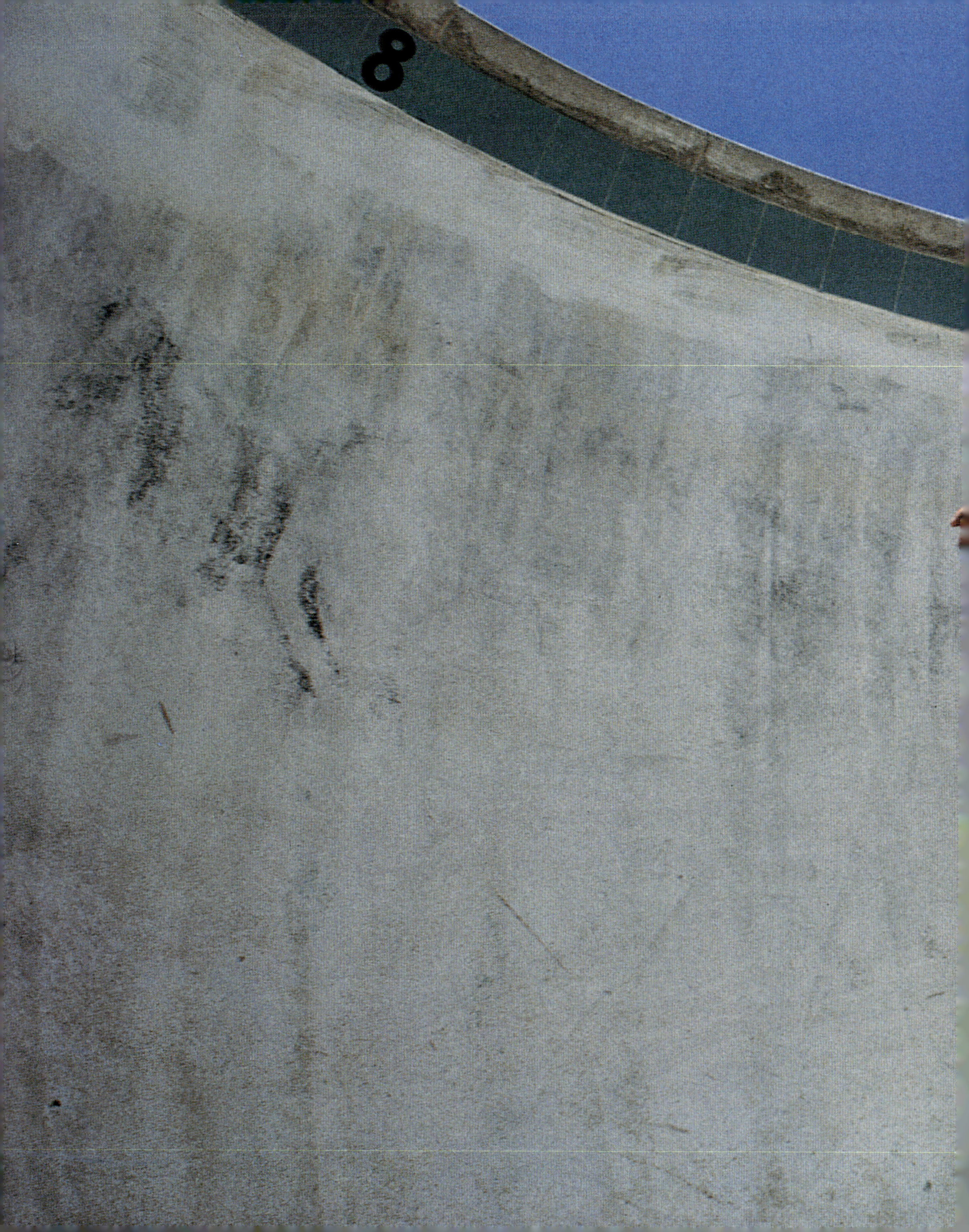
8

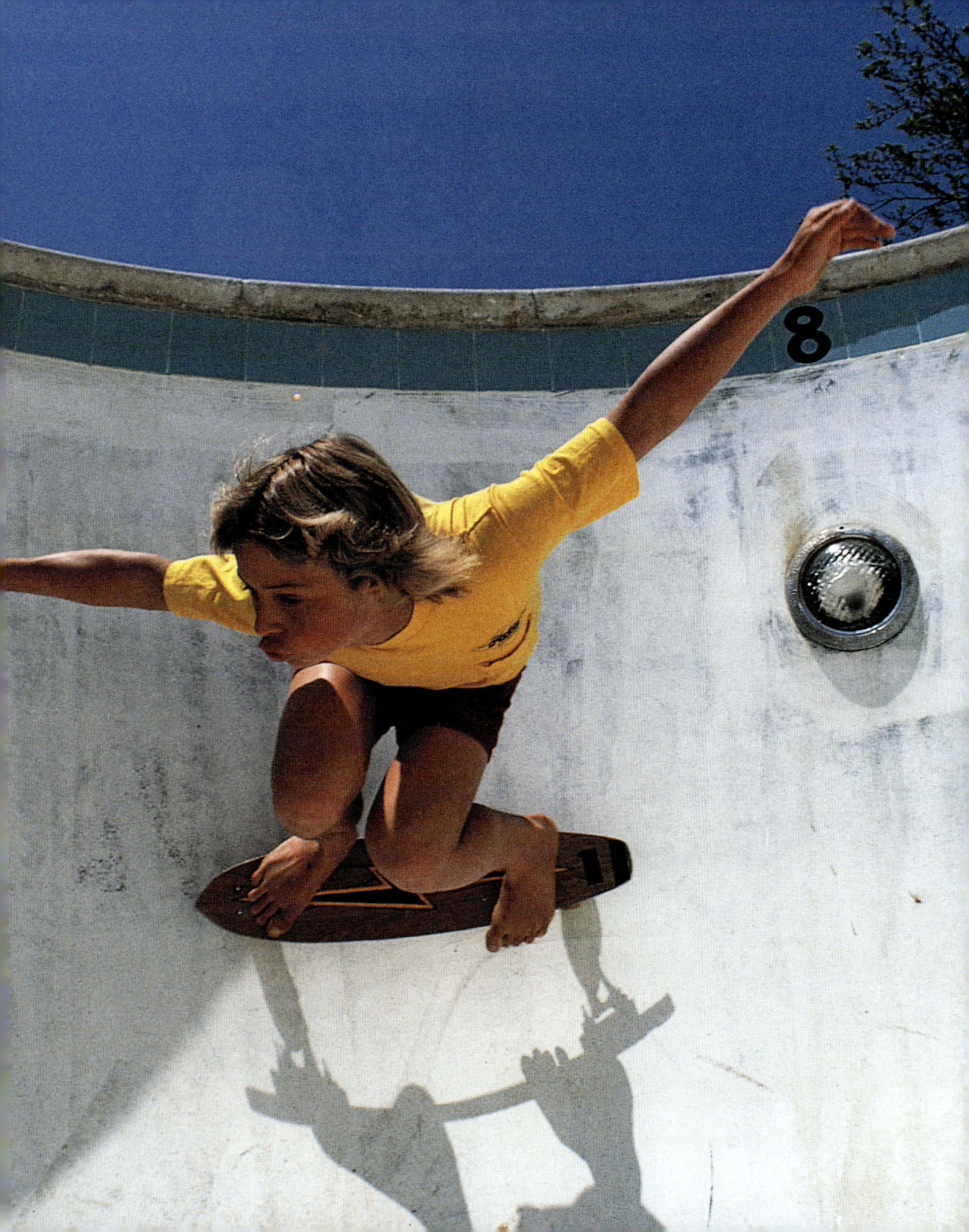
8

Wheels

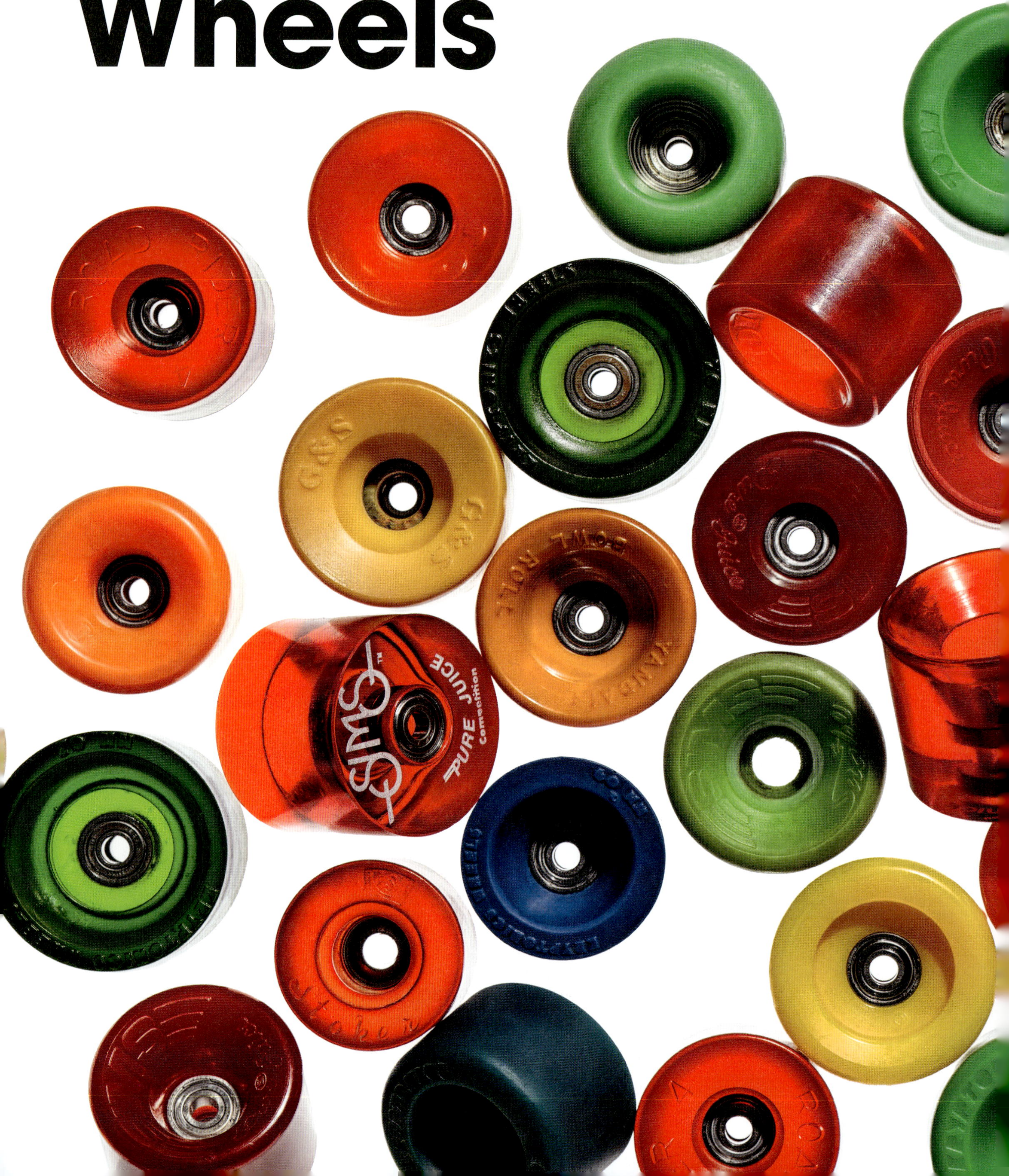

Few things have shaped skateboarding as profoundly as the changes in the materials used to make wheels. In the 1960s, for instance, the sport's boom was cut short by the comically inadequate clay wheels that were commonly available. They rattled, slipped, shattered, and registered even the smallest pebble. As a result, they held skateboarding back, too.

Of course, things did not end there, as skateboarding is, in essence, a discipline dedicated to overcoming obstacles. When urethane wheels emerged in the early 1970s, they solved the sport's wheel problem and ushered in new ways of skating. Legend has it that it all began when the founders of Cadillac Wheels, no relation to the carmaker, stumbled upon a forgotten inventory of urethane roller skate wheels. By repurposing these discarded items, they changed the physics and future of skateboarding.

After this turn, the sport became quieter, faster, and grippier. Skaters could suddenly roll across rough concrete, drop into reservoirs, or carve in drained pools without the constant fear of wheel bite. Urethane did not just make skating better; it changed the way we skate. It made progression possible.

Wheel innovation subsequently exploded. Brands appeared across California and beyond, each with its own formulas, shapes, colors, sizes, and ambitions. Some of those wheels sit in my collection today, each one a testament to the urethane revolution. What follows is my own perspective on these wheels, their stories, personalities, and the roles they played in shaping the sport in the 1970s.

Cadillac

Cadillac Wheels emerged as the leading brand almost by chance. In the early 1970s, skaters experimenting with urethane roller skate wheels discovered that, mounted on a board, urethane wheels rolled faster, gripped harder, absorbed vibration, and made speed feel controllable in a way that old-style clay wheels could not.

Recognizing the implications, Cadillac Wheels adapted urethane for skateboarding. The result was the most important technical leap in the history of the sport. Downhill racing, slalom, pool skating, and vertical ramp riding all became possible because wheels could finally be trusted.

The name "Cadillac," referencing the golden age of comfortable, powerful automobiles, captured the feeling perfectly. Like the cars, the ride these wheels gave was smooth and effortless. You did not need to understand the science behind this new material to appreciate its advantages over brittle old clay. One push was enough.

Stoker by Roller Sports

Stoker wheels are fascinating because they represent both the beginning and the rebirth of urethane. Most skaters know the Cadillac story, but few also know that Roller Sports had, in fact, been making urethane wheels for roller skates during the 1960s. It was these very wheels that the founders of Cadillac Wheels later stumbled upon, realizing they were ideal for skateboarding, and eventually set up their own production. The rest is history. Even today, however, Roller Sports does not receive the recognition it deserves.

Once Cadillac's urethane wheels became popular, Roller Sports followed suit. The brand's Stoker wheels quickly became the choice for downhill and slalom skaters. Stoker wheels had a certain boldness: solid, dependable wheels that were popular in competitions between 1975 and 1976. The company's glory days were short-lived, but transformative nevertheless.

Road Rider

As skateboard brands go, Road Rider was central to skateboarding in the 1970s. With its unique urethane formula and introducing precision-shielded bearings, the company offered skaters unrivaled speed, grip, and control.

The Road Rider 4, a preferred slalom wheel, was followed by the slalom specific Road Rider's Henry Hester signature wheel, introduced in 1976. Their success and popularity meant that even professional skaters sponsored by other companies preferred them. The wheels represented a leap forward in what urethane could do, and their success had a ripple effect across the company's wider ecosystem. Road Rider's sister brand, Park Rider, used the same molds to pour a harder urethane formula, creating a dedicated wheel for bowl riders. More significantly, Road Rider's commercial success helped fuel the rise of its other sister company, Santa Cruz Skateboards, a name that remains synonymous with the sport to this day. In that sense, Road Rider did not just make great wheels. It helped lay the groundwork for one of skateboarding's most enduring empires.

Kryptonics

Founded in Boulder, Colorado, Kryptonics entered the scene in 1976 with clear, color-coded wheels available in multiple sizes and durometers. The company also introduced the first truly systematic approach to wheel choice: a product line built around rider needs rather than marketing intuition.
A year later, its breakthrough came with the second-generation Star Trac line. A family of wheels that became gospel for an entire generation of dedicated users, they came in three varieties: Red, ultrasoft and smooth; Blue, balanced, versatile, the perfect "ride everything" wheel; and Green, fast, grippy, and designed for pools and ramps.

The lore surrounding these wheels is vast. Even at the time, skaters discussed using their first Kryptonics in terms approaching the devotional. The silence, the glide, and the sense of floating above the ground they provided meant that the Star Trac range transformed how skateboarders felt about their sport in toto. Few other wheels of this era conjure such nostalgia.

Yandall by Gordon & Smith

Made by FibreFlex's parent company, Gordon & Smith (G&S), Yandall Bowl Roll wheels occupy a unique place in the history of skateboarding during the 1970s. Born from the influence of racer Chris Yandall, whose fast footwork popularized slalom riding, they helped build, alongside Bo Tuff decks, the brand's reputation as one of the sport's great innovators.

Released in variants designed to be ridden on both slalom courses and vert ramps, the 1977 Yandall Bowl Roll line became a respected choice among serious slalom and vert riders. The Yandalls remained in catalogs until 1979, serving as a consistent, dependable wheel in a rapidly accelerating market. Today, they represent the diversity of G&S's ambitions during a period when companies were flooding the market with multiple models to satisfy proliferating demand.

Sims Wheels

The winner of the 1975 World Skateboarding Championship, held in Los Angeles, Tom Sims, understood what set an exceptional skateboard wheel apart from a good one. Armed with this knowledge, his eponymous company produced a range of models, including the Competition, Bowl Rider, and Pure Juice, for different riding styles. From speed to grip to versatility, Sims catered to every need.

The company's most revolutionary models were the Snakes and their successor, the Snakes

Conical. Released in fall 1978, they hit the shelves when skateboarding was dramatically changing. Boards suddenly went over 10 inches, or 25 cm, wide, and vert ramp skating exploded. Wheels needed to adapt. The Snakes offered riders a wider contact patch, increased grip, and a shape that would easily slide past the coping (edges).

The Snakes marked an evolutionary shift in skateboard wheel technology. Broad, powerful, and built for extreme riding, they were created with an understanding of the sport that only a champion like Tom Sims could marshal.

<u>OJs</u>

Owned by NHS, the same company behind Road Rider, OJ Wheels was uniquely positioned for success when it entered the market in 1976. Its bright orange urethane instantly became part of skateboarding's visual language in the late 1970s, one that continues to influence how modern skateboard wheels look today.

OJ launched with three models: the Slalom, the larger Hot Juice, and the largest Super Juice, which was quickly snapped up by riders in the burgeoning vert ramp scene. What set the company apart from its competition was its knack for capturing youthful energy. Not only were the wheels agile and reliable, but the brand felt fun and performance-driven as well. Today, half a century later, OJ is still making wheels and remains one of the biggest skate brands in the world, a testament to the clarity of these early designs.

<u>Powerflex</u>

Founded in 1975 in Huntington Beach, California, by the well-known surfer and skateboarder Bob Ballou and his brothers, Powerflex's skate team in the 1970s rivaled that of the revered Z-Boys of Venice and Santa Monica, also known as Dogtown and now famously commemorated in film. While Powerflex may not yet have received the celluloid treatment, its legacy lives on in its much-loved wheel design. The rainbow palette of the company's initial wheel range stood out in magazines and shops, making them instantly recognizable.

Then, in the summer of 1977, the brand launched the Powerflex 5, its most revered model. Even used by skaters from rival teams, for example, Shogo Kubo of the Z-Boys, the wheel found success across multiple disciplines as bowl and freestyle riding became more inventive and vert skaters pushed the limits of what then seemed possible. In doing so, Powerflex managed something rare: a wheel that was both innovative and culturally resonant, yet also sustained its popularity in a competitive market.

<u>YoYo Wheels by Gordon & Smith</u>

Few pieces of skateboard equipment in the 1970s were as widely regarded or culturally significant as Gordon & Smith's YoYo wheels. Designed by professional rider Steve Cathey, YoYo wheels introduced a rounded outer edge that increased traction and created a uniquely forgiving ride.

Early Yo-Yo models came in red, yellow, and striking half-red, half-yellow versions, making them a popular all-around choice. G&S's best-loved model, however, was its 1978 white YoYo wheel. Used by freestyle, slalom, pool, and ramp skaters alike, its reputation for smoothness and grip meant it was adopted across almost every discipline. Later that year, the company's orange model began to appear in catalogs and ads, a harder, snappier wheel that added speed without sacrificing the signature bouncy YoYo ride. But for many skaters and collectors, the white YoYos were never bested.

<u>G&S Wonkers Wheels</u>

The G&S Wonkers, sub-manufactured by Kryptonics, were launched in late 1977 or early 1978. Available in two sizes and two durometers, or colorways, a soft pale orange model and a firmer yellow one, they had a somewhat traditional shape at a time when the wheel market was rapidly evolving.

Upon release, the line drew its share of critics, with some suggesting the Wonkers were outdated and stuck in the past. Many of these naysayers were caught up in the fashion for specialized wheels tailored to vert ramps and similar terrain. But performance is not always the whole story. The softer orange Wonkers, for instance, became highly regarded among skaters who simply wanted a cruising wheel: smooth, forgiving, and always a pleasure to ride. In essence, the Wonkers are a reminder that even wheels considered démodé at the time could still play an important role.

Bennett Super Gator Wheels

Released in summer 1978, Bennett's Super Gator wheels epitomize the brand's inventive spirit. Their tapered design offered a clever concept: reduced resistance while riding straight, achieved by narrowing the contact patch, while retaining full grip during turns as the wheel flexed onto its wider profile.

It was bold, different, and unmistakably experimental. While the market in the late 1970s did not fully embrace the concept, the Super Gators stand out today as one of the more imaginative attempts to rethink wheel geometry, proof that innovation often thrives in the margins.

Double Conical Wheels by Gyro

By late 1978, the landscape of skateboarding equipment was shifting almost weekly. Boards and trucks were becoming wider, and the realities of new terrain, including coping, pool lips, and ramps with vertical sections, demanded a new kind of wheel shape.

With its Double Conical model, from 1979, Gyro was one of the first skateboard equipment companies to produce wheels with a conical inner edge that prevented them from catching on coping, a design that helped define modern vert skating. This shape, also eventually adopted by all brands, allowed riders to avoid catching on the edge of a ramp or pool and to ride with more confidence, whether skating bowls or ramps of any shape or size. Then as now, the Double Conical represents a new era for skateboarding, one in which wheel design was no longer an afterthought but a fundamental tool for progression.

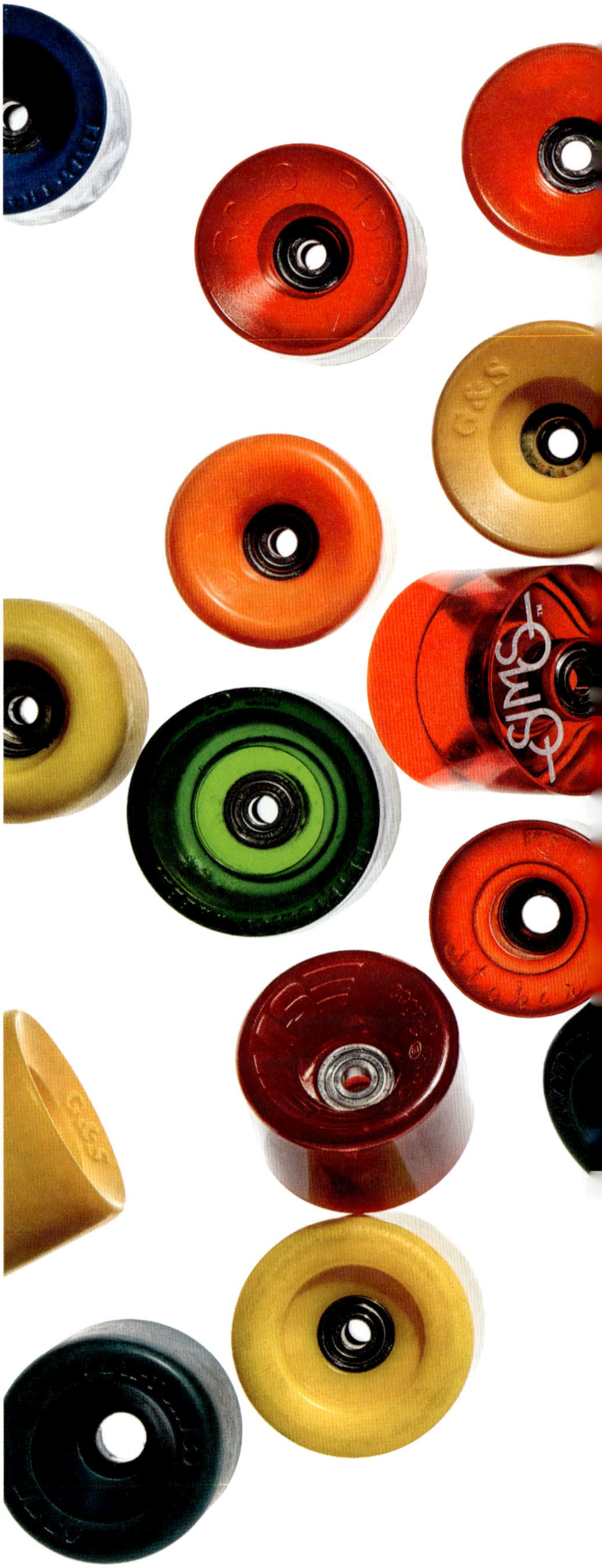

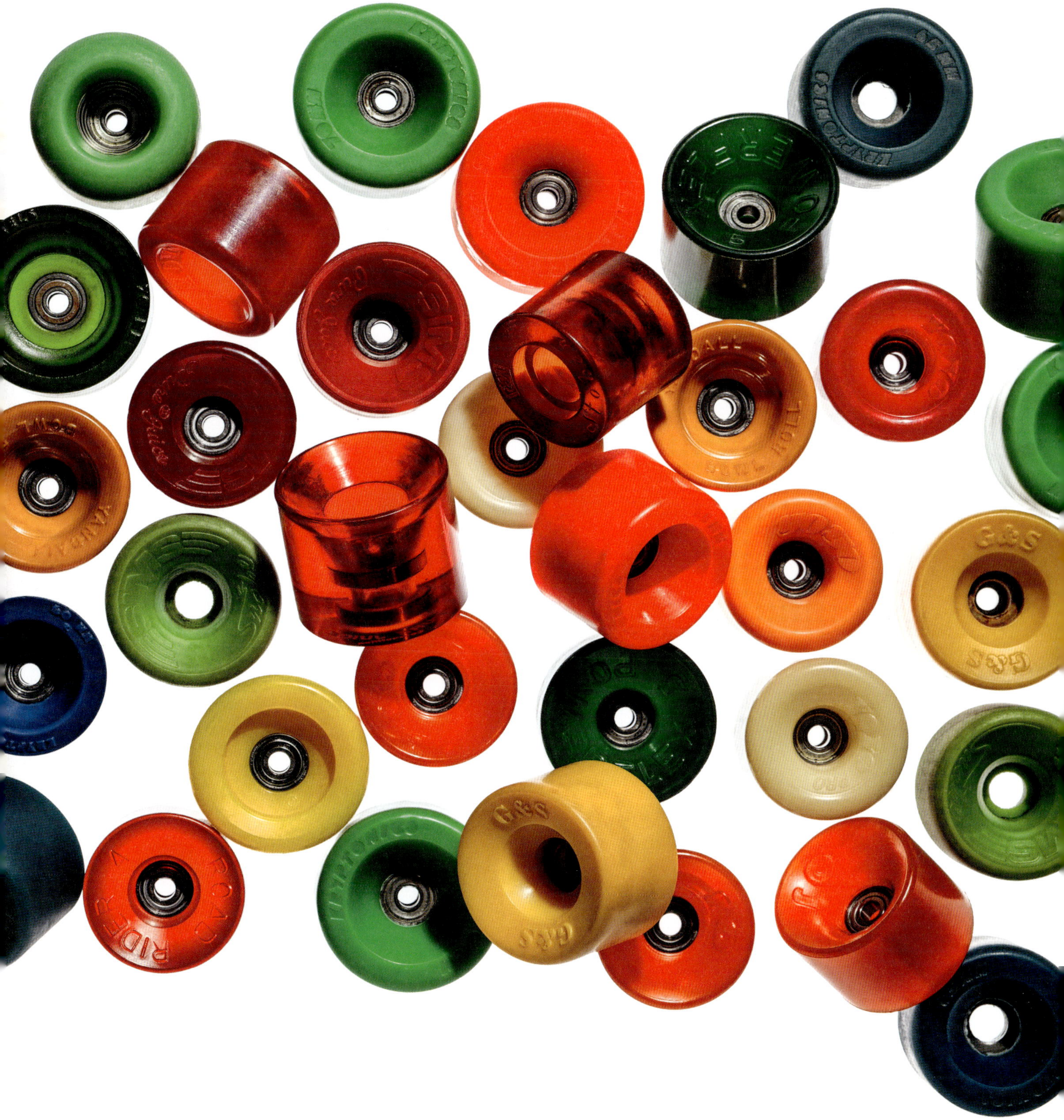
G&S
ROAD RIDER

Trucks

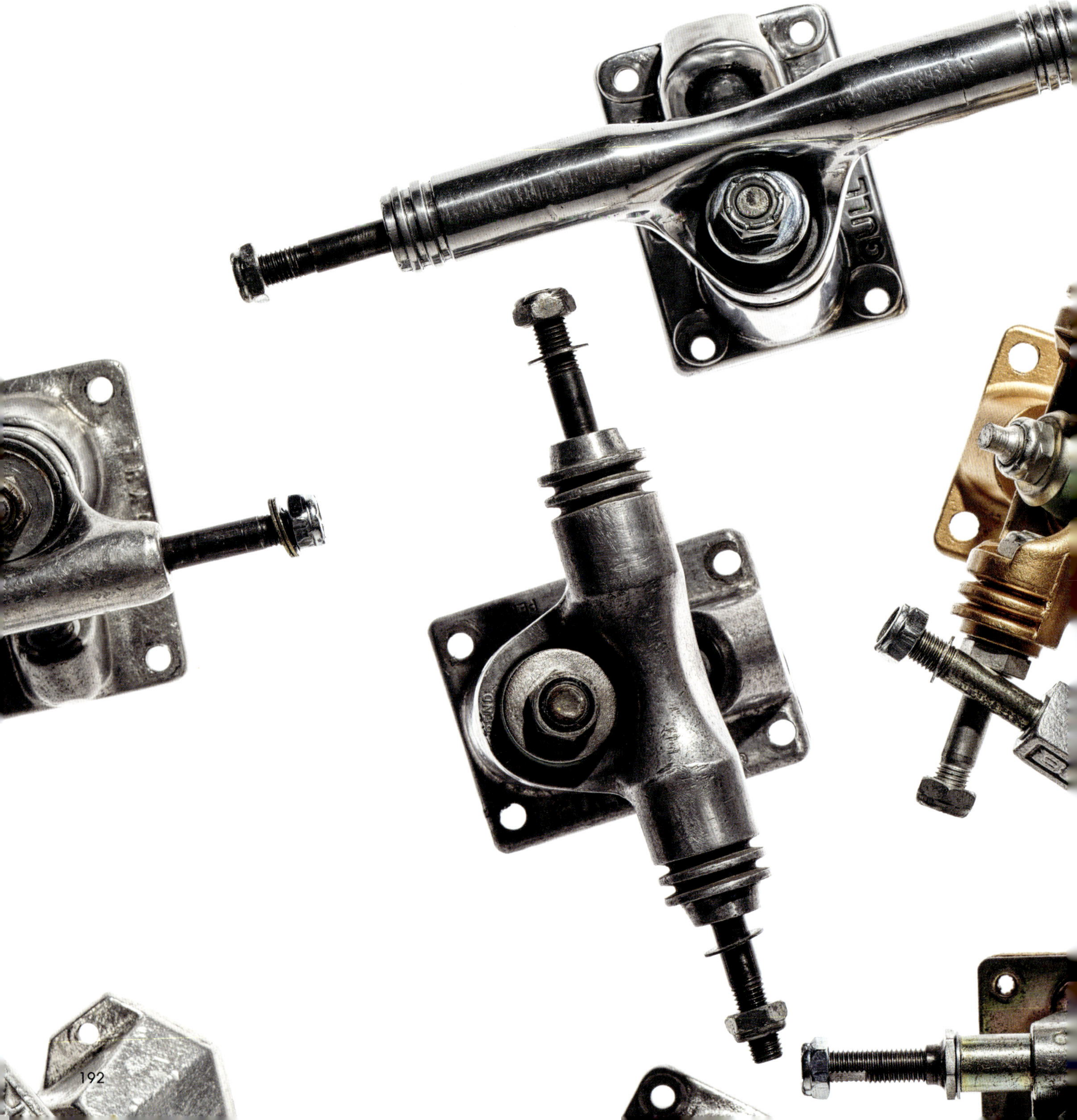

If urethane wheels were the spark that reignited skateboarding in the 1970s, trucks were the fuel that set it ablaze in a cultural and technical revolution. What began as simple roller skate hardware quickly transformed into a new category of mechanical object, evolving as riders pushed their skills and abilities in new environments, including pools, concrete ditches, hills, and skateparks.

While it is hard to imagine now, before the mid-1970s, skateboard trucks were essentially the same as those used on roller skates, albeit mounted on a flat base plate. This meant that boards had to be narrow, and skating styles were limited. But after Bennett introduced the first skateboard-dedicated truck in 1975, everything changed. From there, Tracker set the standard for what a modern skateboard truck could be; ACS introduced precision machining; Gullwing added experimental thinking; and Independent Truck Company brought durability and attitude. Others, including Bahne, Lazer, and Chicago, also played essential roles in the transition from roller skate technology to purpose-built skateboard hardware.

The trucks in my collection, which date from 1975 to 1979, therefore tell this story. Together, they form a mechanical history of skateboarding's most transformative years, a period when engineering met imagination, and when every improvement in design expanded not only the sport's performance but its very identity.

Chicago: The Last of the Roller Skate Adaptations

Chicago trucks represent the closing chapter of skateboarding's improvised beginnings. Produced by the Chicago Roller Skate Company throughout the 1960s, they were essentially roller skate trucks mounted onto metal plates and paired with clay wheels. But for the relatively modest needs and ambitions of skaters at the time, they provided endless satisfaction. Once urethane wheels arrived in the 1970s, however, and skaters began discovering banks, downhill runs, and concrete ditches, the limitations of Chicago trucks became conspicuous. Originally designed for a different sport, their narrow, lean geometry could not offer the stability riders required. Nevertheless, although they had been eclipsed by skateboard-specific designs by the mid-1970s, the brand's legacy as one of the first truck companies remains unquestionable.

Bennett: The First True Skateboard Truck

Ronald Bennett's Hijacker trucks from 1975 marked a major step toward trucks designed exclusively for skateboarding. An engineer from Orange County, California, Bennett examined the physics of turning on a skateboard and created a truck that felt alive beneath the rider's feet. His brand's Big Red Rubber bushings, the rubber components sandwiched between the axle and baseplate, subsequently became iconic, offering smooth, progressive turning, while his lowered kingpin, the central rod that holds the truck together, improved clearance and reduced drag.

Bennett trucks were light and responsive, ideal for slalom, carving, freestyle, and early iterations of skatepark terrain. Although the baseplates could crack under stress, riders accepted the trade-off because the feeling was unmatched. Bennett proved that trucks could be high-performance elements of skateboard technology, engineered with purpose.

Bahne: Custom-Made Steel for a Developing Sport

Bahne, already deeply embedded in skateboard manufacturing through its fiberglass decks, was among the first companies to recognize that roller skate trucks were no longer suited to the sport's demands. This led the company to commission custom-made steel trucks from a foundry in Los Angeles, creating stronger, more consistent hardware capable of supporting both its mass-produced fiberglass boards and the evolving abilities of riders.

Though not as refined as later innovations, Bahne trucks represented a crucial transitional moment, a bridge connecting the era of makeshift solutions with the emerging generation of engineered skateboard trucks.

Tracker Trucks: A Next Step

The arrival of Tracker Trucks in 1975 was a defining shift in the landscape of skateboard equipment. Designed by Larry Balma and Dave Dominy with mold maker Gary Dodds, the Tracker Fultrack broke decisively from the lineage of roller skate trucks. Its geometry, proportions, and reinforced construction reflected what riders needed at that moment: stability, consistency, and strength across slalom, freestyle, downhill, and the newly unfolding world of vertical terrain.

The Fultrack was followed by the Tracker Haftrack and eventually the Midtrack, both tailored for narrower boards and quickly adopted as industry standards. In 1979, the wider Extrack and Sixtrack models were also launched.

Tracker gave skaters trucks that could keep up with the sport's explosive progression, becoming the benchmark for what a modern skateboard truck should look and feel like. In turn, Tracker's innovations helped make possible everything that came next: pools, vert ramps, and the aerial skating that would define the next decade.

ACS: Precision Machining and Industrial Strength

American Cycle Systems, commonly known as ACS, entered skateboarding with unrivaled experience in mechanical design and engineering. Renowned for producing high-quality bicycle components, the company began making skateboard trucks in the mid-1970s using an ultra-durable aluminum-magnesium alloy, finished with industrial precision that became a core part of the brand's identity.

ACS trucks were strong, stylish, and dependable. They especially appealed to downhill racers, slalom riders, and skaters experimenting with fast, aggressive, unpredictable riding styles. While many other skate brands were only beginning to transition from small craft-based businesses to the technical standards of industrial production, ACS was ahead of the curve.

Gullwing: Experimental Vision and Split Axle Ingenuity

Founded in 1976, Gullwing quickly became known for creating inimitable skateboard equipment. Its original split-axle truck allowed the axle ends to flex independently, creating an unusually quick, fluid turning response while maintaining control. Slalom riders unsurprisingly embraced this technology immediately, but it was a hit with skaters across nearly every other discipline as well.

Gullwing trucks also had a visual presence that set them apart from the competition. Organic, futuristic, and almost science fiction in appearance, they looked and rode unlike anything else on the market. The company's willingness to experiment inspired others to follow suit, helping open up the possibilities of truck design beyond what had previously been imagined. In this spirit, Gullwing was also quick to adapt to new demands, releasing models suited to pools and parks while maintaining an inventive spirit.

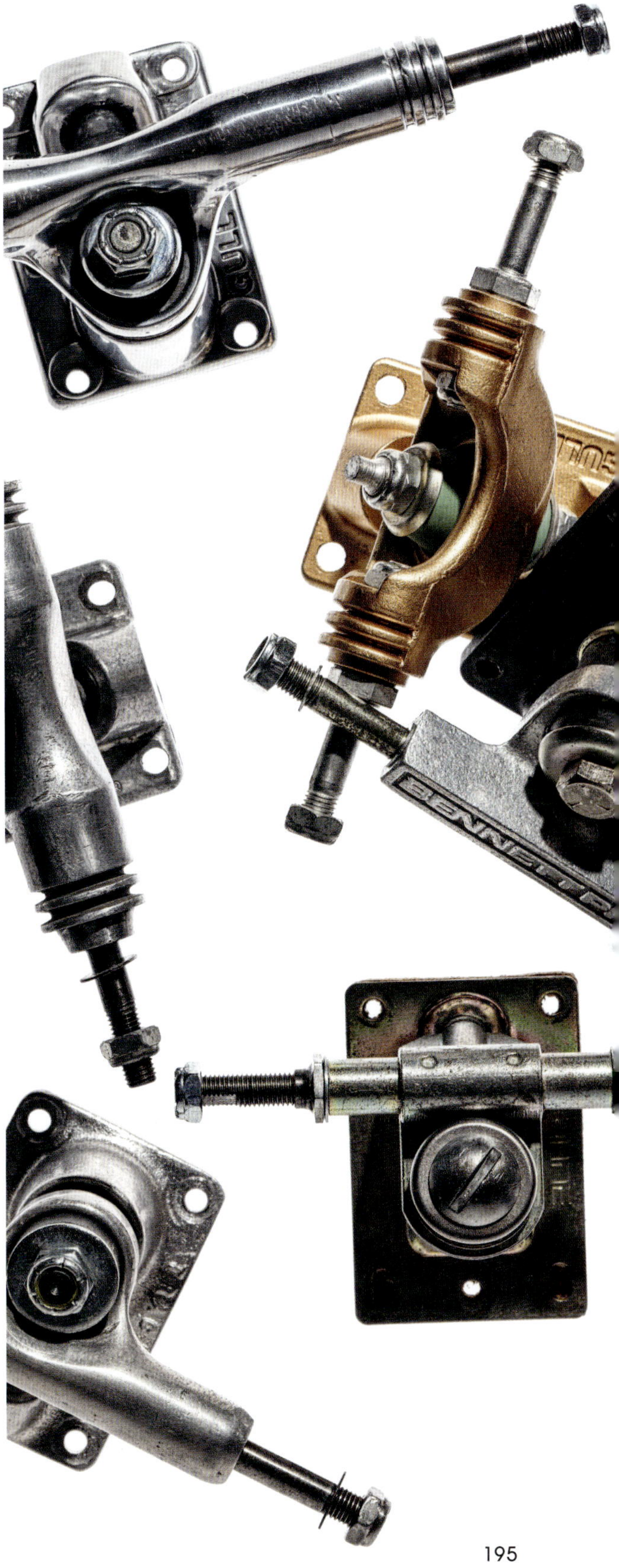

Lazer: Reliable, Egalitarian Sand Cast Character

Lazer Skateboard Trucks filled a unique niche in the late 1970s. Cast in Newport Beach, California, using sand molds, its trucks were more affordable than many competing models, had a distinctive style, and were popular among riders of all stripes, particularly novice skaters looking for a reliable introduction to the sport.

While not the most technically advanced trucks of the decade, they were significant for their angular design and for opening up skateboarding to riders from different backgrounds. Production ended around 1980, but a small revival followed in the 1990s, a testament to the enduring appeal of Lazer's egalitarian vision.

Independent Truck Company: Strength, Precision, and the Beginning of a Dynasty

When Independent Truck Company launched in 1978, its Stage I model immediately stood out. Designed by Richard Novak, Jay Shuirman, and the Ermico foundry team, the truck was built around the principle of eliminating every weakness riders experienced in existing designs. The Stage I thus felt sturdier, turned with great precision, and could withstand fierce impact with concrete, coping, and curved surfaces.

Alongside its reinforced geometry and overall solidity, the thickness of the Stage I made it an instant favorite among riders of bowls, ramps, and other terrain alike. Independent would go on to release a long line of subsequent models, all based on the company's unchanging commitment to dependable performance, an ethos that has made it one of the longest-running brands in skateboarding.

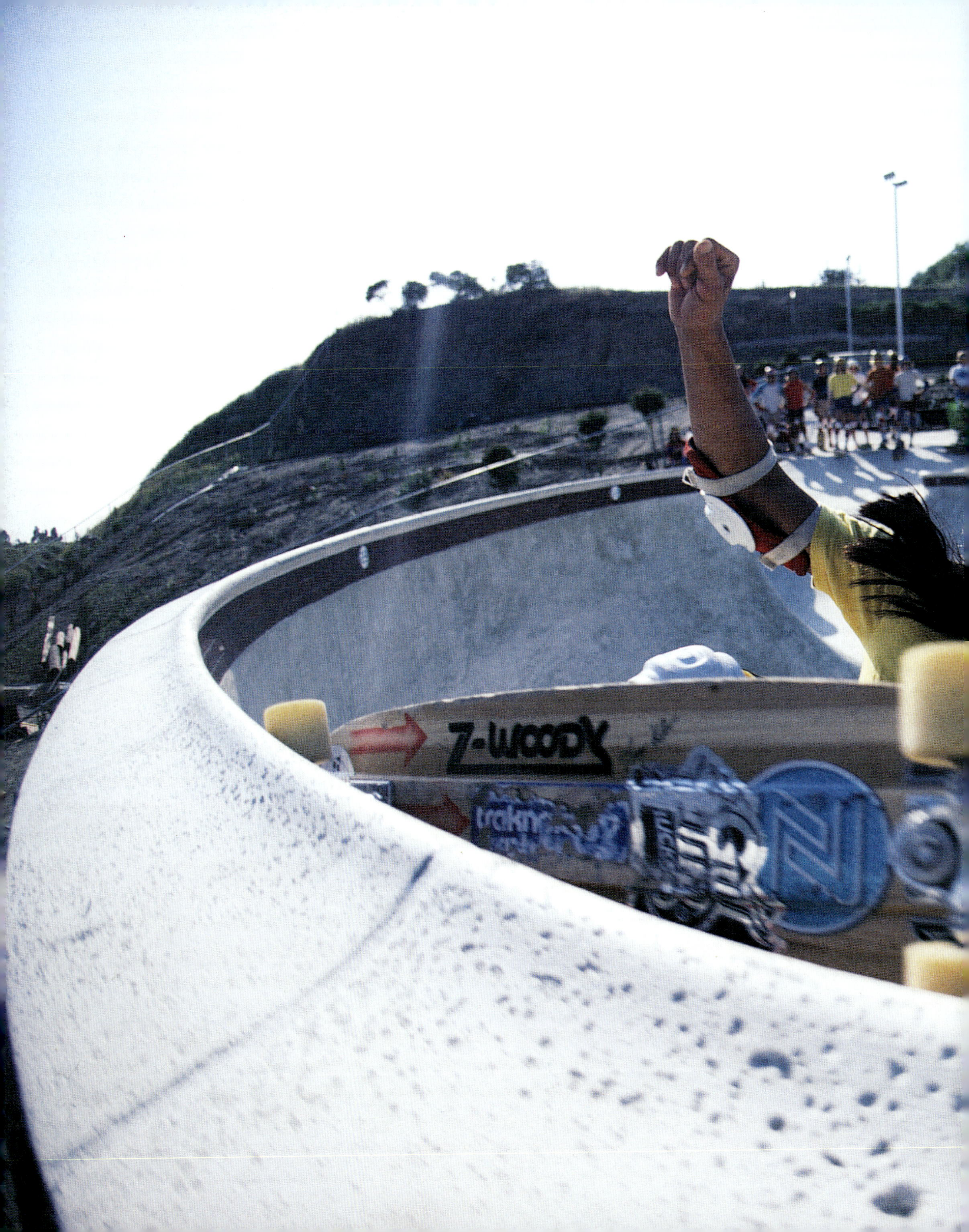
Z-WOODY

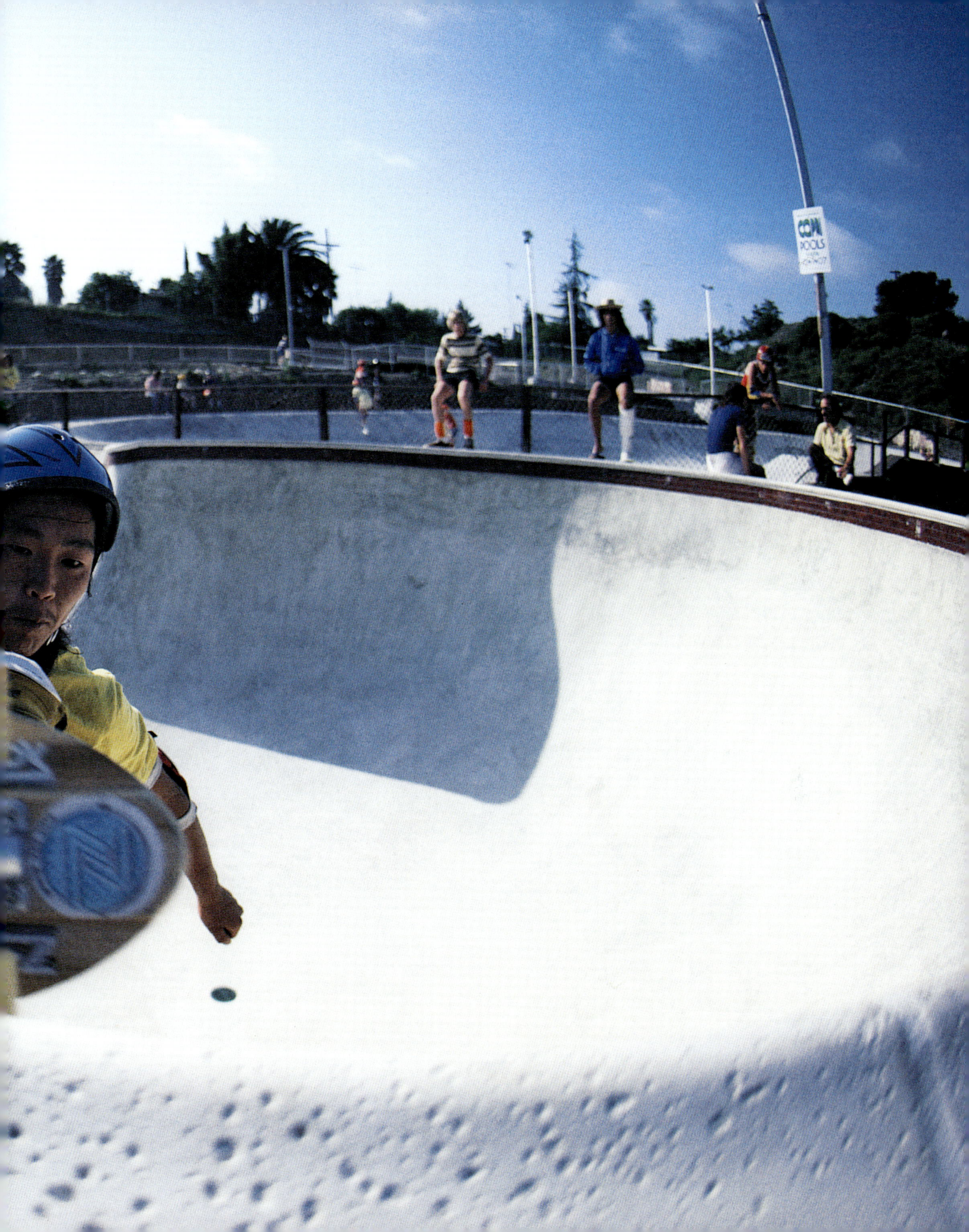
POOLS

Getting There First Came at a Price

As one of the defining brand of skateboarding's golden era, FibreFlex did it all. From producing boards catering to speed-demons riding downhill and slalom to its models designed to please skaters drawn to pools, bowls, ramps, parks, and vertical surfaces, the brand triumphed at everything it put its mind to. Like all good things, it couldn't last. But today, few other skate brands can claim to have influenced the sport as much as FibreFlex.

Today, the FibreFlex boards that exist in collections like mine are portals to the past. Emblems of a brief but electric period in skateboarding's history that encompassed new styles, technological innovation, and evolving identities, these objects are like time capsules – entryways into skateboarding's golden era. Moreover, the reason FibreFlex is such a totem for this period – as I hope this book has demonstrated – is because it was both one of the most successful brands at the time, and one whose dramatic transformations are representative of the equally dramatic changes in the sport in general.

Originally beginning life as a sub-brand of the surf company Gordon & Smith (G&S), FibreFlex carried both its parent company's manufacturing credentials and its surf heritage, which mattered enormously. For those of us who grew up far from Southern California, the surf culture embedded in the G&S and FibreFlex DNA helped us connect the new world of skateboarding with the established world of surfing.

Outside the US, FibreFlex's popularity grew quickly. In Europe, particularly France, Switzerland, the UK, and Scandinavia, the brand had strong traction. It represented both aspiration and authority: a bridge between surf culture and the rapidly modernizing discipline of skateboarding. What wasn't evident at the time, however, was that FibreFlex's heyday would coincide almost exactly with skateboarding's golden era itself: that narrow window of 1975–79 where the company's flexible Bo-Tuff decks – alongside urethane wheels, and the new generation of purpose-built trucks – sparked a revolution in skateboarding.

As a young skater in Sweden in the late '70s, I was barely able to appreciate any of this. Indeed, it was only later, flipping through old ads in *SkateBoarder* magazine, that I realized how deliberately FibreFlex framed itself. The brand was clean-cut, preppy, even. (Occasionally it even branded itself as a "Christ-centered company.") But as skating adopted a more aggressive, punk attitude toward the end of the '70s, this branding potentially worked against it. Like riding styles, the culture was changing too, and by the early 1980s, FibreFlex's image suddenly seemed a little outdated.

That story, however, is beyond the scope of these pages. Indeed, one of the key motivations in assembling my collection has been to examine the precise nature of FibreFlex's transformative contributions to the sport during its glory years – achievemtns that are, frankly, plain for all to see. When FibreFlex relaunched in 1975 with three new models, it reactivated its mid 1960s legacy as one of the first skate companies, and immediately connected with the downhill and slalom boom. Its range of flexy decks, urethane wheels, and tailor-made trucks were perfect for these disciplines, and riders like Henry Hester and Greg Taie dominated races while riding them. Overnight, FibreFlex became synonymous with performance.

Success came fast. With its team's downhill victories piling up, FibreFlex's decks became standard across multiple disciplines. But as riders began exploring new terrain – ditches, pools, ramps – courtesy of the brand's groundbreaking equipment, the sport changed too. Keen to give skaters what they wanted, FibreFlex introduced a new Stifflex range in 1977, designed to meet the needs of these new skaters. Thicker and stiffer, its decks like the Bowlrider and the Steve Cathey Signature board were a step towards riders wanting more power. Production duly soared to 10,000 decks per month.

Things, however, didn't end there. Armed with these stiffer boards, skaters began using them with even greater intensity in pools, bowls, and skateparks. As a result, they not only began demanding even stiffer models but wider decks too. Flexibility was no longer as desirable, so in 1978, FibreFlex released its first rigid boards. Its Teamrider, shaped with input from Doug Saladino and Dennis Martinez, consequently featured five layers of wood ply, and a revised Bowlrider followed the same logic. They were both instant hits, and the brand triumphed once again.

Amid this, vert riding was emerging as a serious, specialized discipline. While FibreFlex's Teamrider and Bowlrider were wide, vert-oriented boards by rivals such as Sims, Alva, Santa Cruz, and even G&S were even wider. FibreFlex responded once more with a new model: the 1979 Dennis Martinez Flying Ace. A huge, pig-shaped board, its bottom layer of Bo-Tuff was at once an homage to the brand's roots and an anxious acknowledgement that the world had moved on.

As detailed elsewhere in this volume, Martinez left FibreFlex shortly after the company released its Flying Aces. Subsequently, even slalom boards began to become rigid too. Skateboarding's golden age was at an end, and with it, FibreFlex's title as one of the sport's leading brand began to pass to other brands, many of which are mentioned in these pages. Few of them, however, could ever claim to have influenced the future of skateboarding to the degree FibreFlex did in the '70s. For a skate-obsessed kid growing up in Sweden, far away from where all of these unbelievable achievements took place, FibreFlex made a major dent – and still does. For the curious and well-versed skateboard enthusiast alike, I hope this book proves why.

Despite my best efforts to be meticulous, I'm sure there is missing or inaccurate information, and some things have been overlooked or not fully understood. For this, I apologise, as I have tried to stick as closely as possible to the historical record.

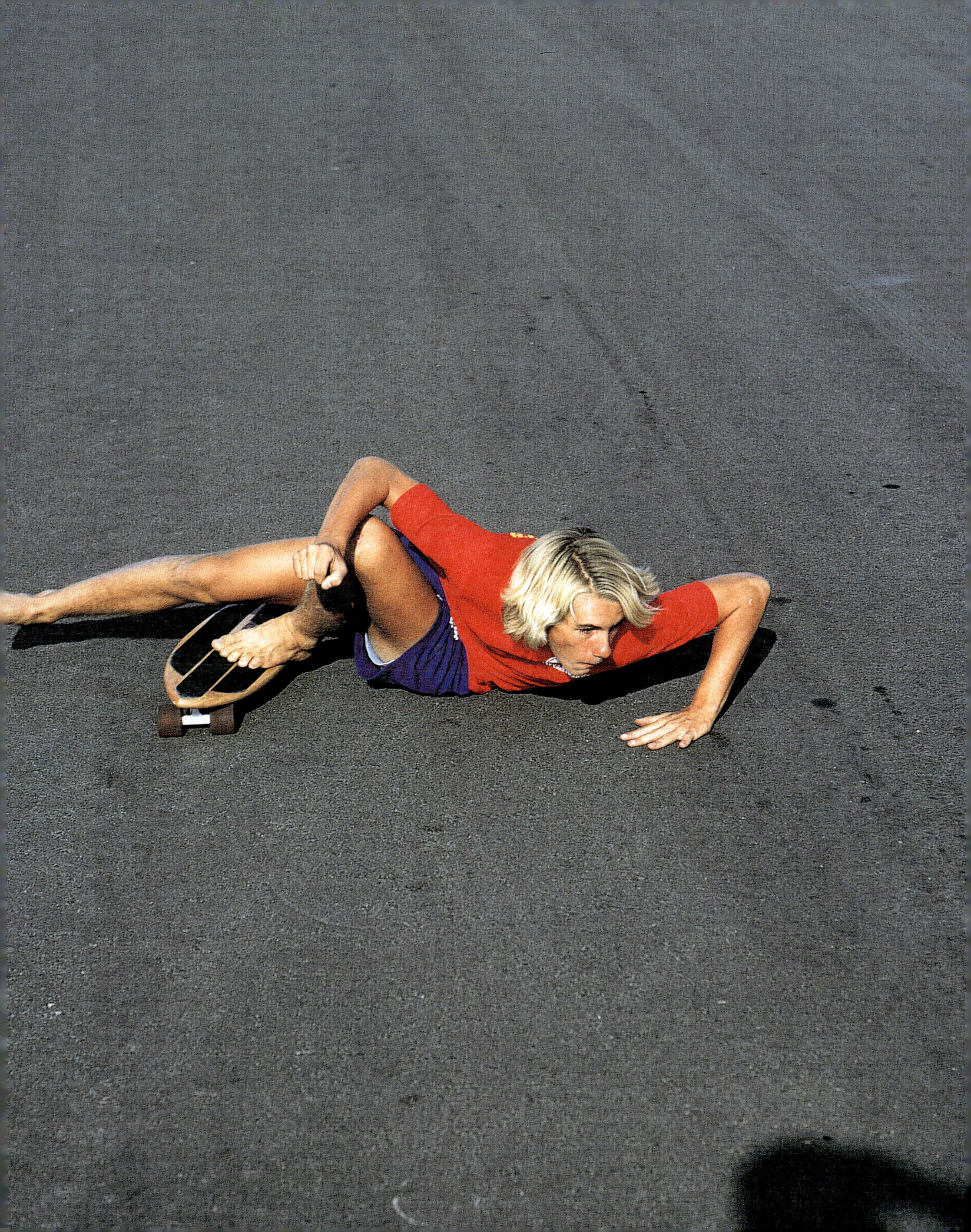

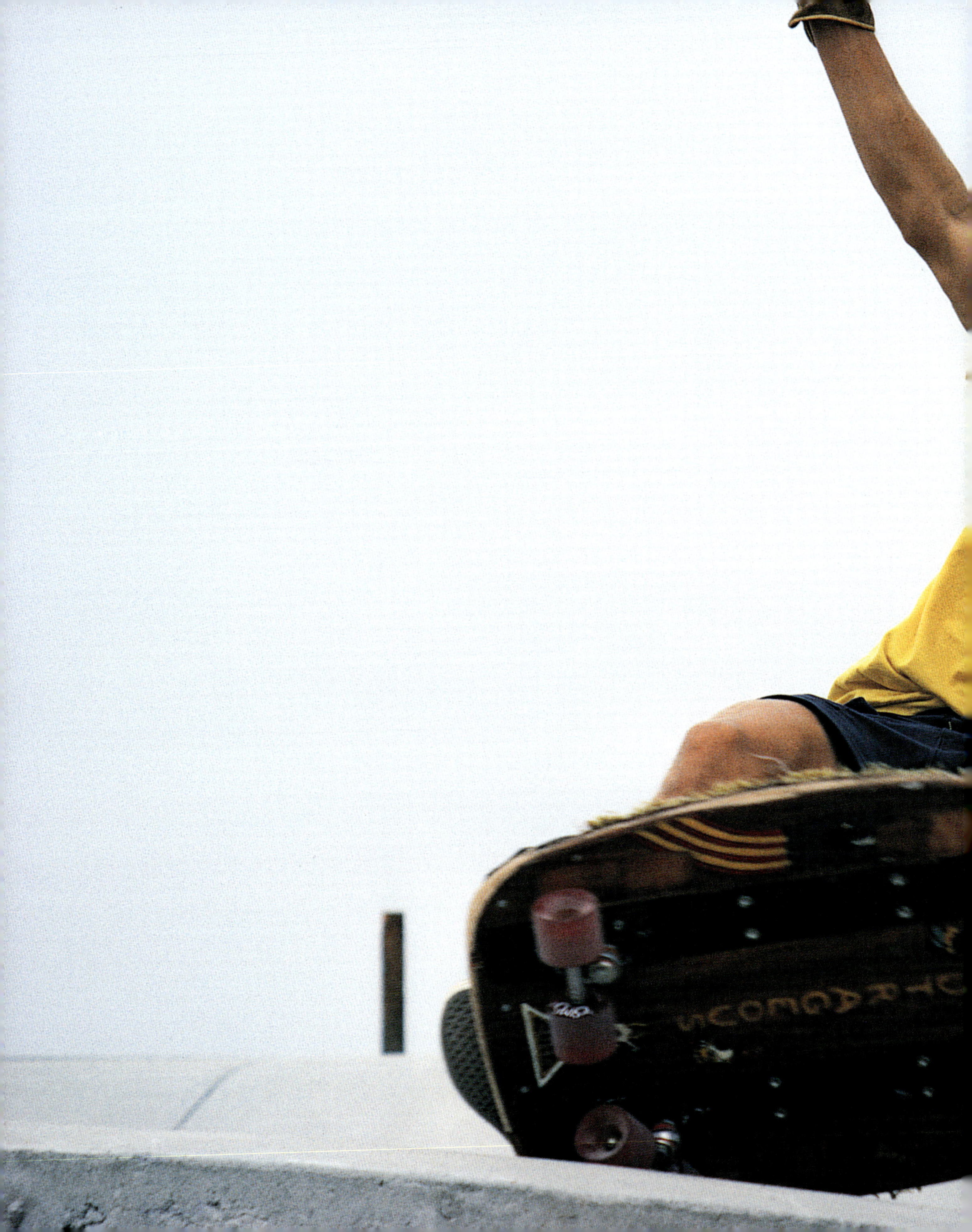

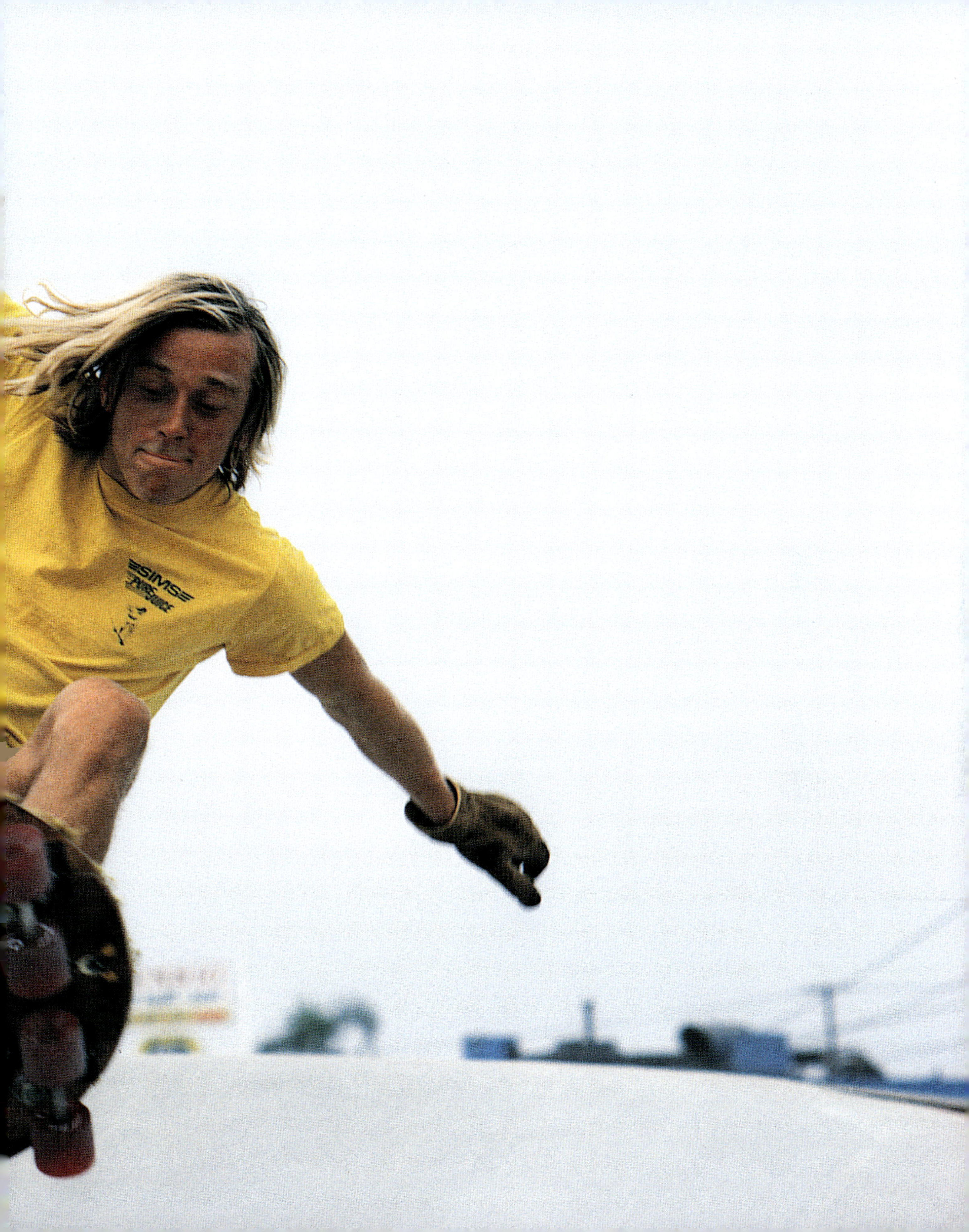
SIMS

Contributors

Stefan Ytterborn
Skateboard Collector and Author

Despite being inspired by the skateboard revolution of the 1970s, particularly its culture, independence, and rapid product evolution, Stefan Ytterborn in fact grew up far away from California, in Stockholm, Sweden.

Although he eagerly took up skateboarding as a teenager, hoping to emulate the heroic exploits of riders captured in photos of *SkateBoarder* magazine, the sport, for him, always represented more than just an athletic activity. Encompassing technological innovation, materials, mechanics, its roots and culture, it conversely provided Ytterborn with an introduction to the idea that how an object appears and functions not only changes the way in which it performs but how people think about it too, a lesson he would carry over into his own career in design.

That early fascination with skateboards, their shapes, constructions, and constant development, became a key component in everything that followed. Over the course of his working life, Ytterborn has founded multiple design- and engineering-driven companies, including POC and CAKE, bringing thousands of products to market across different industries. Behind all of these endeavors, however, is a simple focus on innovation, performance, and purpose, principles he gleaned from the skateboarding brands that drove the sport's golden era in the late '70s.

At heart, this book is an exploration of those ideas, one conducted via his collection of FibreFlex skateboards produced between 1975 and 1979. Through the analysis of each board, as well as the history and context of the brand that made them, *Flex Appeal* becomes Ytterborn's love letter to the era as well as a de facto handbook for deliberate design.

Jörgen Brennicke
Photographer, Co-producer, and Skateboarder

Jörgen Brennicke discovered skateboarding in 1976 at the age of nine, growing up in suburban Stockholm. What began as curiosity quickly became a defining influence, less a sport than a complete world shaped by experimentation, aesthetics, and independence.

His early encounters with skateboarding, from acquiring his first fiberglass board in Berlin to building ramps with friends using intuition rather than instruction, eventually getting his first FibreFlex Freestyle in 1977 – instilled a hands-on mindset rooted in trial, error, and persistence. That same approach would later define his work behind the camera.

Photography emerged as a natural extension of skating, first as a way of documenting friends and sessions, and later evolving into an international career spanning fashion, film, and commercial work. Regardless of context, Brennicke has maintained a consistent perspective: observational, curious, and grounded in making rather than theory.

After decades away from the board, he returned to skateboarding in recent years. Today, he rides pools regularly, closing a circle that continues to inform both his creative work and his way of seeing the world.

David Gonzalez

Designer, Co-producer, and Skateboarder

Born in the 1970s, David Gonzalez came into skateboarding in the early 1980s, at a time when the culture was beginning to spread globally. His first encounters were modest, but the impact came quickly, driven not only by the act of riding, but by the visual and cultural force of the boards themselves.

Graphics, shapes, and the personalities behind them left a lasting impression. Boards were no longer just objects; they carried identity, attitude, and intent. That realization stayed with him.

As his focus shifted toward design, Gonzalez initially worked with Stefan at POC and CAKE and later co-founded a studio, Com Tru, building a career centered on creative direction and product development. While skateboarding receded from everyday life, its influence remained embedded.

Years later, he returned to skating, this time with a different perspective. No longer driven by progression alone, he found renewed meaning in the flow, the environments, and the culture surrounding it. For him, as a dedicated pool rider, skateboarding continues to serve as both a physical practice and a creative reference point.

Michael Brooke

Speaking Partner, Skateboard Historian, Photo Enabler, and Skateboarder

Born in Leeds, England, and raised in Canada, Michael Brooke began skateboarding in 1975 and has remained deeply connected to it ever since. For Brooke, skateboarding has never been a phase, but a constant, one that has informed both his professional path and personal outlook. Over several decades, he has moved across industries, yet consistently returned to documenting and supporting skate culture. He founded *Concrete Wave* magazine and authored the immensely successful book *The Concrete Wave: The History of Skateboarding,* playing a key role in preserving and communicating the sport's legacy to a broader audience.

Beyond publishing, Brooke has also explored skateboarding as a vehicle for social good, most notably through Longboarding for Peace, a grassroots initiative using skateboarding to support community-driven projects around the world.

In more recent years, his work has expanded into questions of reflection, identity, and human behavior. Still, at the core of it all remains skateboarding, both as a lived experience and as a cultural thread running through his life. One of his most valued possessions is an original FibreFlex slalom deck, a tangible link to the era that continues to inspire his work.

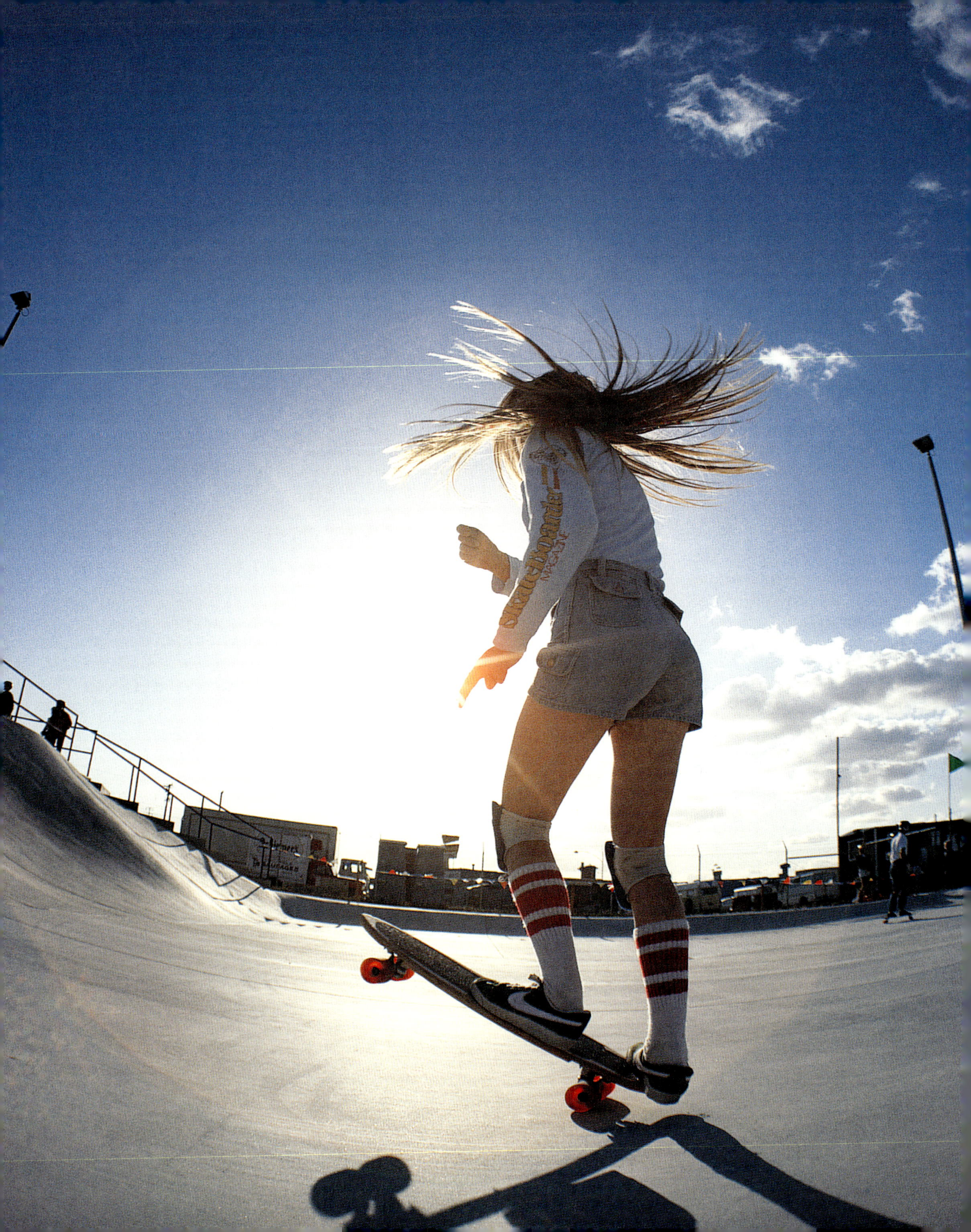

Captions

pp. 4/5: Denis Shufeldt, La Costa 1975
pp. 10/11: Tony Alva, Fruit Bowl 1976
pp. 16/17: The Rampage, Encinitas 1977
pp. 94/95: Murray Estes,
San Marcos Pool 1976
p. 105: Mark Mayers, at his home in
Cornwall, U.K.
p. 109: Steve Cathey
p. 111: Henry Hester
p. 113: Dennis Martinez
p. 114/115: The Arizona Dessert Pipes
p. 119: Carlsbad Skatepark
p. 121: Concrete Wave Skatepark
p. 123: Skatopia Skatepark & Gregg Weaver
p. 125: The Pipeline & Tom Inouye
p. 127: Oasis Skatepark Amazing Egg
p. 129: Skateboard Heaven & Dennis Martinez
p. 131: Marina del Rey Skatepark
p. 133: Surf the Earth & Steve Cathey
p. 135: Del Mar Skate Ranch & Tom Inouye
p. 139: Tony Alva at Wallos, Hawaii, USA
p. 141: The Arizona Desert Pipelines
p. 143: La Costa & Steve Cathey
p. 145: Chris Strople at
Tom Stewarts Ramp, Encinitas
p. 147: Stacy Peralta at the Dog Bowl
p. 149: Kent Senatore at the
Turning Point Ramp
pp. 150/151: Tom Sims at Concrete Wave
p. 155: Bruce Logan at Del Mar
p. 157: Gregg Weaver at the
Worlds Long Beach
p. 159: Paul Cullen at the Carlsbad Skatepark
p. 161: Catalina Classic & Bobby Piercy
"the Turner Guy"
p. 163: Signal Hill
p. 165: Steve Olson at the Hester Series
p. 167: Alan "Ollie" Gelfand at Del Mar
pp. 184/185: : Gregg Weaver, SkateBoarder
magazine relaunch cover
pp. 196/197: Shogo Kubo
p. 201: Jay Adams
pp. 202/203: Lonnie Toft
p. 206: Laura Thornhill

Image Credits

Photos by Warren Bolster, courtesy of
Concrete Wave Editions: pp. 4/5, 10/11, 16/17, 94/95, 109–115, 119, 121, 123, 125, 135, 139, 141, 143, 145, 150/151, 155, 157, 159, 161, 163, 165, 184/185, 196/197, 201, 202/203, 206

Photos by Jörgen Brennicke: pp. 20–23, 26–93, 105, 170–181, 186–195

Sketch by Stefan Ytterborn: p. 25

Photo by S. Nok: p. 127

Photos by Glen E Friedman: pp. 129, 147, 149, 167

Photo by © Chuck Saccio | Dreamstime.com: p. 131

Photo by Steve Cathey: p. 133

Gratitudes

THANKS to fellow collectors, enablers, friends: Aaron Wagner, Ally Barr, Chris Bara, Dave Lober, Dee Eggington, Dennis Allgeier, Dennis Martinez, Doug Saladino, Eric Starkey, Fernando Linhares, Gael Vuillemin, Gareth Hambrook, Glen E Friedman, Harvey Gallant, Henry Hester, Höglund, Ian Stothard, Jeronimo Ayres, Joachim Leonhardt, Johan L-n, Jon Welton, Jonny Uren, Justin Fletcher, Mark Manbars Baxley, Michael Hollamby, Mike Foley, Ministro Leo Herrera, Ole Cosmus, Omar Mata, Pacific Coast Vintage, Peter Gill, Steve Cathey, Stuart Geer, Terence Sideras

Imprint

Flex Appeal
The Changing Face of '70s
Skateboard Culture

This book was edited and designed
by gestalten.

Edited by Iris Hempelmann and
François-Luc Giraldeau
With Contributing Editor Stefan Ytterborn

Text by Stefan Ytterborn
Copy edited by Huw Nesbitt

Editorial management by Lars Pietzschmann

Art Direction by David Gonzalez
Design, layout and cover by StudioNearMe

Original photography by Jörgen Brennicke

Production management by
Martin Bretschneider

Typefaces: Neue Haas Grotesk by
Christian Schwartz, Berton Hasebe,
Eduard Hoffmann, Max Miedinger,
ITC Avant Garde Gothic by Herb Lubalin,
Tom Carnase, André Gürtler,
Christian Mengelt, Erich Gschwind

Printed by FINIDR, s. r. o., Český Těšín
Made in Europe

Published by gestalten, Berlin 2026
ISBN 978-3-96704-238-2
1st printing, 2026

For more information and to order books,
please visit www.gestalten.com

Die Gestalten Verlag GmbH & Co. KG
Mariannenstrasse 9–10
10999 Berlin, Germany
hello@gestalten.com

Bibliographic information published by the Deutsche Nationalbibliothek
The Deutsche Nationalbibliothek lists this publication in the Deutsche Nationalbibliografie;

detailed bibliographic data is available online at www.dnb.de

This book was printed on paper certified according to the standards of the FSC®.

MIX
Paper | Supporting responsible forestry
FSC® C014138